THE TEMPO OF MODERN LIFE

THE TEMPO
OF MODERN LIFE

BY JAMES TRUSLOW ADAMS

Essay Index Reprint Series

 BOOKS FOR LIBRARIES PRESS
FREEPORT, NEW YORK

11-19-87

First Published 1931
Reprinted 1970

STANDARD BOOK NUMBER:
8369-1691-3

LIBRARY OF CONGRESS CATALOG CARD NUMBER:
74-121444

PRINTED IN THE UNITED STATES OF AMERICA

PREFACE

ALTHOUGH all of the essays grouped in this volume deal with one or another aspect of the contemporary scene, it is hoped that their interest may transcend the passing moment. Every moment is compact of past and future as well as of the present; there are abiding as well as fleeting phases of all our problems, and the author has been more interested in the former than the latter. All sound criticism demands standards, and standards imply a permanent element. It is the presence or absence of this core of permanence that establishes criticism as transitory or lasting, and it is with the modest hope that these essays may belong to some extent to the more lasting sort that they have been gathered into book form.

JAMES TRUSLOW ADAMS

New York City, 1931.

v

CONTENTS

vii

I

1. VALUES AND STANDARDS

FOR THE THOUGHTFUL historian there are few subjects more fascinating than a bitter controversy which suddenly rolls up like a crashing thunderstorm in the social sky. The interest lies in the fact that the ostensible topic in dispute is as a rule merely like the lightning, something made visible for a moment but telling us nothing of that tension of unseen forces which has brought the storm about. It is the historian's amusing task to discover the forces. In the American Revolution the lightning was "no taxation without representation," and in the Civil War it was the slavery question; but in each instance there had been a tension of many social forces for several decades prior to the outburst of the storm which sent men scuttling.

In the past few years we have had two minor controversies in America which seemed to the casual onlooker as different as any two mild storms could be, and yet which broke out from almost identical tensions of intellectual forces behind the clouds—the "Monkey Trial" at Dayton, Tennessee, and the sudden "Humanistic" ballyhoo in New York and a few other Eastern points, the latter astounding a world which could not quite understand why prosperity-bitten Americans should without warning rise up and belabor each other on the subject of an illy-defined "Humanism." (I think capitals were always used.) When the first controversy broke on us, the "Humanists" and "Anti-Humanists" both had a jolly laugh at the shirt-sleeved mountaineers who were trying to prevent by law the teaching of evolution in their schools. What the mountaineers thought of the second controversy, if they thought of it at all, history has not yet recorded.

However different the setting and contestants, the real causes of these two squabbles were identical. The mountaineers had a certain set of intellectual and moral values in life. As a result of education they had seen their children abandoning these values without apparently substituting anything better. Education was somehow to blame, it seemed, and the chief stress in education was laid on science. *Ergo,* science must be curbed because the standards were of approved value and must be saved. "Evolution" was merely the lightning. The forces behind were those of moral and intellectual order, and those of sheer and destructive anarchy, as seen by the mountaineers. In the same way, the "Humanistic" hullabaloo emerged from the tension of the same forces as seen by the participants in that unedifying spectacle. It was order and standards against anarchy.

Both controversies were conducted with equal lack of intelligence. The Daytonians took a wholly unintelligent view of science when in its *proper* sphere; and the

Easterners just as unintelligent a one of it when in its *improper* sphere. On the whole, I preferred the Dayton show, though naturally disagreeing wholly with the Daytonian point of view as to remedies. There was less cleverness than in New York but a refreshing discovery that there were people still left who believed that life was worthwhile and that ideas (even wrongly selected) did matter tremendously and were not mere chips in an intellectual poker game.

I mention these two controversies because they indicated that under the surface of our disillusioned and weary post-war age there is evidently a good deal more personal preoccupation with the problem of standards than might otherwise have been thought. When Tennessee mountaineers flock down to fight over the question in a court of law, and Eastern illuminati hire New York's Town Hall to debate it, something is stirring. This has been confirmed by letters received from strangers, mostly boys in or just out of college, which have come to me steadily for many months past.

"Events have made us young ones," writes one of the most recent of these, "a little more realistic than previous generations. . . . Nevertheless our idealism needs a main stream into which to flow. At present each man of character or intellect has within himself the impulse toward heroism and improvement, but all this spiritual strength flows in separate little brooklets which trickle alone and sometimes dry up." They need something, he adds, by which they "may achieve some unity of feeling

13

and effort," and he ends by suggesting that "if there are such things as permanent values based on laws which defy disobedience, it ought to be possible to incorporate these values into a set of standards which would be authoritative in the charting of conduct." This letter is merely typical of many which indicate a growing need and search for values by which to chart conduct.

*

As one sits in front of the fire, quite aware that one is not a "great thinker" but nevertheless that one has to have a developing philosophy of life for oneself and has these letters to answer, one ponders a good deal in the light of fifty years' experience of a rather unusually varied existence. *Are* there values and standards? If so, how are they to be found? And when found what are we to do with them?

Let us avoid one source of confusion at the outset. When I speak of values and standards I do not mean a specific code of conduct. A gold dollar, for example, to maintain its value must have 25.8 grains of gold in it, but it may be a cube or flat, octagonal, square or round. It may be stamped with a buffalo, an eagle, a rooster, or President Harding. Those conditions of form are dictated by custom, caprice, convenience, or whatnot. By experimenting through many centuries and in many lands, it has been found that a flat, round coin is so much better in every respect than any other form that it has become accepted universally, though the design varies infinitely on it. What I am discussing in this article is the gold which gives value; not the form or design in which it is embodied.

With the great changes which came to society with the industrial revolution and applied science, many of the items in our codes of conduct began to suffer strain and to be questioned. With Darwin's evolutionary doctrine and other scientific discoveries or hypotheses, the theology of the Christian religion, which happened to be ours, was made so suspect as to undermine the sanctions which our code of morals had derived from its connection with religion. Then came the comparative study of codes of conduct or morality in anthropology, and Einstein's doctrine of relativity, which latter has had a tremendous influence upon tens of thousands of us who probably have a most inexact if not erroneous notion of its meaning. It was thus a very stormy Cape Horn which we had to round, and many dumped over their belief in standards and values to lighten ship. But, to adopt Daytonian language for the moment, Jonah, who had also been cast over in a storm, got ashore by a circuitous route and lived to make many repent.

Perhaps because it is the newest and most intellectually exclusive of the above influences, that of relativity has counted most of late in causing many to be confused as to standards. For example, my friend Henry Hazlitt of *The Nation,* whom I hold in intellectual respect usually and personal affection always, had a provocative article entitled "Standards (Loud Cheers)" in his journal recently. He allows only two meanings to standards, *viz.* "standards (loud cheers)" and standards in "a simple indicative sense." The first I should agree with him in discarding. He thus would leave me only the second; and what this is, is devastatingly shown by his next statement.

"In its simple, indicative sense," he says, "it is obvious that the charge that a given critic or group of critics has no standards is never true. A critic's standards may be low, they may shift with every book he writes about or even in the course of a single review, but standards, *in the sense of implied comparison,* he must have (italics mine). If a play reviewer on one of the dailies remarks that a play is good, he probably means that it is better than the average play of the season; if he remarks it is excellent, he may mean that it is one of the five or six best of the season; if he pronounces it superb, he may mean that it is the best of the season. Such standards are not high, but they are sensible." Mr. Hazlitt ends his article by saying that the literary critic's "standards in literature, in brief, will not be essentially different from his standards in life," thus extending his definition of literary standards to all standards.

If this is all true, there would evidently be no such thing as absolute standards left. They would melt into a mere "more" or "less," even if we had, as Hazlitt says, "a clear idea of just what standard is implied in the reviewer's judgment." But I do not believe that all this is true, and I may add that Mr. Hazlitt himself does not act on it. It is not even, as he says, "sensible."

In the first place, we would not be able to understand the critic at all unless we had that "clear idea" of what his little bit of relativity, instead of a standard, stemmed from as a base. If all his terms are used by him relatively only, it is essential that we know to what they are relative. How much simpler, instead of having to provide us with his personal yardstick each time, to employ words in "standard" English meanings! It is not necessary, as the "Anti-Humanists" seem to think, that otherwise we can use only Æschylus or Shakespeare as bases. Our humanity is a broad leveler which makes reasonable words understood on our own level. The demands of modern advertising and the outshrieking of each other in superlatives, as well as the needs of the business manager of a newspaper dependent on advertising, may make it impossible for a critic to use the English language with precision and decorum, but assuredly so careful a thinker as Mr. Hazlitt should not enact that damnable condition into a philosophic doctrine.

Let us apply one test to this theory. Let us suppose New York produces twenty plays in a season of which nineteen are deplorable, without interest to the playgoer or any quality of excellence in construction, plot, lines, or acting. The twentieth play is moderately good. Would the best two of the deplorable ones and the one passable one really become, by any stretching of language, even if we knew the critic's yardstick, respectively "good," "excellent" and "superb"? If Mr. Hazlitt came back to New York from some backward western town and I asked him whether there was any good architecture there, would he think over ten atrocities in the way of public buildings and, having recollected that the jail was the least offensive, tell me that it was "superb"? He would not. He would have in mind an international standard of good architecture for several centuries, and tell me the truth; nor in doing so would he have in mind, on the other hand, the Parthenon or the older *fléche* of Chartres Cathedral. But he would have in mind a standard not limited to 1931 Kokomo or wherever he had been. In other words, he would have in mind a standard not limited to a single week or one village.

Let us take another example. Business (and most Americans are business men) has a very definite standard of excellence, that of profit. If I asked a theoretical relativist in standards if a certain company were a "profitable" concern he would not reply that it was superbly profitable on the ground (which he would leave me to discover elsewhere) that it had lost only half a million dollars in a year in which its competitors had lost two millions. If he said it was profitable he would mean it had left a real profit, or else he would tell me it was profitable relatively but unprofitable actually.

*

I have labored this point somewhat at length because the conception of relativity has for many played ducks and drakes with their conception of any absolute standards. Of course everything bears some relation to everything else, and in a sense everything may be considered relatively, but as we have seen in the instances cited above, and particularly clearly—because mathematically—in the case of the word *profit*, there *is* a lower limit below which a standard can no longer be used as a measure of comparison positively but only as a negative. In other words, there is something absolute and not merely relative about standards; otherwise we could pursue the "more" or "less" perpetually down the scale, with no zero point between profit or loss, good or bad, virtue or vice. Moreover, to continue the business example, a concern may be said to be profitable without our having in mind the earnings of U. S. Steel, Standard Oil, or American Telephone. Somewhere between reasonable earnings and the beginning of a deficit, it may be said to be profitable. In the same way, without thinking of the Parthenon or Shakespeare, a building or a play may be said to be good, or even "superb"; but there is also for them a lower level below which such use of words becomes false. This is what the relativists seem to fail to see, and if I cite Mr. Hazlitt it is only because he has said so clearly what many of them appear to be groping after without his capacity for clear expression.

Mr. Hazlitt got his terms "standards (loud cheers)" from Eddington's amusing use of "reality—loud cheers," but lest the reader of *The Nation* might get the impression that Sir A. S. Eddington would endorse Mr. Hazlitt,

I may quote from a recent interview with the former in the London *Observer*. In reply to a question, Eddington replied: "I believe that science, like art, enables mankind to approach nearer to the realization of the absolute values that alone can give an aim and meaning to life."

"Then you believe in absolute values?"

"I think we all do in practice."

When asked whether a man should try to lead a perfectly balanced or a specialized life, he answered that he preferred a specialized life with plenty of other interests, and that "a life spent in complete devotion to an absolute value is a good life."

The more we consider life, the more it seems to me that we must agree that in practice we all do accept absolute standards, and know what we mean by them. These standards in the drama are not the absolute standards, which the "Anti-Humanists" would allow us as our only ones, Æschylus, Molière, Shakespeare *et al.* Neither are they the relativist standards, of the same "Anti-Humanists," of the score of plays being given between Forty-second Street and Sixtieth Street in New York City in the first six weeks of the 1931 theatrical season. They are absolute standards but based upon the reasonable possibilities, achievements, and expectations of humanity over a long period of time and in many places. If this view should leave me nothing to stand on but the hyphen between Humanist and Anti, I am quite content. It seems to me, as to Eddington, the bridge to common sense. I would be much inclined to sit on such a bridge and attend to my fishing while I cried "a plague on both your houses" to either end.

The critic who has no absolute standards at all is likely to lose·himself in a confusion of relativities and debauched tastes. This does not mean at all that he should insist upon or look for any Byzantine rigidities of form or expression. Absolute value may be and has been found in a vast number of each. Because he knows the value of gold there is no reason, though there may be much temptation for the lazy-minded, to insist upon its being in the form of a small flat round disk. But if he has no sense of the value of "gold," he is likely to fail as a critic. In the same way a business man is likely to fail if he does not believe in the absolute value of a profit. If, to paraphrase Mr. Hazlitt, his standards shift with every business he tries or even in the course of a single job, he will not last long. In precisely the same way, we have to have clear notions of absolute values in our intellectual, emotional, and spiritual life if we are not to flounder about as failures, if we are to achieve, as my young correspondent writes, "some unity of feeling and effort."

This first question of whether there *are* standards and values merges into the second one of how we are to discover them, for I believe that to a considerable extent they are discovered intuitively, and hence, for all the purposes of practical life, they do exist. This is true, at least, for the higher types of men, and it is for them only that I am writing at the moment. In the past the lower types have largely had to be coerced by material or spiritual fears into conforming to the standards and values of the higher. How in future the lower type will be handled is a question outside the immediate scope of this discussion.

The value envisaged and worked for by the business man is given him by intuition. It is direct. He needs no revelation or authority or science to tell him that his value is a profit and not deficit. In the same way the values of art come to the critic and ourselves largely by intuition, though for us who are not creative our standards may constantly rise by seeing the best of all ages. There is as much variety in form and expression among a painting by Hokusai and one by Rembrandt, the Ludovisi throne, the bust of Queen Nefertete and the *Thinker* by Rodin, a play by Æschylus and one by Eugene O'Neill, as the most rabid relativist "Anti-Humanist" could desire to give scope to new genius should such arise, but there is in all of these the pure gold which gives value. Under such variety we recognize it instinctively.

In the same way the higher of us do recognize values in human life and conduct. Whatever biology might have to say of the two bodies as functioning organisms we recognize that on the plane of self-conscious human life the character of George Washington was of higher value than that of Benedict Arnold, that of Lincoln than that of Jim Fisk, that of Father Damien than that of Al Capone. We could continue indefinitely

22

to point out such obvious intuitions. In fact if we considered carefully a hundred men in history or our own acquaintance, listed their characteristics and achievements, and reacted to them intuitively and tabulated the results, we would have gone far toward establishing a set and scale of values. Clearly this would have to be done by an intelligent person and one capable of responding to what was of value, just as a critic has got to be capable of responding to æsthetic values if he is to grow. But, as I have just stated, this is the type for whom I am writing at the moment.

*

I do not think that, on the whole, although science may help to interpret some aspects of ourselves to us, it is going to help very greatly in arriving at determinations of values for our lives and establishing scales for them, certainly not at present. For one thing, as yet at least, science is at its best at the levels farthest remote from our minds and conduct. As we pass up from astronomy and chemistry through biology to sociology and psychology we come to more and more inadequate data, confused conclusions among inextricable complexity, and a welter of unproved hypotheses and conflicting opinions. The existence of a permanent self is even denied and we are asked to contemplate "ourselves" as transient states of mind or mere reactions to passing stimuli.

Whatever may be the "truth" of all this—that

23

elusive "truth" which seems to grow ever more wraithlike the nearer we approach to it—the plain everyday fact on which we base our conduct is that we do regard ourselves as permanent and developing entities. We make money with the idea of enjoying it in old age or a year hence, and the values of all things in life must be considered in relation to this permanent, developing core of "self," "soul," or what you will, and not in relation to a mere transient state of mind or instantaneous reaction. To do the latter would prevent any planned life at all.

Apart from this, science is too apt to keep close to the physical and the partial. Even the psychiatrist and the psychoanalyst are too likely to overstress a single factor instead of seeing our lives whole. We are extremely complicated beings on the plane of self-consciousness, whatever scientifically we may be, and our lasting happiness and satisfactions are dependent upon a vast variety of resultants of conduct and environment. The psychoanalyst may rightly diagnose that a certain repression at one stage may account for a certain neurosis at another, and such knowledge may have its medical use, but for the vast majority of fairly normal people life is made up of an infinite number of strands. We do not react solely to sex any more than we do to religion, climate, or the economic motive. One cannot with a scalpel isolate one factor. That is the besetting sin of the crank, the faddist, and the too-enthusiastic scientific specialist. Science may become increasingly useful as a

24

tool to help us to attain to the things which we believe to have value. I do not think it will help us to decide on values.

Nor in our present mood and intellectual climate can we rely for an index of values upon authority, whatever form it may take. To be sure, our business man in pursuit of his limited but clearly defined value does almost precisely what the religious man did in former times. He follows the voices of his great leaders—Morgan, Ford, or others—with reverent attention. He has his textbooks and his lives of the men who have succeeded as he is trying to do. In conventions and smaller meetings, he joins for inspiration and helpful thought with others whose strivings are akin to his. This is nothing but preachers and theologians, sacred writings, lives of the saints, and church congregations all over again, but when it comes to ethical questions we live in an age which apparently does not enjoy and derives little benefit from such machinery.

The change is not, as a recent clerical writer asserted, due to democracy, because the machinery has not been discarded by us but has been taken over complete by business. It is due to change of taste or something else. The fact remains that, at present, of the many seeking some scale of values and the means of making their lives conform to them, few can bring themselves to accept authorities or share in group discussions for inspiration. We do not do it that way. We have preferred individual thinking and experimentation, which perhaps has been a very good thing for a while, both for testing the real values and for introducing variety in forms from which some more consonant to modern needs may arise.

But if one may judge by the letters and magazine articles of the personal confession sort, a great many are discovering that the old values somehow persist and that the old forms are more convenient than they had thought. In many cases, though not all, it is as if, having got bored and fed up with all coins being made in flat round disks, we had been trying cubes, or stars, or octagons, and discovered that after all the round coins, evolved nobody knows how from countless experiments in the past centuries, did have their reason for being just that shape after all.

*

But if we leave authority and past experience out of the question, to satisfy our present desire to settle things by and for ourselves, how are we to find what are the values of existence? It seems to me we have only two means of doing so—by intuition, as I have said, and by the use of our intelligence. The intelligent man or woman of any age who is really trying seriously to establish values for himself or herself will certainly discover many by such simple processes of intuition as I have suggested above. They cannot confront two such differing characters as, say, Lincoln, or the unstable, egoistically ambitious libertine Aaron Burr, and not confess

26

honestly wherein Lincoln is the nobler and more worthy one. In the same way if they consider one man who yields to every gust of passion or to cheap ambition easily gained, or to winning satisfactions that the lowest natures would be content with, and on the other hand another of opposite sort, they cannot but honestly consider the qualities of the latter of higher value than those of the former. Intuitions honestly sought and honestly recognized would carry one a good way on the path.

A trained intelligence also honestly used should carry us a good way farther. I am not concerning myself here with forms. I am not advocating any choice between the lives of artists, business men, priests, politicians, professional men, or whatnot. One man's food might be another man's poison. But building on our intuitions, intelligence can help us to rise above the moment or the single act. It can play the part which, before it fell on evil days, philosophy was supposed to play—that of coordinating all the branches of knowledge into a reasonable synthesis, the making of scattered parts into a coherent whole.

Intelligence should enable us to see that we have got to establish our values with reference, first, to the whole of our being—all our tastes, desires, capacities— and, secondly, to the whole of our lives in point of time and not any one period or episode. It is precisely here that in the absence of a synthesizing philosophy, the individual sciences are most likely to fail us. They are too much like medical specialists who try to understand

27

our whole organism by the way of eyes or teeth or glands. Intelligence will also, lead us to see that in considering what may be of value from the standpoint of the whole being and the entire life, we shall often have to set a lower against a higher value, a transient one against an abiding one.

The other day I was talking to a friend, now about forty-five and with three children ranging up to fifteen. He occupies a high, important, and interesting but not very well paid post, and has as sound a scale of values and as great contentment in his life as anyone I know. He told me that when he and his wife were married, they determined that the union should be for life; that whatever irritations might come, they would consider them in the light of the greater adventure of a spiritual partnership which they were going to do their best to carry on to the end with ever-increasing satisfaction. They knew that the sexual side counted heavily but also that age would come when other things would also count, and they were going to prepare for an old age of mutual love, trust, confidence, and the sense of life-long loyalty borne toward each other, as well as for the days of youth. Since they preferred other things in life, such as simplicity of living and hospitality, reading, leisure for each other and the children when they might come, to those things which they could have if they struggled harder to make money in a less interesting career than the man had chosen, they deliberately set themselves to be contented without the things large incomes brought so that

28

money troubles should not be a source of friction in the home. And so he went on.

Here were a man and woman who established their scale of values on the intelligent basis of their whole mutual interest and the whole of their lives, not any segmented slice of either. When looking at things in that way, it is obvious that one has to choose between whole sets of values. A man or woman, for example, who prefers a succession of amours to a life relationship chosen for what it may give, is not choosing between values of the same sort, merely differing in degree of intensity, but between wholly different ones; and the choice has to be made deliberately and intelligently.

With regard to many of our choices, intelligence has to answer questions of a searching sort. Will the act or course of conduct weaken or strengthen will and character? Is it the result of drifting or intelligent volition? Will it make me more or less capable of guiding and controlling my life later? Is the satisfaction it promises transient or permanent? Is it going to increase or decrease my ability to enjoy a higher and more permanently satisfying range of values? Is it going to make me more or less capable of being, in the long run, the sort of person I should like to be? The list could be extended far.

Are such standards and values, in the words of my young correspondent "based on laws which defy disobedience"? I think it reasonably positive that they are. Many people slip through life by luck, denying their own values at times, without notable disaster, just as some people may contract typhoid and pull through where others succumb. Nevertheless we cannot acquire typhoid germs without risk. Let us take, for example, the value of insistence upon intellectual integrity. The law of intellectual integrity would seem to defy disobedience in that if we continually flout it we become incapable of seeing things clearly and become one of those who, as we say, unconsciously deceive themselves.

In many choices between lower and higher values, or transient and permanent ones, a law would seem to be inevitable as that in the physical world which says that two bodies cannot occupy the same place at the same time. If, as above, a succession of love affairs are preferred to marriage, one simply cannot expect to have the set of values at the end which grow from a lifelong loyalty. For my own part, I believe that in determining values for ourselves, as in any other pursuit of knowledge, we should not disdain wholly the wisdom accumulated in the past; but if we will have none of that, then I can see nothing for it but an honest play of intelligence among our intuitions. If this is carried on with intellectual integrity, I believe it will bring us to much the same point as we should have reached by the other method, only it may satisfy us better in the present temper of our age.

To a considerable extent the older generation abandoned its traditional values and declined the intellectual task of establishing others. One result has been the complete confusion in our educational system. Because that generation which is solely responsible for our colleges and universities has no standard of values, it has been unable to define the ends of education; and with no comprehension of aims, there can be nothing but a muddle in method. Happily, youth, which first revolted against forms, is now revolting against this lack of values, which is much more fundamental. Forms will vary with different values and may even vary with the same value. It is not the form, the particular item in a social code, which counts, but the values clothed in the forms. Without a scale of values we are as hopelessly at sea to direct our course as a business man would be who did not know whether he was trying to make a loss or a profit.

To answer the last question—what are we going to do with our scale of values when we have achieved it?— I should say: stand by it to the uttermost possible. At present the whole social and economic machine is so geared as to make that an undertaking of extreme difficulty, but unless the newer generation can base a scale of values on what derives from the best of our whole natures and the consideration of our entire lives, and can swing our educational system, our business and social life around to them, I see no hope for anything but a muddle and chaos which will drown our human personalities in a dehumanized whirl of production and consumption of things without human value.

That youth, and to some extent the older generation, is now searching hearts on the problem of values, is I believe true. That these values can be found is also true. The problem is how many, after considering these values in terms of their whole lives, like my friend, will have the courage to organize all parts of their lives so as to give the values play in face of the almost insuperable opposition of a society which does not recognize them.

The most deadly weapon in the struggle is the cost of living when the college graduate has been about seven years out of college. At that point I fully recognize that the question is apt to be mercilessly shifted from that of a life based on humane values to life on any reasonable terms unless the sufferer conforms to the standards of the dehumanized economic system which seems to have us all in its grip. The existence of that barrier is perhaps the most fatal indictment that can be brought against our entire American civilization. If enough can gallantly surmount it to capture in time our universities and in other ways make their influence felt on our economic and social ideals, we may be able to rebuild a civilization in which a scale of humane values may again be established and win an authority now lacking.

There *are* such standards and values. They can be found. The chief problem is how can the present whirling life of our country be made to provide scope for those who wish to base a sane and intelligent life on such values without warping their every energy not to the making of an undesired great fortune but merely a decent living. That is the problem, unhappily bequeathed to them, of the new generation; and for their own sakes and their children's sakes, it is the biggest that they have to face. If the problem cannot in time be resolved, we cannot be said to have a civilization. That is not a civilization but merely a herd existence in which those who have in youth the vision of a humane life based on the higher values of all man's history are ground underfoot by the galloping horses of our machines rushing madly and uncontrolled.

2. OUR CHANGING CHARACTERISTICS

THERE ARE FEW things more difficult to generalize about without danger of valid objections than national character. The exceptions to any generalization at once begin to appear destructively numerous. A concept of a Frenchman must include not only such diverse types as the Gascon, the Parisian, and the Breton, but also the innumerable differences between individuals of these and other types in what is a rather small country which for long has been culturally and politically unified.

When we attempt the task in America it would seem to be hopeless. Who *is* an American? Is he the descendant of a Boston Brahman, of a Georgia cotton planter, or a newly arrived Armenian, Hungarian, or Italian? Is the typical American a clerk on the fifty-fourth story of a Wall Street office building or a farm hand of the Machine Age guiding in isolation a power plow along a furrow which stretches endlessly over the horizon? Is he a scientist working for pitiful pay and the love of science in some government bureau in Washington, or a one hundred per cent go-getter in a Chamber of Commerce whose ideas of progress are limited to increase of wealth and population? Is he Hamilton or Jefferson, Lincoln or Harding, Roosevelt or Coolidge, Emerson or Barnum?

The task of defining national character in such a conflicting welter of opposites is dismaying enough, and yet a fairly clear notion is of prime importance for any number of very practical purposes. The modern business man doing business on a national scale, making mass appeal to our whole hundred and twenty millions at once; the statesman, domestic or foreign, trying to forecast the success or failure of an idea or a policy; the genuine patriot interested in the highest development of his civilization—these and others must all take account of that real if vague concept which we call the national character. It is from the third point of view that we are concerned with the topic in the present article.

*

There are many signs that our world is approaching a new and critical stage. Deeply embedded in the structure of the universe there is a power or force that is continually at work molding chaos into cosmos, formlessness into forms. These forms, or patterns, belong to the spiritual as well as to the physical plane of reality. A scale of values, an ethical system, a philosophy of life appear to be as "natural" and inevitable a part of the web and woof of that strange and inexplicable phantasmagoria that we call the universe as are crystals,

35

corals, or living embodiments of the form-producing force in the plant or animal body.

For generations now we have been witnessing the gradual breakdown of old forms until we have reached the very nadir of formlessness in our whole spiritual life. But there are, as I have said, many indications that we are about to witness a new stage, the embryo stage of new forms.

For the most part this play of cosmic forces is independent of consciousness or will in individuals. The atoms know not and care not why or how they combine to make quartz crystals or a living cell of protoplasm. To a greater extent than we care to admit, perhaps, the higher forms—our scales of values, our philosophies—are also independent of conscious molding by ourselves. They are not wholly so, however, and if, as has recently been said, more and more of us here in America as elsewhere "are looking for a new set of controlling ideas capable of restoring value to human existence," is it evidence of the interplay between the blind form-making force of physical nature and the consciousness of man? What these ideas will be will depend largely upon the soil in which they will be rooted, the soil of our national character.

It is also clear that the form in which life, either physical or spiritual, is embodied is of transcendent importance for the individual. If living cells are arranged in the form of a bird, both the powers and limitations of the individual are wholly different from those of the individual when they are arranged in the form of a fish. Similarly in the spiritual world, powers and limitations depend largely upon the forms within which the spirit has its being. Because they are so largely intangible, we are likely to lose sight of the fact that these forms— scales of values, systems of thought, philosophies of life —all afford the spirit peculiar powers and impose peculiar limits.

What of the new forms? Arising from and in large part molded by the national character, are they likely to afford wider scope for man's highest aspirations, to enlarge the powers of the spirit, or to place limits and bind them closer to the earth? What of the national character itself?

Let us for the present discussion avoid the more difficult problem of a complete analysis and seek to establish a trend, often a simpler task, in the spiritual as in the physical world. Are our characteristics changing, and, if so, in what direction? Can we, in the first place, establish any definite points of reference which will be tangible and certain? I think we can.

*

Man expresses himself in his arts, and among these none is more illuminating than the earliest and most practical, that of architecture. It is one, moreover, in which we as Americans excel.

We need not greatly concern ourselves with the

inchoate beginnings of our nationality in the first few generations of early settlement in the wilderness of the Atlantic seaboard. The physical tasks were almost overwhelmingly hard and there was little opportunity for a distinctly American expression of either old or new spiritual life. By the time there was, we find that the spirit of the colonies had expressed itself in an architectural form, characteristic with minor variations throughout all of them.

When we speak of "colonial architecture," what at once comes to our mind is the home, the dwelling house of Georgian type, modeled on the English but with a delicacy and refinement surpassing most of the models overseas. From New England to the Far South these homes had outwardly a perfection of form and inwardly a proportion, a refinement of detail, a simplicity that all clearly sprang from the spirit of the time.

We may note quickly in passing several points in regard to them. The high point of the architecture was domestic. They were homes. They had an air of spaciousness, of dignity. They were aristocratic in the best sense. They were restrained and disciplined. Display or vulgarity were unthinkable in connection with them. They evidenced an ordered and stratified society. They held peace and rest. They were simple, unostentatious, and profoundly satisfying. They were shelters for a quiet life, alien from haste.

Let us, using the same architectural measure, pass

38

from this first flowering of the American spirit to the very instant of to-day. The great contribution of twentieth-century America to the art of building is the skyscraper, of which we may take the office building as both the earliest and most typical example. What are some of its usual characteristics?

The buildings are commercial, not domestic. Their very *raison d'être* is financial, the desire to get the most money possible from a given plot of ground. Their bulk is huge but they are not spacious, save perhaps for their entrance halls in some instances. They are democratic in the physical sense of herding within their walls thousands of persons of every possible sort. In their primary insistence upon mere size and height regardless of every other element, they are undisciplined and unrestrained. Peace or rest are unthinkable within their walls with the incessant movement of thousands of hurrying individuals, and elevators moving at incredible speed.

They are lavish in their ostentation of expense on the ground floor, bare and unsatisfying above. A "front" of vulgar cost is built to hide the emptiness of the countless floors beyond the reach of the first casual glance from the street. Yet every small and growing community cries for them and we hold them to the world as our characteristic achievement in art, as our most significant contribution in that most tell-tale of all arts, the housing of man's chief interest.

*

Here, then, we have two points of reference tangible enough to be noted by all men, because they are physical in structure, yet full of spiritual implications for our task. When we turn to other means of establishing our trend, such as literature, newspapers, our methods of living, the wants we create and strive to satisfy, our social ways of contact, our national ideals as expressed in political campaigns and policies, and other means less obvious than the buildings in which we live or work or express our spiritual aspirations, what do we find? I think we find the same trends indicated above, amplified and emphasized.

It is, if I may repeat myself to prevent misunderstanding, only with these trends and not with the whole complex national character that I am here concerned. As a historian, and with no wish to make a case but only to report what I find, certain trends in the past century appear to me to be clearly indicated. Let me note them just as from time to time I have jotted them down, without at first trying either to order or explain them.

These trends are the substitution of self-expression for self-discipline; of the concept of prosperity for that of liberty; of restlessness for rest; of spending for saving; of show for solidity; of desire for the new or novel in place of affection for the old and tried; of dependence for self-reliance; of gregariousness for solitude; of luxury for simplicity; of ostentation for restraint; of success for integrity; of national for local; of easy generosity for wise giving; of preferring impressions to thought, facts to ideas; of democracy for aristocracy; of the mediocre for the excellent.

For the most part I do not think any observer would quarrel with the validity of most of the above list. Discipline, self or other, has almost completely vanished from our life. In earlier days it was amply provided by school, family, and social life, by ideals and religious beliefs. To-day it is not only absent in all these quarters but is preached against by psychologists and sociologists, decried by the new pedagogy, and even legislated against in school and prison.

Nothing is imposed any longer, from learning one's ABC's to honoring one's parents. Everything is elective, from college courses to marital fidelity. The man or woman who casts all discipline to the winds for the sake of transient gratification of selfish desires, who denies obligations and duties, is no longer considered a libertine or a cad but merely a modernist pursuing the legitimate end of self-expression.

For a considerable time evidence has been accumulating that the national rallying cry has become an economic balance sheet. Perhaps one of the chief values of the whole prohibition muddle has been to serve as a mirror for the American soul. In the arguments advanced for and against, in the spiritual tone of the discussion, we can see all too well reflected the moving ideals of the American people, and the argument that carries most weight would clearly appear to be that of prosperity. Balanced against this, the questions of personal liberty, class legislation, or constitutional propriety are but as straw weighed against iron.

Prohibition is only one of the many mirrors that reflect the same truth. In innumerable cases of business practice and of legislation it has become evident that when personal freedom and initiative have to be balanced against the prosperity of the moment according to the business methods of the moment, prosperity wins. The one liberty that is still valued is the liberty to exploit and to acquire. That liberty will be defended to the death, but other liberties, such as freedom of thought and speech, have become pale and unreal ghosts, academic questions of no interest to the practical man.

Who cares in the slightest about the innumerable cases of encroachment on personal liberties on the part of both state and Federal governments in the past ten years so long as business is good? Who cares about the methods employed by our police? Who is willing to give thought to the treatment frequently meted out to foreigners by our immigration officials—treatment that could hardly be surpassed by the old Russian régime at its worst, treatment that we could not stand a moment if accorded to *our* citizens by any foreign government? No, personal liberty as a rallying cry to-day receives no answer. But we will elect any man President who will promise us prosperity.

*

There is as little question of our growing restlessness. By rail, boat, automobile, or plane we are as restless as a swarm of gnats in a summer sunbeam. "We don't know where we're going but we're on our way" is the cry of all. Even the babies get their rest by traveling at forty miles an hour swung in cradles in Ford cars. That much of the movement is mere restlessness and does not spring from a desire to see and learn may easily be observed by watching the speed of our new tourists when they travel and listening to their comments when they have to stop to look at anything. As for the "nature" they claim to go to see, they are ruining our whole countryside with appalling indifference.

The home itself has yielded and has ceased to afford any sense of permanence and security. In the old days a home was expected to serve for generations. In the South, frequently property was entailed and the family was assured of a continuing center where it could cluster. A year ago, on October first, a hundred thousand families in New York City moved from one apartment to another, in many instances for no better reason than that they were bored with the one they had occupied a twelve-month. Our multimillionaires build palaces, and in a few years abandon them to country clubs or office buildings.

As for thrift and saving, with the entire complex of spiritual satisfactions that go with an assured future, they have not only notoriously been thrown overboard but are vigorously denounced by advertising experts like Bruce Barton and great industrial leaders like Henry

43

Ford. "We should use, not save," the latter teaches the American people while they mortgage their homes, if they own them, to buy his cars. On every side we are being taught not to save but to borrow. The self-respect and satisfaction of the man of a generation ago who did not owe a penny in the world is being replaced by the social-respect and deep dissatisfaction of the man who has borrowed to the limit to live on the most expensive scale that hard cash and bank credit will allow.

With this has naturally come a preference for show to solidity. A witty and observing foreigner has said that Americans put all their goods in the shop window. In every vein the insidious poison is at work. A man who toiled and saved to own his home would see to it that it was well built and substantial. The man who expects to move every year cares for nothing more than that the roof will not fall until he gets out, provided the appearance is attractive. In an advertisement of houses for sale in a New York suburb recently one of the great advantages pointed out was that the roofs were guaranteed for three years.

The first thing that every business firm thinks of is show. Its office or shop must look as if there were unlimited resources behind it. Even a savings bank, whose real solidity should be seen in its list of investments, and whose object is to encourage thrift, will squander hugely on marbles and bronze in its banking room to impress the depositor.

The same motive is at work in our intellectual life.

44

One has only to glance at the advertisements of the classics, of language courses, of "five foot shelves" and note the motives that are appealed to for desiring culture. Nor are our schools and colleges exempt from the same poison. The insistence on degrees after a teacher's name, the regulating of wage scales in accordance with them, the insistence on a professor's publishing something which can be listed, are as much part of the same trend as is the clerk's wanting to be cultured so as to pass from a grilled window to an assistant-assistant executive's desk.

*

We could expand the above examples almost indefinitely and continue through the remainder of the list. But it is all obvious enough to anyone who will observe with fresh eyes, and ponder. Both for those who may agree or disagree with me, let us pass to some of the other questions that arise in connection with the trends I have noted. Do they in any way hang together? Do they make a unified whole or are they self-contradictory and hence probably mistaken? Do they derive from any conditions in our history that would make them natural and probable, or are they opposed to those conditions? If they are real, do they represent a transient phase or a permanent alteration in our character?

As we study them carefully, it seems to me that they do hang together remarkably and ominously well. A person, for example, who is restless, rather than one who

45

cares for rest and permanence, would naturally prefer the new to the old, the novel for the tried, impressions instead of difficult and sustained thought. Both these characteristics, again, naturally cohere with the desire for show rather than solidity, and for self-expression rather than self-discipline.

With these same qualities would go the love of gregariousness rather than solitude, of luxury rather than simplicity, and, easily belonging to the same type of character, we would find the desire to spend ousting the desire to save, and the substitution of prosperity for liberty and of success for integrity. With such a succession of substitutions, that of dependence for self-reliance is not only natural but inevitable, and so with the other items in the trend. They all fit into a psychological whole. There is no self-contradiction to be found among them.

But is there any connection to be found between them and our history? Are they qualities that might be found to have developed with more or less logical and psychological necessity from the conditions of American life which have separated the period of the colonial home from that of the seventy-story office building? I think here again we find confirmation rather than contradiction.

I have no intention to rival Mr. Coolidge by writing the history of America in five hundred words. All I can do in this chapter is to point to certain facts and influences.

Until well into the eighteenth century, there had

been no very great change in the character of the American to mark him off from his English cousin. The wilderness and remoteness had, indeed, had some effect, but this was small compared with the later effects of what we have come to call "the West." Leaving out a few minor strains—such as the Dutch, Swedes, and the earlier Germans—the settlers were almost wholly British, who sought, in a somewhat freer atmosphere and with somewhat wider economic opportunity, to reproduce the life they had left.

The continent open to them was of limited extent. Beyond a comparatively narrow strip lay the long barrier of the Appalachians and the claims of the French. The strip itself contained no great natural resources to arouse cupidity or feverish activity. The character of the colonists had become a little more democratic, a little more pliant, a little more rebellious and self-reliant than that of their cousins of similar social ranks at home. That was all. They might differ with the majority of both Englishmen and Parliament over questions of politics and economics, but those were differences of interest and policy, not of character.

There lay ahead, however, the operation of two factors that were to prove of enormous influence—the exploitation of the American continent, and the immigration from Europe. We cannot here trace this influence step by step chronologically, but we must summarize it. "The West"—there were successively many of them—

47

unlike the colonial America, was of almost limitless extent and wealth. There were whole empires of farm land and forest, mines that made fortunes for the lucky almost overnight, reservoirs of gas and oil that spawned cities and millionaires.

All did not happen in a day, but it did happen within what might almost be the span of one long life. In ages past an Oriental conqueror might sack the riches of a rival's state, a king of Spain might draw gold from a Peruvian hoard, but never before had such boundless opportunities for sudden wealth been opened to the fortunate among a whole population which could join in the race unhampered.

In the rush for opportunity, old ties and loyalties were broken. A restlessness entered the American blood that has remained in it ever since. In American legend, the frontier has become the Land of Romance and we are bid to think of the pioneers as empire-builders. A very few may have dreamed of the future glory of America rather than of private gain, but it is well not to gild too much the plain truth, which is that in the vast majority of instances, the rush was for riches to be made as quickly as might be. In the killing of a million buffaloes a year, in the total destruction of forests without replanting, in the whole of the story in all its aspects there were few thoughts for a national destiny not linked with immediate personal gain at any expense to the nation. In this orgy of exploitation it is not difficult to discover the soil in which some of the elements of the changed trend in American character had its roots.

*

Another factor was also at work which combined with the above in its effects. The racial homogeneity of our earlier colonial days was broken by the millions of immigrants who came to us of racial stocks other than our own. Our first character had been that of seventeenth- and eighteenth-century Englishmen, not greatly altered until the Revolution. It was unified and stable, but the West and Europe both operated to undermine its stability.

On the one hand, the influence of the West, with the loosening of old bonds, its peculiar population, and its opportunities of limitless expansion and wealth greatly altered old ideals and standards of value. On the other, the steady infusion in large numbers of Germans, Irish, Swedes, Norwegians, Jews, Russians, Italians, Greeks, and other races also bore a conspicuous part in making the national character less uniform and stable. I am not concerned with their several contributions of value, but merely with the fact that the introduction of such foreign swarms tended to destroy a unified national character.

By the latter part of the nineteenth century, two things had thus happened. In the first place, the real America had become the West, and its traits were be-

49

coming dominant. One of these was restlessness, not only a willingness but a desire to try any new place or thing and make a complete break with the old. Moreover, although the frontier may breed some fine qualities, it is a good deal like the farm in the respect that although it may be a fine place to come from, it is a soul-killing place in which to remain. It bred emotion rather than thought, and to a considerable extent substituted new material values for the spiritual ones of the older America.

In the rush for wealth—whether won from forests or mines; farms tilled, raped, and abandoned for fresher soil; real estate values from fast-growing cities; lands fraudulently obtained from a complaisant government—restraint, self-discipline, thought for the future ceased to be virtues. With all this came a vast optimism, a belief that everything would become bigger and better, and, because the standards of success were economic, better because bigger. Wealth was the goal, and the faster things got bigger—towns, cities, the piles of slain buffaloes, the area of forests destroyed—the quicker one's personal wealth accumulated. Statistics took on a new significance and spelled the letters of one's private fate.

At the same time, by the latter half of the nineteenth century another thing had happened, as we have said. Partly from the effects of the West and partly from immigration, the old, stable American-English character had become unstable, soft, pliant, something which could be easily molded by new influences. It could readily take the impress of an emotion, a leader, a new invention. It was full of possibility, both of good and evil.

Suddenly this new, unformed, malleable national character, already warped to a large degree toward material values, was called upon to feel the full force of the influences flowing from the fruition of the Industrial Revolution. Invention followed invention with startling rapidity. Life itself became infinitely more mobile. Scientists, engineers, manufacturers threw at the public contrivance after contrivance of the most far-reaching influence upon man's personal and social life without a thought of what that influence might be beyond the profit of the moment to the individual manufacturer.

Choice became bewildering in its complexity. The national character had become unstable. It was in a real sense unformed and immature, far more so than it had been a century earlier. It had also lost belief in the necessity of restraint and discipline. It had accepted material standards and ideals. It was in far more danger of being overwhelmed by the ideals of a new, raw, and crude Machine Age than was perhaps any other nation of the civilized group.

With an ingenuity that would have been fiendish had it not been so unthinking and ignorant, the leaders of the new era used every resource of modern psychology to warp the unformed character of the people, to provide the greatest possible profit to the individuals and corporations that made and purveyed the new "goods." Our best and worst qualities, our love of wife and children, our national pride, our self-respect, our snobbery, our fear of social opinion, our neglect of the future, our lack of self-restraint and discipline, our love of mere physical comfort have all been played upon to make mush of our characters in order that big business might thrive. Even our national government, whether wittingly or not, undertook to inflame our American love of gambling and our desire to "get rich quick" regardless of effect on character.

*

Taking all the molding influences of the past century and more into account, it is little wonder, perhaps, that our national characteristics exhibit the trend noted. The situation, serious as it is, might be less so had it occurred at a time when the spiritual forms in the world at large—its scales of values, its ethical systems, its philosophies of life—were intact. But as we have noted, they have been largely destroyed; and at the very time when new forms are in process of arising, largely to be molded by the national characters of the peoples among whom they arise, our own is in the state pictured above. The question whether our new characteristics are temporary or permanent thus becomes of acute significance.

Race is a word of such vague and undefined content as to be of slight help to us, but if we take the whole history of the Western nations from which we derive, I think we may say that the characteristics noted above may be classed as acquired and not inherited. Biologists

52

consider such not to be permanent and heritable, though the analogy with biology again is so vague as to afford little comfort.

More hopeful, I think, is the fact that these new characteristics appear to have derived directly from circumstances, and that these circumstances themselves have been in large part such as have passed and will not recur again. Immigration and "the West" have ceased to be continuing factors in our development. Their effects remain and must be dealt with, but neither factor will continue to intensify them. The tides of immigration have been shut off. There is significance in the fact that "the Wests" which won under Jefferson, Jackson, and Lincoln were defeated in 1896 under Bryan.

"The West" of to-day is a new West in which conditions, and to a large extent ideals, are different. Yet its greatest contribution to our national life and character remains that broadening and deepening of the dream of a better and a richer life for all of every class which was the cause of its earlier victories and which goes far to redeem its less noble influences. The nation as a whole is entering upon a new era in which all the conditions will be different from any experienced heretofore. Territory, resources, opportunities are none of them any longer unexploited and boundless. What the future may hold, we cannot tell, but in fundamental influences it will be different from the past. The menacing factor that remains is that of mass production and the machine.

Also, we have spoken thus far only of the trend in

53

characteristics, not of our character as a whole. In that there are certain noble traits which remain unaltered, or have matured and strengthened. It is possible, now the warping influences of the past century have to some extent disappeared, that the national character may develop around them as a core, that we shall forget in manhood the wild oats sown in our youth.

But age acquires no value save through thought and discipline. If we cannot reinstate those, we are in danger of hampering rather than aiding in that reconstruction of the spiritual life of man that is the inevitable and most vital task now before the nations. We must either forward or retard it. We are too great to live aloof. We could not if we would, and upon the trend of our character depends to a great extent the future of the world.

Nor let us forget that although fortune has poured her favors in our lap, there is a Nemesis that dogs the steps of all, and we cannot lightly scorn the growing enmity of half the world. Are we to treat the Machine Age and mass production only as a new and different "West," or are we at last, in growing up, to learn wisdom and restraint? Are we going to change the trend in our character or is it to become fixed in its present form, a danger to ourselves and a menace to mankind? Few questions could be more difficult to answer or more pregnant with consequence.

3. DIMINISHING RETURNS
IN MODERN LIFE

THROUGH INCREASING knowledge of natural laws man has enormously increased his control over his environment. This is so obvious as to make any amplification of the simple statement unnecessary. Our type of culture to-day is based solely on power, the power hidden in coal, steam, electricity, or the chemical combination of atoms, and is due to our having discovered and utilized natural laws. Because of the enormous increase in our control over the environment due to such knowledge, we have come instinctively to think of the discovery of each additional law as enlarging the possible scope of human life and activities. We never think of them as indicating limits. The changes realized have been so overwhelming that the possibilities have come to appear illimitable, and scant attention is paid to those laws which put definite limits to our advance in any desired direction. They are brushed aside, and any discussion of them is as unpopular as was conservative economic reasoning at the top of the recent bull market. Unfortunately, the unpopular laws as well as the popular ones are ceaselessly at work, as the enthusiastic speculators found, and disregard of them is bound to end in trouble. Laws are merely formulations of the ways in which things invariably and inevitably happen or act; and to get in the way of a law of nature which does not work the way we should like, and to insist on having our own way is about as futile as for a cow on the track to dispute the right of way with the Chicago Flyer at sixty miles an hour. The laws of nature do not work for us. All we can do is to find out how they work, to make use of some of those going in our direction, and to get out of the way of others as fast as we can.

So far, most of the laws discovered belong to the physical sciences. Psychology, economics, politics, sociology, and the others are grievously behind. Any astronomer can predict with absolute accuracy just where every star in the heavens will be at half-past eleven to-night. He can make no such prediction about his young daughter. From this fact—that one group of sciences has got entirely out of step with another—our civilization is becoming warped out of shape. For a good many centuries, in spite of defects, the social and political life of peoples fitted on the material base almost as neatly as the top layer of a chocolate cake fits on the bottom. To-day the top layer has altered little, but the bottom one, the material base of our life, has gone spinning, with grave danger of ruining the cake and losing the chocolate. The cake is, in fact, acting like a thing bewitched, and if we are to make it stick together again we have got to do something with the upper layer, for the under one has clearly gone too far to get it back in its old place if we would.

56

It is clear that we have got to know a great deal more about psychology and sociology than we do now, keeping them "ologies" and not making them "isms." Our chemists and engineers will look after our T.N.T.'s and dynamos, but we must learn how to use them, and come to some new terms with our ethics, politics, and social life in the largest sense. A chemist who tried to make T.N.T. according to his emotions and not his science might bring it off but, a million to one, would more likely be brought off himself. It is the same with our social and institutional life. If, on the scale of modern nations, we try to adjust them only to our vague emotions and callow aspirations, something very violent and unpleasant can be rather certainly predicted. We must hunt for laws to guide us— Nature's, not lobbyists'. It is also essential to find the unpopular as well as the popular ones, those which tell us what we cannot do as well as those which tell us what we can. The Garden of Eden and the flaming sword were myths—excellent ones, by the way; but a definite limit here and there to self-expression and undirected aspirations is not. I do not pretend to be a scientist, but when one observes the cow on the track and the Chicago Flyer coming one does not have to be one to predict that something is going to happen immediately to the cow. I wish, in a word, to call attention to what is an apparent law, and about as unpopular a one as could exist.

*

Economists, observing the way things happen, have established what they call "the Law of Diminishing Returns." I shall not try to give it in scientific terms or bother with graphs. Briefly it is that working in a given direction there is a point up to which profit increases and beyond which it inevitably declines. Let us illustrate this with a few examples comprehensible to every practical man. I once lived in a farming community. The farmers would figure very carefully how much to spend per acre in fertilizer. Twenty-five dollars per acre would increase the value of the crop so much, less cost of fertilizer. Fifty dollars would do so to a greater extent, as would a hundred dollars; but two hundred would not. There was a point at which the cost of fertilizing, profitable up to then, overtook the increased value of the crop, and became unprofitable. The wise farmer, who knew his land, his fertilizer, and his crop, knew just how far to go and where to stop to get the last dollar out of all three—perhaps I should say cent.

Let us turn to another great industry, mining. Gold is found in rock, a very small amount of gold to a fearsome amount of rock. To extract it requires costly machinery and labor. Up to a certain point an increase in outlay on the best machinery will pay, but beyond that it will not. There is a relation between the percentage of gold in the rock and the cost of getting at it, as I once found out.

Let us consider our pet toy, the skyscraper. I used to have an office at 2 Wall Street. Across the street there was a lot with a four-story building on it, forty feet square. It has been called the most valuable piece of real estate in the world. Indeed, I was told as a boy many years ago that the then owner was asked what he would take for it, and answered that his price was the sixteen hundred square feet covered with gold dollars. This was figured out, and the offer made, whereupon he smiled and answered, "I meant, stood on edge." However that may be, it did change hands, and a high building was put on it which became known as "the chimney." I have forgotten how high it was, but here is the point: its height was limited by the fact that it could have only one elevator; and architects tell us that although up to a certain point every floor you add to a building increases the rental, there is a point, given a certain ground space, at which the space required for elevators to carry people to the added floors will offset the increased rental space gained by adding such floors, which sounds reasonable. Of course, you can buy the adjoining lots, tear down the old buildings, and build a higher, but the limit is the city block, and there is a point at which the increased rental space will be offset by the increased lost elevator space.

Let us take one more illustration. Everyone who builds a house for himself has the same problems I had. There was the question, for example, of the cost of the copper sheathing I was to put around my windows and the copper gutters under my piazza floor. Knowing I wished to cut cost as much as might be, the architect suggested copper of a certain thickness and cost. The builder suggested that it would last only so many years, whereas the shingling and piazza floors would last longer. If I spent more on the copper I should save in the long run. I, therefore, added to the weight, but it was quite obvious that there was a point beyond which to add to the weight and cost would cease to be profitable and prove merely loss. It was our job to determine that point.

Perhaps these illustrations have made my basic point clear. Let us now work toward somewhat broader problems.

I suppose it will make me seem antediluvian to the young generation but I well remember when taxis were introduced into New York. As a matter of fact, it was not so long ago in spite of the fact that most young people to-day cannot imagine Peter Stuyvesant getting about in any other way. At first they were a great help in saving time. When one was in a great hurry one took a taxi and swept along Fifth Avenue at what seemed a terrific rate. But taxis multiplied like rabbits in Australia with the result that to-day when I am really in a hurry I now have to walk to get from Thirty-Third Street to Forty-Second. It once took me twenty-five minutes in a taxi. In other words, as a time-saver, when there were few taxis and few of us used them, they served their purpose admirably. Now that there are, apparently, millions of them and the millions use them, they are of no use, for that purpose, to anybody. It is not that the mob has got what a few used to have, but that nobody has got anything, in this particular aspect.

In 1913 I built a house at the east end of Long

Island. Cars, of course, were coming into use by then but there were still comparatively few of them. Ten years before that the only way to get to that beautiful bit of wild scenery, Montauk Point, had been to take a train to Amagansett, and then get a "rig" to drive one across the mosquito-infested Napeague Beach and about ten miles or more on to Montauk, a slow nag plowing through heavy sand. The road was improved, and I had my modest little car. It was delightful to make Montauk in an hour, without mosquitoes, and enjoy the beauty and solitude without all the old discomfort. But what has happened? The last holiday I was at home before I sold my place there were said to be two thousand cars at the Point. I admit that according to the Declaration of Independence and the New Testament there was no reason why only a privileged few should enjoy the solitude and beauty of the Point. Theoretically there is no reason why the whole million cars of New York State should not have been there instead of the half dozen of the earlier days.

Theory, however, has nothing to do with it. The plain fact is that those eight thousand people, allowing only four to a car, were not sharing what I had enjoyed before. There were no longer the empty spaces, the moorland hanging over-cliff to the sea. Instead of solitude, there were eight thousand people; instead of bare rolling downs, there was a landscape littered with lunch boxes, papers, and ginger ale bottles by the thousand. I have not the slightest objection to people enjoying themselves as they will. *De gustibus non est disputandum.* The point is that

61

by the mere fact that eight thousand people tried to enjoy the solitude and beauty of Montauk at once, the solitude and beauty evaporated. They did not get what I had had. It was simply that none of us got it. I am not discussing whether it is better for eight thousand people to have what our English cousins call "ginger-pop" and sandwiches in a mob and the fresh air than that a few should enjoy the stillness of what used to be one of the few unspoiled spots in New York, or not. The point is that "the many" did not get what the "the few" had had. Up to a certain number they might have done so. Beyond that the law began to work; and to turn eight thousand people loose on a quiet beauty spot of nature and expect returns was as absurd as for a farmer to put a thousand dollars' worth of fertilizer on every acre, or for the owner of 1 Wall Street to have built fifty stories on forty square feet only to find that all his floor space was taken up with elevator shafts instead of offices to rent. What the many got was something entirely different from what the few had got. Which of these, for the whole human race for generations to come, might be the better would baffle the mathematics of even an Einstein to figure out.

Let us take the old English inn, one of the most delightful places, when it is good, in which a wayfarer can find rest and simple comfort at a reasonable cost. It is clear that an increasing number of guests, up to a certain point, adds to the value of the inn for the guests themselves. One which had only a stray guest every few weeks, and did not pay, could not offer the facilities and ready service of one that was daily prepared for the few guests who could be relied upon to turn up from somewhere. If, however, there are too many, the place ceases to be one of comfort. If we succeed in getting a room only once in a dozen times; if every chair in the lounge is occupied; if we have to wait an hour for a meal until the mob ahead of us has eaten, not only is our comfort destroyed but that of everyone else. If, as would inevitably happen in America, the owner should add to the building, and then again, until, as I have seen so often in the last thirty years, a comfortable inn has grown into a huge caravansary housing hundreds of guests, the inn has really ceased to exist. The old Mitre at Oxford, for example, could conceivably have added a couple of hundred rooms and changed the small coffee room with its dozen chairs by the fire into a lounge that would seat a hundred. But by doing so it would have subtly ceased to exist, and the three hundred tourists who would put up at it to get the flavor of the old Mitre would seek in vain for something which their own numbers had destroyed. They would get shelter and meals but they would not get the Mitre.

In the rise of a city there is a point up to which the gain in comfort and interest is steady. We get paved streets, sewers, lights, better schools and shops, a few good theaters, perhaps, as in most European cities, an opera, a museum, and so on. Traffic is easy, people are not too crowded in their housing, can live comparatively near their work, and the advantages have not been counter-weighted with serious disadvantages. But as the city growth continues, as in the greatest of modern cities, the disadvantages begin to weigh more and more heavily. It becomes more and more difficult to secure decent living space at any price that most can pay. Land becomes so valuable that houses give way to apartments, and large apartments are subdivided into small ones, in the process we have come to know so well. People have to live farther and farther from their work, while, owing to traffic congestion, it becomes harder and harder to reach office or home. Owing to increasing costs of all sorts, the expense of doing business mounts. For many, the point has been reached at which the law has worked and the return for living in a city has begun to diminish. Individuals move into the suburbs. Factories, in many cases, move to smaller towns.

*

Let us look at labor-saving devices in the home. In order to avoid complicating the case with any question as to man's and woman's work, let us suppose a woman is earning her own income and running her home herself. The labor-saving devices she can install are already innumerable, and almost every month brings a new one. She can put in an electric washing machine, a dishwasher, vacuum cleaners, electric refrigerator, and so on indefinitely. Every one of these things is admirable in itself and undeniably saves her trouble in connection with its specific function. But there is another point. A vacuum cleaner is infinitely preferable to a broom, but it costs about sixty times as much; old-fashioned dish-washing was boring and hard on the hands but cost nothing, whereas a dish-washer is expensive; the new refrigerators are much handier than the older type, but whereas they used to cost, say, about thirty dollars, the new cost about three hundred. Garbage incinerators and various delightful and tricky contrivances in the newer apartments save trouble but mean higher rents to be paid. Now somewhere along the line there is a point up to which it will save this woman labor to work so that she can pay for all these labor-saving devices; but somewhere the law we are discussing will begin to work, and she will begin to expend so much energy and anxiety in trying to make the extra money needed to save labor in one department of her life that she is expending more than her nature permits in another. The devices, although still saving labor in one sphere, have so added to it in another that, taking life as a whole, they have ceased to function profitably.

The law works in the same way with a lot of our modern contrivances to give pleasure. Up to a certain point the possession of our modern toys, radios, cars, and so on adds to our pleasure, as do increasing numbers of bathrooms, increased luxury in hotels for those who like it, more gorgeous theaters, more costly scenery, and magnificent offices and shops; but there comes a point at which the increasing and in many cases intolerable burden of cost necessitated by these advances in number and quality of things used becomes so great as to destroy the pleasure or offset it by a still greater anxiety. In some cases the result will be to deprive the person of the pleasure entirely. For example, the opera of to-day in New York is far better than that of fifty years ago. For the ordinary music lover, who is apt not to be a hard-headed successful maker of money, there was a point somewhere where the increase in quality was not neutralized by the increase in cost; but there was also the fatal point at which the law began to work and at which the cost became so great that for him the opera, as a regularly recurring pleasure in his life, ceased to exist as completely as though there had been none at all.

Let us consider another type of case, that of the birth and up-bringing of children. The medical care surrounding childbirth is infinitely better than a generation ago, and about fifteen times as costly. The opportunities for the child in school, summer camp, mental and physical activities of all sorts are also far greater and more costly. Somewhere along the line there was a point up to which these new advantages were clear gain, like the fertilizing by the farmer, but a point was reached at which the added cost has resulted not in better and happier children but in many a family not being able to afford one. By trying to make the child, like the opera, too fine and luxurious, it has in all too many cases ceased to exist at all.

Take the involved problem of woman in business. For a while it seemed all clear gain that the unmarried woman not financially independent, the widow who had to support children and herself—all, in a word, who had to earn money—should have the whole business field open to them. But it was impossible to draw a line at which money-making ceased to be necessary and was merely desirable. As business opportunity for those who needed it became wider, more and more flocked to offices. The competition for jobs with men became keener, and as married women added their earnings to those of their husbands, the standard of living in such households was raised. The burden on the man who was trying to support a home single-handed in competition with the "two-worker" homes became greater. It may be asked, for the women themselves, whether the point is not being reached at which the law is beginning to work. On the one hand, the lower type that used to do household work is not only competing with the cheaper-paid type of man in factory or office but has thrown the manual labor of the household, which she used to do, on the higher-type woman who is capable, given time and strength, of doing something more worthwhile for social life as a whole than cooking and cleaning. On the other hand, the steadily increasing strain to maintain the single-worker home is forcing more and more women who would much rather be in the home than out of it to go to work; and the vicious tendencies are strengthened while the competition becomes fiercer and fiercer. There would seem to be already clearly indicated the working of the law and the fact that there is a point somewhere at which the gain to woman of having business open to her will be offset by the loss.

*

Let us finally consider briefly the problem of democratic government, simplifying it as much as possible. If we have government solely by an oligarchy, an aristocracy, or an upper class, there will be evils. With the best intentions, it will be to some extent a class government. It is obvious that there will be gain if other classes or interests have representation. In all modern democratic countries this representation has been given and steadily increased until we have practically universal suffrage, tempered by influences wielded by certain groups, influences losing power as democracy increases. With universal suffrage, however, the control of votes lies with the laboring class, which is the most numerous. As this class comes to realize and exert its power, the legislation becomes again class legislation, of which we have a glaring example in the steadily widening and increasing dole in England. What we do is to substitute one class for another, the so-called lower for the so-called upper. Both classes when in power will unconsciously think in terms of their own class, but the upper class is bound to have a better understanding of the extreme complexity of modern civilization, and the exercise of their power has limits in the very numbers of the lower class. A socialist government, for example, might well lay a capital levy of fifty per cent regardless of the fact that it would mean ruin for the whole country, poor as well as rich, whereas the upper class would never think of making a "labor-levy," taking fifty per cent of the labor of the country free. Somewhere along the line increased representation was an all-round gain, but we reach the point where the law begins to work, and increased representation, instead of doing away with the evils of a class government, begins to substitute the evils of government by another, and on the whole, for governing purposes, a less able class.

The possible existence of this law in all social life is not a mere theory to be toyed with. It is of just as much practical importance to us in considering our institutions as it is to the farmer in considering his fertilizing. Consider, for example, the situation in English education at this very moment. I take England rather than America because we have ignored the possibility of such a law entirely, as well as a certain range of human values, whereas in England those values, if not the law, are recognized by many. There seems to be a general impression at home that English education for the masses is a very poor affair, so far as it may be existent at all. Of course, this is not the case. There is a good system of public education, and every child has to attend school up to the age of fourteen, soon to be made sixteen. There are also the great and rapidly growing "provincial" universities, access to which is practically as easy as to our own, State and other. There is no difficulty in England for a poor boy, if he has a mind, to get an education including a university course.

But obviously, a boy from a meager home background, who has to count on his education (and his degree) getting him a remunerative job in as few days after graduation as may be possible, requires and will insist upon a different sort of education from one whose home background is rich in the best sense, that is one who has opportunities for good social and mental contacts, travel and other sorts of informal education outside his school and university, and who, while expecting to make a career later, does not have to look upon his education as narrowly heading toward some very special remunerative job but can regard it as a general broadening and developing of his mind and all his nature. That, in the past, has been the ideal of the great endowed schools like Eton and Harrow, and the universities of Oxford and, to a lesser extent, Cambridge. Such a group of students and such an ideal have created a certain type of teaching and a certain atmosphere, alien to that in most American institutions and to the public "job-training" institutions in England. To anyone who wishes to understand the situation and problem better than it can be touched upon briefly here, I commend a small volume called *Isis, or the Future of Oxford,* in the excellent "Today and Tomorrow" series, which should be read by American educators as well as English Labor politicians.

There is at present a good deal of agitation in England on this subject, the agitators claiming that the special atmosphere and opportunities of Eton, Harrow, Oxford, Cambridge, and such places, should not be confined only to the few but should be enjoyed by the many and that, in some way, the State should make it possible by financial acts of some sort for large numbers of the poorer classes to attend these institutions. A few do now, but it is quite clear, if the Laborites have their way, that the law we have been discussing will also have *its* way, and that instead of the masses enjoying Eton and Oxford, Eton and Oxford will merely evaporate. Swamped with students of the same type as those who now attend the State schools and universities, they will become like them; and instead of the many enjoying the privileges of the few, those privileges will have disappeared for everyone.

In some of the above instances I have, perhaps, stretched the strict letter of the Law of Diminishing Returns but I have, I think, indicated that there is some general law at work that is worth our studying and recognizing. It appears to be a very unfortunate one for idealists, but we do not make the universe. Such as it is we have to accept it and work with it, not against it. It is to be regretted that, having found a profitable lead, we cannot follow that lead forever but instead find that it invariably turns back on itself at some stage and gets us into trouble. It is also to be regretted that everyone cannot have everything, that eight thousand people, for example, cannot enjoy the same solitude at the same spot at once, but there seems to be something in the foundation of the universe that prohibits it, and there is no use in our insisting that the contrary is true and that the thing is possible. The cow can insist that it has as much right to follow the track in its direction as the Chicago Flyer has in its, but that does not prevent the catastrophe to the cow.

In the last century and a half we have heard a great deal about rights—"natural rights," the rights of man, woman's rights. The word is an unfortunate one for it carries an implication that somehow the universe is back of the human wishes and desires embodied in the word "right." There are, of course, no "natural rights." Nature knows nothing of rights. She knows only laws. Man, on the other hand, has ideals and aspirations. These, however, can be fulfilled only when they run with, not counter to, nature's laws, and there is no use blinking that fact.

Because a hundred dollars an acre in fertilizer will double the crop, it does not follow that five hundred dollars will quintuple it. Because a thirty-story building on a given lot is more profitable than a ten, and sixty is more profitable than thirty, it does not follow that a hundred is more profitable than sixty. Because a hundred motor cars on a given road will give people pleasure, it does not follow that a thousand will give ten times the number pleasure. Because twenty people can enjoy a beauty spot, it does not follow that two thousand can. Because going into business may benefit some women, it does not follow that it will benefit all. Because government becomes juster if the laboring class has some votes, it does not follow that it will become still juster if we give them still more. Unfortunately the reverse seems true.

There seems to be a law also that although up to a certain point we can increase the number of people who can have, see, and enjoy, if we go beyond a certain point, instead of giving everybody everything, nobody has anything. A Labor Government could destroy Eton and Oxford. They could not, with all the power in the world, give Eton and Oxford to the mob. The universe would say "you are paying no attention to my laws," and the real Eton and Oxford would disappear under the very eyes of the mob which had gone to look for them.

Is it not time that we recognized more clearly the law, or perhaps two laws, hinted at in this article? They are laws that are unfortunately hostile to many of man's aspirations and especially to much of the democratic doctrine, but that has nothing to do with their existence and power. If they are there we have got to recognize them or suffer the consequences. We have refused so far to recognize them for the simple and childish reason that we do not like their implications. We do so to some extent in our economic life but not in our social and political. May not we account in some part, at least, for the rise and fall of civilizations in the past by the working of these laws that man has declined to recognize, the law, if we separate them, that returns increase up to a certain point and then decline, and the law that if too many people strive to enjoy the same good, that good disappears? The farmer, the miner, or the business man studies to find the exact point at which, according to the Law of Diminishing Returns, advantage begins to turn into disadvantage. If there is any chance of regulating society scientifically and saving it from the recurring cycle of the rise and fall, have we not got to seek the same point for our political and social tendencies as our "practical" men do for our economics? If the farmer, the miner, and the manufacturer pay no attention to this law, they go bankrupt and are sold up. If society pays no more attention to it in the future than in the past, it will do likewise, as it has a thousand times before, and no amount of declaiming about "rights" will save it for a moment longer than the law will take to work out its own inevitable end. The rights of man, the rights of labor, the rights of woman as expressions of ideals to be worked out in harmony with nature's laws are beneficent concepts. When, however, they are proclaimed as superior to her laws they are of no more avail than the twittering of sparrows on the roof when Ætna breaks loose and the lava flows over the house.

4. THE TEMPO OF MODERN LIFE

THE NEWLY ARRIVED tourist from Europe to America receives a vast number of rather staggering impressions. Landing annually there myself, I also receive a great number, but they are in a different key from those of the foreigner. America being my own land and New York my "home town," its skyscrapers, its taxi-drivers, speak-easies, and Sunday newspapers have no novelty. They have long ceased to strike me as extraordinary. But there is one thing that never fails to strike me annually, and as unequivocally, one might say as brutally, as it does the foreigner. That is the abrupt change in the tempo of life. The trip itself in no way prepares one for it. I have made it so often that it is not in itself at all an exciting event. The six days at sea, spent mostly in sleeping, eating and reading, merely prolong, and even lower the tempo of living I left in London where my work for the most part keeps me now. But from the moment I have won my way, in fierce fight, into a taxi at the dock, I am conscious of an overwhelming change. The most recent French author to write a book on us after a few weeks' trip, in which his admiration is expressed with a violence only equalled by its lack of critical quality, notes that *"le rythme du pays tout entier est à cent quand le nôtre est à dix"*: "the rhythm of the whole country is a hundred while ours is ten." As the rhythm of London is distinctly slower than that of Paris, it is quite evident why in passing from my quiet flat off Campden Hill to a fifteenth-story room over-looking Forty-second Street I find this difference in tempo almost appalling. On my return to Europe, of course, the impression is as strong, only reversed. "On landing in England," one of the ladies of my party remarked last time, "I always feel as though someone had put a cool hand on my forehead." When we landed some weeks ago and drove to our flat through Trafalgar Square there was a larger crowd collected than I had ever seen there before. Amy Johnson, for the moment the idol of the people after her flight to Australia, had just passed on her way to be received by the King. But the contrast with New York, seven days behind us, was little short of amazing. "How strangely quiet it is," my wife said; "it's just like Sunday."

I doubt if there were any such difference noticeable in the eighteenth century. At least the book-writing traveler, whom we have always had with us, did not at that period make comments which would indicate marked difference between the pace of life here and abroad. By 1835, however, we find De Tocqueville writing that "no sooner do you set your foot upon American ground than you are stunned by a kind of tumult; a confused clamor

76

is heard on every side; and a thousand simultaneous voices demand the satisfaction of their social wants." From that day to this the difference has been markedly increasing.

But if there is a vast difference in tempo between Europe and America, there is also as great a one between the life of our own generation on each side of the water and that of our respective fathers and grandfathers on each side. It is true that some forms of nervous and useless hustle date from longer ago than we might think. One of the most characteristic scenes in America may be witnessed any morning at the Lackawanna or Erie stations on the Jersey shore when scores of commuters leap from their trains and join in a mad flight for the Tube, where the trains run to Manhattan, I believe, on a three-minute schedule. To most of those whose coat-tails fly in the breeze and whose hearts before long will begin to act queerly, the three minutes can really be of slight importance. It is merely instinctive reaction to the thought of *a* train to be caught, though a leisurely walk to the next one would serve their purpose as well and their hearts better. In Allen Nevin's delightful history of editorial writing, I find, however, that when the Fulton Ferry was new, and the fastest means of transport between Brooklyn and Manhattan, a similar scene could be witnessed daily at the slip. On the whole, nevertheless, if one thinks over the sort of life led in innumerable homes a generation ago, the fact of an immense speeding up in the process of living is clear and true. People then, as we say, "had time." Now, no one "has time." Why not? Is there really a speeding-up process at work throughout the world? And if there is, what does it consist in and what are its effects to be?

Some years ago, in a noteworthy effort to establish history on a scientific basis, Henry Adams attempted to fit certain phenomena of society into the laws of physics. He himself was quite aware of the extremely tentative nature of his suggestions, and I need not here discuss the reasons for what I believe to have been his failure, which I give elsewhere in this book. Even if Adams did not succeed, his work was immensely interesting, and I believe will receive more attention in the future than it has in the past. In his effort to bring some sort of order out of the multitudinous "facts" of human history, Adams was struck by the very point which we are considering, that is, the change in tempo, which he chose to call, in terms of physics, "acceleration." Using man's consumption of power, and the physical law of squares, as data and method, he tried to plot a curve of man's destiny. I will not here involve the reader farther in Adams's theory. He made the mistake of using concepts in one field of thought that belonged only to another. But that there is some law of acceleration at work in the universe as applied to man would seem to be true. I shall merely try to give some of the indications without myself attempting in turn any expression of them in physical laws.

*

No one knows where or when some lower form of being first took on distinctly human characteristics. It has been estimated that the Java Ape Man, *Pithecanthropus*, lived a half-million years ago. A million years have been given to the skull recently found in China. Whatever validity these guesses may or may not have, we can safely give man several hundred thousand years before he rises above the stage of stone implements and hunting. During this long period he was called on to make few adjustments to any change in environment. These were probably called forth by the terrific changes in climate due to the periods of Arctic cold, alternating with far longer periods of tropical heat. As Professor Coleman says in his *Ice Ages*, "these short spells of trial and stress meant far more for the development of the world's inhabitants than all the long periods of ease and sloth when the earth was a hothouse." He adds that, "it may be that the races of civilized men are merely evanescent phenomena bound up with the bracing climate of a brief ice-age, to sink, after a few more thousand years, into a state of tropical sloth and barbarism when the world shall have fallen back into its usual relaxing warmth and moisture, the East African conditions which have been so customary in the past." However this may be, the tempo of change, due to climate, which was all to which the hunting, eating, sleeping, breeding man of these hundreds of thousands of years had to adjust himself, was a rhythm in which

79

swings could be measured in tens of thousands of years. It was a tempo of inconceivable slowness.

As he made discoveries—fire, smelting of copper and iron, the wheel, agriculture, domestication of animals —the tempo quickened a bit, but vast spaces of time were still allowed for adjustments. Even when we get into the historical period of recorded history—a mere few thousand years compared with the hundreds of thousands behind it—we find a slow rhythm in such major social phenomena as the rise and fall of empires and civilizations. In the Far East, discarding centuries of earlier myth, we have reliable history of China for over two thousand years, and find Japan paying tribute to her before Augustus defeated Antony and Cleopatra at the battle of Actium. And Japan and China remained almost unchanged till yesterday. The civilzation in Crete can be traced from 3000 B.C. to its decadence about 1100 B.C. The art history of Egypt extends from 4000 B.C. until she was finally conquered in 525 B.C. If national periods of two and three thousand years seem long to us, yet they were brief compared to the long pulsations of climate in the dawn of man. The pulse was beating faster. The tempo of life was increasing.

I need not trace the changes in the Middle Ages and down to the nineteenth century—the introduction of gunpowder, the invention of printing, the new scientific ideas, later the discovery of America, and the opening of a new world on all sides. They are familiar to every schoolboy. The tempo of life, the need for constant readjustment was showing another great increase for the individual and for society. But even so, what we may call this third period in the history of the acceleration of our life was still slow in comparison with that next in store. A few events will give us a rough measure for the tempo prevailing in it. The thirteenth century saw the invention of the mariner's compass; the fourteenth that of gunpowder; the fifteenth, printing and the discovery of America; the sixteenth, the circumnavigation of the globe and the invention of the spinning wheel; the seventeenth, the telescope, Galileo's trial, and the first newspaper; the end of the eighteenth, the spinning jenny and the cotton gin. Each century was bringing an important invention or two, and the human mind was being called on to make increasingly rapid adjustments to new modes of thought. But the population of the world was still overwhelmingly agricultural in occupation, and the speed of communication, when there was any, was still limited to the tempo of the past ten thousand years—that of a horse by land and a sailing ship by sea. With the first successful use of the steam locomotive in 1804 and the steamboat in 1807, a new era dawned. During the next century every decade brought its discoveries which in their aggregate have completely altered the entire social structure, occupational life, and intellectual outlook of mankind. In a very general way, intended to be merely suggestive and not accurate, we may denote "wave lengths" in the tempo of life in the four periods as 30,000; 3000; 100; 10.

There are indications that in our own period, the fourth, we are not yet at the end of the process, and that the tempo is still being quickened. Take, for example, the length of the business cycle, which is the resultant of a great mass of social and psychological factors. During the nineteenth century its length was about twenty years, but many economists are of the opinion, which seems to be borne out by the facts, that under the conditions under which we now live we must expect short, sharp setbacks at much more frequent intervals; that is, that the business rhythm is essentially a faster one. The investor with long experience is fully conscious of the effect of our faster tempo. A decade or two may be all that embraces the life of a great and colossally profitable industry from its beginning to its decadence, as for example the bicycle industry of the 1890's, and the automobile industry, which has been the marvel of the world for two decades but which would seem now to be facing the much retarded pace of replacement sales instead of installation ones. The same speeding up has taken place in the life of the workman, not only in the speeding up of his daily work but in concentrating his working life between school and forty or forty-five years of age, and cutting down what was often a lifelong relation to his employer to a daily or weekly wage contract.

The reader can follow out the process for himself in almost every department of life. In art and literature "periods" follow one another with such rapidity as to be in danger of telescoping, and assume the air of mere fads.

In public taste the same quickening of rhythm is notable. Publishers will tell you that the life of a book is now considerably shorter than twenty years ago and that the profit to be made from it, if made, must be made much more quickly. The tempo of life varies with occupation and location, being slowest on the farm, though with radio and automobile, it has been greatly speeded up there. For the general tempo of our country, therefore, (and the same is more or less true of others), it is notable that whereas in 1790 about ninety per cent of the entire population lived on farms, in 1925 only twenty-five per cent did so. The tempo of their mental life, as of the population at large of all classes, may be measured by the length of time it has taken for revolutionary ideas to be taken into the intellectual outlook of the general public. Copernicus published his *De Revolutionibus Orbium Coelestium* in 1543, and I think we may say that it was a century and a half before his theory had really permeated the thinking mass. Darwin published his *Origin of Species* in 1859, and it was perhaps forty years or so before evolution was generally recognized as safe and respectable doctrine. It was hardly a few months after Einstein proclaimed his theory of relativity before it was beginning to be taken up into the general discussions and outlook of vast numbers of people, even if in a half-understood way. We may also note that whole nations, with a total population of well on to a billion, such as India, China, and Japan, have suddenly had the tempo of their lives altered from that of the very beginning of the historic period to that of the fastest pulse beat of the West. The alteration in the position of woman has been less a change in tempo perhaps than a mere added source of confusion.

But I need not labor the point longer. It seems to me that as we survey the entire past of man the fact emerges clearly that his life shows a perpetually increasing tempo. The movement grows always faster, never slower. The phenomenon would appear to be a law of nature, though our knowledge is not of a sufficiently exact sort to enable us to establish reference points for the plotting of an accurate curve. Such a curve, however, if we accept roughly the four periods noted above, would show a very long, slowly ascending line for the first period; a sharp upward swing at the beginning of the historic period, and a more rapidly ascending line for a shorter length; another sharp deflection upward around the Middle Ages, and a yet shorter rising line; and lastly, for us to-day, a very sharp upward turn and a very short but almost vertically rising line to 1930. Given that much, the makers of graphs may amuse themselves by plotting it into our future. The optimists might not be satisfied with the result, but after all we must not press the graphic representation too far. Let us try to search the more immediate future a little without the aid of the law of squares.

*

At this point, if the reader has followed me thus far, he may ask just what do we mean, after all, by the "tempo of life"? Perhaps a clearer definition would be wise before we attempt to appraise the effect of an accelerated tempo on man. Whether any more "events" are happening in the universe now than in earlier times would lead us into unfathomable bogs of metaphysics, but for our purpose it is enough to grant that more events are happening to each man of which he is conscious. In other words, a resident of New York to-day is getting more sensations and of a more varied sort than the Neanderthal or early man of several hundreds of thousands of years ago. Owing to this number and variety of sensations and his constantly shifting environment, modern man is also called upon to make a far greater number of adjustments to the universe than was his remote relative in the caves and forests of Germany or Java. It is the number of these sensations and adjustments in a given time that makes the tempo of life. As the number and variety of sensations increase, the time which we have for reacting to and digesting them becomes less, as it does also for adjusting ourselves to our environment when that alters at an advancing rate. The rhythm of our life becomes quicker, the wave lengths, to borrow a physical concept, of that kind of force which is our mental life grow shorter. If I am right in what I have outlined in a somewhat vague and general fashion above, our mental life has altered its

85

rhythm four times, each time the wave length of the force growing shorter, the vibration more rapid. Does this have any effect upon us? I think there is no question but what it does.

Rhythm in the universe is fundamental in its effect upon our minds. For example, certain rhythmical waves of energy (to use a loose term), of long wave length and low frequency, make themselves known to us as heat; increase the rhythm a little by shortening the wave length and increasing the frequency, and we become aware of them as color; continue the process, and we get electricity; do so again, and we get a phenomenon which we can use but cannot perceive by our senses, the X-rays; and so on. A change of rhythm, whatever it may be in reality, is for us a change in essential nature.

I do not wish to press physical concepts too far and so I suggest an effect of rhythm which we encounter whenever we read poetry, and, though we are less conscious of it, prose. Certain sorts of thought or emotion go with certain rhythms. Let us take at haphazard two quotations from Shakespeare. The first is in the rhythm of "Yankee Doodle."

King Stephen was a worthy peer,
His breeches cost him but a crown;
He held them sixpence all too dear,
With that he called the tailor down.

Now let us take another:

86

To die, to sleep;
To sleep: perchance to dream: ay, there's the rub;
For in that sleep of death what dreams may come
When we have shuffled off this mortail coil,
Must give us pause. . . .

Neither of these series of thoughts could be expressed in the rhythm of the other without profoundly altering its effect on us. There is something in ourselves, some long-established rhythm of our own, which reacts in various ways to the rhythms of the outer world. A marked alteration in the tempo of life might, therefore, be expected to alter profoundly, possibly disastrously, our reactions. To use an extreme example: if, owing to a sudden shift, heat waves became sensed by us as light, and electricity as heat, and light as X-rays, we should become so completely out of adjustment that the result would be a breakdown. To a lesser but a real extent, the same result comes from a sudden change in the tempo of our lives. We are all familiar with the effect which sudden wealth is apt to have upon its acquirer. It is because there has been for him a sudden change in tempo—a great increase in the number and variety of sensations and in the number of called-for adjustments.

One marked effect, both for good and evil, in a rapidly changing environment is the difficulty or impossibility of acquiring habits. To cite a simple example, last year I knew where almost everything I wanted in New York was—my broker, bank, the Consolidated ticket office, my friends' homes and telephone numbers. When I was there this year almost every one had shifted. I had to learn them all over again. My habits had become utterly useless, indeed, worse, for they led me in wrong directions. This break-up of habit may have had the advantage of leading me to new places and buildings, but, on the other hand, life becomes too wearing and impossible without habits. We have to perform a great many acts as easily as walking or eating or we waste an enormous amount of energy for nothing, just as we should if we had to watch over our stomachs for an hour after each meal to see that they digested properly. A considerable habit-pattern is essential for the release of our minds for more important things. The illustration which I have drawn from mere changes in street addresses may be extended to our whole intellectual life and our system of ethics. A certain fluidity in habits is healthful. Too complete a breakdown of the habit-patterns may spell disaster.

Too violent a change in tempo and a too-constantly changing environment tends also to impair the power of concentration on which most of man's highest satisfactions and his chance of improvement depend. As we rise in the scale from the lowest forms of sensual to the highest spiritual and intellectual enjoyments, the need for concentration is correspondingly increased. I do not mean that sense enjoyments do not play a very important rôle in our life and mental health. They do. Our body also plays an essential one in permitting us

88

to function at all as self-conscious beings; but the human race would not have advanced far had it never risen above the performance of mere bodily functions and the enjoyment of sensations, nor will either the individual or the race advance which retrogrades in the power of concentrated thought. It is impossible or very difficult for most people to concentrate and think except with a certain amount of leisure and freedom from intrusion, whether the intrusion be that of a visitor or a distracting sensation. If I may illustrate by my personal experience, I may say that I have, I believe, a fair power of concentration due in part to my having had to learn to work in all sorts of places and under all sorts of conditions. On the other hand, I am, I suppose, attuned to the rhythm of life of my earlier American days, a rhythm about like that of England to-day. In passing from the tempo of life there, where my work keeps me a good deal of the time, to America I am at once conscious of increasing difficulty in concentrating and of a marked difference in the kind and quality of my work, a difference which my publishers recognize as well. I react at home to an incredible number of passing impressions but find it hard to sit quietly and ponder them over. In other words, a hailstorm of sensations—they may be merely noises—and an unaccustomed increase in the general tempo are bound to produce in most people the complex of what we call "the tired business man." Losing the power of concentration in thought, we sink lower and lower to live our lives on the plane of sensation.

Some change, as rest, is essential, and when by evening
we are weary of the sensations to which we have been
accustomed all day, there is nothing left to change to—
in a life lived on the plane of sensation—but other sensations. Once we have made the simple division of sensations into agreeable and disagreeable, the scale of value
for them becomes purely quantitative, and we prefer
the more intense to the less intense. The consequence
is that such a life tends to become a mere search for
more and more exciting sensations, undermining yet
more our power of concentration in thought. Relief from
fatigue and ennui is sought in mere excitation of our
nerves, as in speeding cars or emotional movies.

Such a life tends to break down the individual personality, and merge all individuals in the mob. People
are much alike in their primitive emotions, as they are
in their bodily organs and functions. It is only when they
rise into the realms of thought and will that they develop
into marked individuals. A suddenly accelerated tempo
thus has a strong tendency to lower the whole population to the level of the mob, and to melt down the variety
of personalities into a gelatinous mass of humanity
flavored with a few pungent sensations.

As I noted above with regard to habit, a certain
fluidity is desirable so as to prevent our habit-patterns
from attaining too great a rigidity, and our type of civilization from petrifying. A change in environment is also
good in so far as it stirs, without breaking down, our
power of thought and will. As I have tried to show else-

where in this volume, however, there is at work in nature a law of diminishing returns. This law indicates that all tendencies and forces operating on our human life, although they may operate beneficially for a while, always attain to a point at which the returns begin to diminish, the benefit is lost, and the effect of operation may even become disastrous. At the present stage in our history we are faced by the very serious problem as to whether those forces which throughout man's career have been steadily increasing the rhythm or tempo of his life, and which have operated beneficially so far, have reached the point of the diminishing return.

There is no use closing our eyes to the possibilty that this may be so. There is a good deal of evidence that maladjustment to the new tempo is reaching the point of possible breakdown. We may cite a few figures which indicate the effects of the altered rhythm on our nervous systems. The great increase of nervous disorders of all sorts is notable, but I have no statistics at hand for them as an entire group. We may note, however, that between 1920 and 1927 the deaths from heart disease per hundred thousand population in America, pre-eminently the land of hustle, increased steadily from 137 to 241. Both in England and America the increase in the ratios of insanity have long been alarming. It was estimated even before the War that if the steady rate of increase shown in England and Wales were maintained, the entire population would have become insane in two centuries more. In the United

States between 1880 and 1923, the latest date I have, the number of patients in hospitals for mental disease tripled, rising, without break, from 81 to 245 per 100,000. The continuation of any such tendencies is appalling to contemplate. Between 1889 and 1927 the number of divorces per thousand marriages rose steadily from 60 to 160. In the large American cities to which the population drift is strongly marked, the rate of homicides rose from 3.4 in 1900 to 10.1 in 1927. New York, with a population of ten millions in the metropolitan area, is planning for a population of twenty millions within another generation. Within the past generation the figures indicating the instability of the home, the instability of man's mind, and those for the most serious crime against his person have all tripled. Even making all allowances, we have here alarming evidence of increasing maladjustment to the new tempo of life. We might, without statistical help, pursue this maladjustment in its other effects, such as the enormous increase in the machinery of life, politically and economically, without corresponding increases in our ability to foresee, manage, and control, with a resultant increase in stability of the whole social structure. Or we might note the increase in mob spirit and mob influence, the increasing emergence of mob psychology as a determining factor in social life. But enough has been indicated to show the seriousness of the situation.

A friend of mine, a distinguished explorer and anthropologist, once spent a couple of years among the savages of the upper Amazon. On one occasion he was suddenly called out to civilization, and, with the help of the chief and a train of attendants, he attempted a forced march of three days through the jungle to the nearest settlement. Without grumbling the party made extraordinary speed for the first day and the second. On the third morning, however, when it was time to start, my friend found all the natives sitting on their haunches, looking very solemn and making no preparation to leave. On asking the chief what the trouble was he received the answer, "They are waiting. They cannot move farther until their souls have caught up with their bodies." I can think of no better illustration of our own plight to-day. Is there any way of letting our souls, so to say, catch up again with our bodies, or attuning ourselves to the new tempo of life?

We certainly cannot do it so easily as the Amazonian savages. They could reduce the tempo by the simple process of sitting still. We cannot. As I have pointed out, the speeding-up process in human life appears to be imbedded in the universe. The "wave lengths" of our life have been steadily getting shorter, the rhythm faster, by a process over which we have no control. It has been going on for hundreds of thousands of years, with perhaps the four periods of marked acceleration to which I have called attention. Scientific discovery, whether cause or effect of the latest acceleration in tempo, cannot be halted without a complete collapse of our civilization which is based upon it. We must now go on, seeking new inventions, new sources of power, or crash—a civilization in a nose dive. What, then, are the possibilities?

*

There is, of course, the one that scientific discovery will cease to progress, that new discoveries will come less frequently, that we shall use up our present sources of power without discovering the new ones our captains of industry so confidently but ignorantly predict. That cure would, in the end, be almost worse than the disease. It would entail an almost unthinkable cataclysm.

The only hope would seem to lie in the possibility of our adjusting ourselves to the shorter wave length, the swiftened tempo of our existence, as the race has in the past. It is possible that with each succeeding increasing in tempo man's powers of adjustment have also been quickened, and that the sinister phenomena we see at present are merely the wreckage of a period of change. It is either that or, like a fly-wheel which turns faster and faster until it reaches the rate at which it breaks to pieces, human society and the human mind may also explode into bits.

If we are to become adjusted, it is evident that in some way we have got to order our lives differently. We have got to bring back, in the new, quickened tempo, some sense of leisure, and secure for ourselves a respite from the hailstorm of sensation and need for constant adjustment, some new habit patterns, that will enable

94

us to control ourselves nervously, to rise above the plane of sensation, and to concentrate on the things of the spirit. Only thus can we regain control of our individuality and our lives in the whirling flux into which we shall otherwise dissolve. This calls for an intelligent ordering of our existence, for selection from among the goods of life, for the exercise of self-control—in a word, for intelligence and will.

For this I think we can look only, or mainly, to the younger generation among the privileged classes. I use the whole phrase advisedly. The older generation is too set in certain ways of living, in certain requirements of life, too involved in the whole economic system of creating new wants to make new business to make more money to supply all their old wants plus the new ones, to be of much assistance in the great adjustment that is ahead. On the other hand, the lower or unprivileged classes (I use the term in no snobbish sense) are everywhere and in all countries too dazzled by their new toys and new power, too confused by their new wealth of sensation, too untrained in the higher values of life, to be of assistance either. One need only watch the crowds on Broadway, the block-long queues waiting admission to the hundred cinemas of London, the aimless, shuffling masses nightly walking the Kulverstraat in Amsterdam, and similar crowds in every large city, to realize that if they revolt on finding their lives devoid of satisfaction it will be only to secure a yet greater share in the life of sensation.

The hopeful point to-day is that the revolt of intel-

95

ligent and trained youth is not for mere independence or for money-making but for a better ordering of their whole lives for regaining in some way the chance to become fully rounded human beings and not mere cogs in a machine. In many cases they think they are fighting the older generation. What they are really fighting against is the time-spirit, the increased tempo of life. The older generation has merely been mired in the historic process like antediluvian monsters that have floundered into an asphalt lake.

The effort to reorganize life by selection and emphasis so as to regain leisure and personality and to rise above the mob-complex of sensation is a race between adjustment and collapse. The life of the human spirit has been an amazing adventure from the start. Nobody knows why it has any place in the universe. Nobody knows what it is. But it has been going on for hundreds of thousands of years. It has been attacked by all sorts of forces, within and without humanity itself. So far it has won its battles, and it has always been led to victory by a select band. Speed and the power to give direction have been in the few; the weight of mass in the many. Both speed and mass are now colossal. If the balance can be maintained, all may yet be well, in spite of the quantitative increase in each. But if the few pass spiritually over to the many, only mass without direction will remain. This has happened to too great an extent in our America in the past few generations. The few, like the many, have given themselves over to material goods and the pleasure of sensation. Abandoning themselves to the pursuit of rapid wealth, worshipping physical comfort and spurious luxury, overwhelmed by the multitude of distractions afforded by every new toy of science, they have tended to lose their sense of human values. It is precisely in the rejection by the younger generation of the standards of values of the older generation, in so far as those standards have debased human values, that I believe the hope of the world lies to-day. Mistakes will be made. They always have been by every generation, and the wine of the new freedom has been too strong for many a head. But if the younger generation—as the more intelligent among it seem determined to do—will re-establish a scale of human values and select from among the wealth of material provided for it those factors that alone conduce to the enjoyment of those values, even in the new tempo of life, leisure and deep satisfactions may again return for all, and mankind may once again have made its adjustment to the new rhythm forced upon it. With each change of tempo man's mind has become somewhat different, and has itself become quickened in proportion to the tempo. With each change the period allowed for readjustment becomes shorter, rhythm vastly faster. The corners must be turned more and more quickly if the process continues. The plotting of the curve may before many generations be followed with tense nerves. Will the law of diminishing returns begin to be felt in the law of increasing tempo? Or will the latter, like the former, at some point, as seems to be indicated, turn back upon itself? Have we attained that point already, or is the younger generation destined to carry the line still forward for a while? Perhaps no greater crisis ever faced adventurous youth. Democracy may be a passing experiment in the struggle for happiness. It is at any rate a mere tool which may or not in the long run prove useful. It is not to make the world safe for that that the fight with the cosmic force of the time-spirit must be waged. It is for any continued possibility of sane, contented, rounded human lives for as many as may be who can learn to live them. If the intelligent youth of the new generation cannot make the adjustments to the new tempo, cannot create a new social life of human value within the rhythmic framework of the new tempo, democracy and all other catchwords of our day will signify as little as the last moaning of the wind when the ship has sunk below the waves.

II

1. KENSINGTON GARDENS AND LAFAYETTE SQUARE

MAKING MY FIRST European tour at the receptive if somewhat unappreciative age of three, I have been repeating the crossing at steadily decreasing intervals ever since, annually now for many years. London and Paris are as familiar to me as New York and Washington, and Amsterdam more so than Boston. Not that I am not tolerably well acquainted with my native country. If I did not see America first, I have at least been in all but five of the States, and in most of the larger cities from Maine to Oregon, and from Texas to Minnesota. I did indeed visit Vienna before I did Butte, Montana, and, if for understandable reasons I have returned to Vienna whereas I have not to Butte, I trust it will not be imputed unto me as unrighteousness. Nor have I merely scrambled over several tens of thousands of miles of the U. S. A. while living, and making a living, there. When, for example, I went to Idaho, it was not for scenery but to travel up and down the line of a bankrupt railway in the cab of my own engine (with a rifle for possible game), and to make a report upon how the unfortunate owners could best recoup their loss. When I went through twenty-odd States, some years ago, it was to find out at first hand from every possible type of American business man what conditions were. If in the past few years both my work and acquaintance have changed, and if I now see somewhat more of scholars and writers than of business types, that has simply rounded out an experience. I have been a member of the Farmer's Grange and of the Massachusetts Historical Society. The first convention I ever attended was a cattlemen's in Ft. Worth, Texas; the last was a meeting of the American Historical Association; and both were essential to know America.

Two years ago I decided that I knew my homeland moderately well as long resident and native son. I knew Europe as a tourist, to be sure a frequent and somewhat leisurely one, but still a tourist. I had been in many of the countries, had sometimes stayed for months at a time in a few of the larger cities, and had scattered acquaintances from the Arno to the Thames, but I had lived only in hotel bedrooms and with no more impedimenta than would go in handbags. Clearly a foreigner who came to New York for a couple of months, put up at a conveniently located hotel, went sight-seeing, and was dined and wined or watered by a gradually made acquaintance would get many impressions, but he would not live himself into the life as he would if he made a home and stayed for some years. The inference was clear, and so my wife and I left our comfortable London hotel, took a flat overlooking Kensington Gardens, lined the walls with my library, and "settled in." We have not been visiting London. We have been living, and making a living, here, acquiring all the new impressions that we hoped to gain therefrom. Our first year is ended, and in a few months we are going to America. The library, pictures, and Queen Anne mahogany are soon to be packed and put in storage, and as I sit looking about the large, high-ceilinged room, with its books and fire, so different from the tiny one which we had for the same price on Brooklyn Heights last year, I have been trying to sort out my impressions as a resident.

All the old charms we felt as tourists are still as potent as ever, familiarity having bred no contempt but merely greater affection. The galleries, the buildings, the quaint bits, the delight of old streets and associations, the parks, all those things that belong to the receptive tourist, persist with as great an attraction for the resident. I shall not dwell on certain advantages of a physical sort, such as the relief for old strap-hangers of the New York subway to find an "underground" that is swift but never crowded and in which a seat is almost invariably waiting; or the pleasure of being able to go to and from most of one's destinations on the top of a bus in the fresh air, passing much of the way by lawns and trees. As I sit and think, what I am trying to discover are not the comforts but the more subtle effects of living here on mind and spirit.

There is at least one such effect which is very marked, and which explains in part what I had not before been able to understand in the English mind. We have scholars in America, even in politics, and there is no more attractive type to be found in any country than the cultivated American gentleman. But, comparing type for type in the two countries, I have always found, or thought I have, a wider range of interest, a more philosophical playing with ideas, in the Englishman of any given type than in his American cousin. I pointed to this once elsewhere when comparing our scholars in politics with the English: our Lodge, Roosevelt, Wilson with their Balfour, Morley, Haldane, or Smuts. The Englishman seems to range over wider and more philosophical fields than the American. It is not simply the difference between the amateur and professional spirit which accounts for so much in the differing attitudes of cultivated men in either country. Smuts, as soldier, statesman, administrator, and philosopher, cannot be considered as merely amateur. His is no shallow versatility. But it has always been somewhat of a marvel to me since boyhood how men could accomplish so much in such varied fields, how they could even, to pose the problem in its simplest term, find the time.

Take, for example, Lord Haldane. Working up from comparative poverty, borrowing money to begin his career, he developed a law practice which not only brought him in a hundred thousand dollars a year but was extremely distinguished and complex. Once in a single fortnight he had to argue appeals from various parts of the world involving the Buddhist law of Burma, the Maori law of New Zealand, the old French law of Quebec, the

Roman-Dutch law of South Africa, the Mohammedan and Hindu laws of India, the Scotch law, and the Norman Custom of the Island of Jersey. He spent much time in Parliament, occupied many public offices, leading up to Lord Chancellor, and was pronounced by Kitchener to be the "greatest Secretary of State for War that England ever had"; yet his published works include nineteen volumes, mostly philosophical, such as his "Pathway to Reality," "Reign of Relativity," "Philosophy of Humanism," his three-volume translation of Schopenhauer, and so on.

The scholars in politics that we have had have been mostly American historians, such as the three mentioned above. The type of mind called for in the writing of such books as Lodge's "English Colonies in America," Roosevelt's "Winning of the West," or Wilson's "History of the American People" is entirely different from that called for by the works of Morley, Haldane, Balfour, or Smuts. The minds of these latter are in direct line with the wider culture of the Renaissance.

I have named only the scholars in politics, but the same comparison holds good among men of mind in other departments of national life. We do not expect an American professor of astronomy to reinforce a scientific point with a quotation from Shakespeare or Milton or to pass readily from hydrodynamic equations to poetry, as does Eddington. In pondering over such men while in America, I had mournfully come to the conclusion that there was something different in the texture of the English mind.

As a matter of fact, however, Smuts, though he has spent much time in England, is not English, and the difference applies to the Continental mind as well as to the English. What American statesman of to-day, for example, would leave two such volumes as Clemenceau's *In the Evening of My Thought*?

Going to Europe, year after year, as tourist, I realized, of course, the tremendous mental and æsthetic stimulation to be derived from all that one saw and came into contact with over here. I would return home every time keen on all sorts of new trails, but, at once involved in the great American game of paying one's bills, life closed in again, and "No Thoroughfare" signs were soon seen at the opening of every trail except one's own professional one.

I surely need not say that if I use myself as an illustration it is not with any absurd thought of ranking myself with the minds already mentioned; but something interesting has happened to my own mind over here, as resident, that throws its own small ray of light on my old problem of how the English or European mind accomplished so much in so many fields.

I have done more work over here in quantity, and my editors and publishers tell me better in quality, than I ever did in a year at home. Yet I have actually worked only about seven and a half months in all and in the other five or so, at intervals, have wandered over France, Belgium, Holland, Germany, Austria, Italy, Switzerland, Czecho-Slovakia, Denmark, and Sweden. Ideas have flowed into my mind as never before, and although I have travelled for nearly five months and written over 250,000 words in the other seven, the interesting point is that I have discovered that I have had the time and the inclination for all sorts of reading I could not "get in" in New York. It has not been without surprise that I find myself re-reading Goethe's "Faust," Marcus Aurelius, Epictetus, Sophocles, Æschylus, Shakespeare, and other books that seemed never likely to leave my shelves again at home. I have for the first time read through all of "Paradise Lost" and the whole of Dante as well as a good bit in current science and philosophy. Thinking harder and writing faster than I did at home, there is leisure for all sorts of things. How does it happen?

I think that there are two facts that in part explain it. One is that there is no friction here in daily life. That may seem to be a small matter, but I have come to the conclusion that it is not. At every turn the contacts of life are oiled by good nature and courtesy. Social life here, by which I mean every human contact whether with a subway guard, a shop clerk, a taxi-driver, or one's distinguished hostess, moves as on a perfect bearing. Daily life here is tremendously "efficient" as compared with America, where the friction has become terrific. I could supply numberless details and instances to prove this point, enough to make an essay in themselves, but for lack of space can only assert the plain fact that the whole business of daily life in England instead of wearing one to a frazzle leaves one unfatigued physically and untroubled mentally. In running a car we know well enough that if we forget the oil we shall burn out the bearings. We Americans too often forget the oil in our own daily contacts everywhere, and we wear ourselves out without reason.

But this marvellous ease in daily life, which can be appreciated to the full only by the resident rather than by the tourist, is but the foundation for the ability to indulge in a wider range of interests and a more philosophical outlook. There is another point. We in America are much like people living on a ship. We live, as the passengers and the crew of a vessel, a life of our own and are cut off from the rest of the world. The continuity has been snapped when we left the dock. American history is made to begin in 1492 or 1783 as you please. I recently had an appeal from the Society for the Preservation of New England Antiquities, a society with whose aims I am in hearty sympathy. These "antiquities" date from around 1640 to 1700. I am about to go to Italy where there are houses that have been steadily rented for a thousand years or more. It is true that we were an offshoot of England and that the history of the British Empire back of 1783 is our history, but it is not generally so regarded. What would happen if someone suggested a statue of Edward the Confessor or Oliver Cromwell on Bowling Green? We go back about three hundred years and stop short. History before that is foreign, and we study it with almost the detachment, though not the calm, of a Japanese.

Here, on the other hand, one comes insensibly to feel oneself as a part of the whole stream of western European civilization from the Greeks onward. It is not simply that the tangible monuments are all about one, that twenty minutes from my flat in one direction is Westminster Abbey emblazoning the whole pageant of English history, or that twenty minutes in another are the finest sculptures from the Parthenon. It is something much more subtle than that. It is a sense of continuity, in spite of vast changes and countless revolutions. Here in London, reading Confucius or the Vedas is something like reading the classics at home. I appreciate them intellectually, but they are alien to the whole complex of the civilization about me, something I am separated from in a hundred ways and reach only by pure intellectual process. On the other hand, here, Æschylus, Plato, Marcus Aurelius, or Dante are in the direct line that leads from Athens through Rome and Florence to my flat by Kensington Gardens. Stuart Sherman once pleaded that much greater emphasis should be placed on American literature in our education on the ground that, although it might be thin and inferior to the European, it was better qualified, merely because it was native, to bring home to us the life of people who lived under our own national conditions. The contention had some truth in it, for even great thought loses some of its power to mould us if it is not closely akin to the whole inherited *milieu* of our contemporary thought and outlook. In spite of jealousies and strife, it has been realized since the Great War that there is a unity to the European mind, geographically and historically. That mind has an inestimable advantage over ours in that the greatest literature the world has produced is not alien but akin to it. It does not have to submit itself to the discipline of the second- or third-rate because those alone possess that quality of kinship which has to replace the lack of greatness. The American mind has been disinherited; the European one is a direct heir.

I do not claim that there may not be some compensating advantages in the wholly fresh start that America has, perforce, made; but I do think that until one has really lived here one does not realize how completely fresh that start is, and, in the good old phrase, "you cannot have your pie and eat it too." You cannot have life both ways. You cannot have the advantages of a clean break and keep the advantages of continuity. In America there is a present and a future and a comparatively negligible past. Here there is a present and a future and an immensely important past. The kind of mind unconsciously developed in a two-dimensional world is different from that developed in a three-dimensional one.

And so as I finish this page and turn to my fire to read Robert Bridges's *Testament of Beauty,* which, had it come out last year, I at least would never have had time to read in New York, I wonder if living over here has not to some extent solved for me the problem of the breadth and philosophy of the English mind. One works steadily and hard, but with no friction and with a sense of leisure. One has somehow become Lord of the Manor of one's own soul. One's mind, no longer hurried and harried, no longer crushed and crumpled by a sense of pressure, smooths itself out. Without effort it responds to the tradition of the civilization of which it forms a part—a tradition which is in the best sense philosophical, and which is embodied in tangible shape in a thousand forms about one. In spite of the so-called complexity of an old civilization, life really is simpler here, its outlines clearer. The toys and tools of life, its motors and radios, somehow take their proper place *as* toys and tools, amusing or useful, and the great realities become again realities— life and death, joy and sorrow, art, love, thought, Fate. As one lives in London and contrasts it with New York, it is as though a turbulent flood, carrying all the flotsam and jetsam of needless things and needless struggles, had subsided and left uncovered again the old landscape of the human heart. The problems of that heart begin to occupy one as naturally here as do its toys at home. Homer and Æschylus again become our kin; the flippancy of an Erskine shrivels before the fire of a Marlowe, and Helen once more becomes the beauty that fires men's souls. And so, I step out on my balcony and wonder, as I look over the lawns and trees in Kensington Gardens, how it will all seem when in a few weeks I am once again only one of the million scurrying ants in Times Square, a transitory spark in the blast furnace of American "prosperity," a link in the endless chain of production, distribution, consumption. What, after all, is the best use to make of this dream we call life? The dusk has fallen. The curtains are drawn. The fire glows, and I turn to *The Testament of Beauty*.

KENSINGTON GARDENS, LONDON,
JANUARY, 1930.

I have now been in America for four months, and I try to sort out some of the innumerable impressions which, staccato, I have received in this virile, incomparably hustling, and energetic life. Never before have I been so occupied every instant with activity of one sort or another. It has been enormously interesting. Much of it has been wholly delightful. Most of it has been colored with good nature and kindness. And I am infinitely tired. I have to whip my mind. That, perhaps, at the moment is the clearest impression of all.

Another, an equally clear and more emphatic one, is that I can never more look forward to living again in my birthplace, the city of New York. Nor am I at all singular apparently in my opinion of the impossibility of enjoying a quiet, thoughtful, sane, and nervously wholesome life in what has come to be in effect one vast and hustling business office. Among all my friends over here, who assuredly cannot be accused of any lack of patriotism, I have found only one who has a good word to say for our greatest city, in which one gets the impression of something vast, inhuman, at times sinister, incredibly active, and fantastically insane. Even a banker told me he was sometimes seized with a sensation of terror in it. In view of the fact that the skyscrapers have ruined all the human qualities and comforts of the city, the race to build a higher one every month can only be considered as pathological. What kind of life will be led in the subways and congested bottoms of dark canyons a decade or more hence, if the present trend keeps up, is impossible to forecast. As I looked from my window on the fifteenth floor of the hotel, it was to strain my neck to gaze upward at scores of stories towering above me in the building across the street, or to look northward across a chaotic jumble of roofs and towers as appallingly inhuman as the Grand Canyon or the Bad Lands. There was not a tree or a leaf or anything that suggested the possibility of man or kindly nature having had a hand in the formation of the chaos of steel and stone. It was as ghastly in its way as the dead landscape around Butte.

One need not here be long engaged in the effort to accomplish any of the ordinary business of life to find that a large part of the apparent activity and of one's own exertions is merely costly waste motion. One gets the impression, for example, that all things, even the buildings themselves, are engaged in some strange fantastic dance as unmeaning as the "jerks" of old camp meeting days. While I had been abroad, my safe deposit company had gone out of business owing to a merger. My boxes had had to be transferred and held in another institution until my return, so that one of my first duties was to locate them. That done, I had them taken (under armed guard, of course) to another bank fifty feet away. I had just got them stowed there when, happening to mention that I would be in Europe next January, I was told that my new company would be moving then, and a fresh complexity was put up to me to be solved. A week after I landed, the firm of brokers through whom I make my small investments moved to a new skyscraper. My bank is to move in a few months. Going to where I had last left the Consolidated Ticket Office, I found it had moved five blocks. Going to see an editor, I found that the office had been moved three days before. A moving van company with which I had some business shifted its address in the midst of the transaction. The hotel where I first put up was suddenly sold, and the guests, some of whom had been there for several years, were given one day's notice to leave. Being out of town at the moment, I had to rescue the baggage I had left there, by long distance telephone from Washington. My sister, who had been promised in writing a room there for six weeks, was told on her arrival from Tennessee in the evening, that she would be allowed to spend only the night. My whole list of telephone numbers made up a few months before was useless owing to moved offices and homes or to changes in centrals.

And when one is once in connection with the concern so precariously housed, one's wasted efforts by no means cease. It is not my own complaint alone but, I find, a very common one that in the present over-organization of business the frequency of mistakes has become intolerable. In connection with one simple banking transaction I had to make four separate trips to Wall Street before a successive lot of errors was finally corrected. Another financial institution "lost" $500 for five weeks, only to find at the end that it had had it all the time but in "the wrong department." From another business concern, apparently "highly organized," I had in one day four letters, each from a separate official in a different department but all relating to the same business and all calling for answer. An instance may be cited in connection with this very article. Usually my wife or I do the typing of the final copy, but in this case I employed a stenographer who agreed to copy my eighteen pages at twenty cents a page, or $3.60. She sent in the work, five hours late, with a bill for $10.40, having by wide margins and other contrivances expanded my eighteen pages to twenty-six and doubling the agreed rate per page! After much annoying controversy we compromised on $5.20

Each of these matters taken separately may seem small but as the days go by the amount of wasted energy and mental irritation involved in doing things that should take no energy at all is immense. And this is a matter of no slight concern in a city which calls for more energy than any other I know of in the world for the ordinary business of living even if the machinery worked smoothly For one thing, the excessive cost of living, notably in rent and service, even if one tries to content oneself with a pitiably small modicum of space, privacy, and quiet, puts the ordinary man to a strain of striving that leaves little or no energy for anything else. For a literary man the necessity for a steady output of immense quantity merely to pay bills soon becomes fatal. One could name, in all kindness, many who have or had genuine creative ability and the power to do work of distinction who under the insistent pressure have become merely sluiceways for pouring out copy.

The pressure and restlessness are increased, even in those who are intellectually superior to any wish to "keep up with the Joneses," by the rapid changes in the standards of living and the fact that scarcely anyone has a definite goal. There being no stability in life, there can be none in one's plans. The fact that everyone is engaged in a struggle to make enough money to pay his bills, and that the bills increase annually, and that no one stops at any given point and says he will remain satisfied, creates the sense of some mad whirl of damned souls on the winds of Hell in Dante. That there is much dissatisfaction with this condition is evident enough, but all seem caught in a process in which they are powerless to live sanely. The nervousness engendered and the astounding amount of organization of all sorts, make for increased and largely meaningless engagements and duties. On landing in New York I had to call a committee meeting of three men to consider an important official matter. There was only one hour in the course of the next week when all were free at the same time. Another meeting of four in an evening had to wait for three weeks for the same reason. Everyone complains, but all go on like helpless dogs in a treadmill.

If one wishes to rest and to change the current of his

thought, there is no place where he can do so. There are no quiet spots to which one can retire outdoors, and the richest city in the world is incomparably poor in any means of simple and agreeable recreation. One walks in the midst of hurrying throngs. One may risk a speakeasy. If in desperation one thinks of near-by country, one can find only hotels ranging from ten to eighteen dollars a day in which one can get no benefit unless one plays golf or has a car. There may be others known to the initiated, but whereas in any big city in Europe one can easily run to the country sure of a comfortable inn at a moderate price without any searching, in New York the problem is almost as difficult as finding a good glass of Chambertin. I have discovered it is little wonder that editors complain it is becoming increasingly difficult to get thoughtful, considered, more or less philosophical articles. One of them asked me on landing to give him my idea for articles when I had been here a fortnight. At the expiration of the time I had to confess that although I had never been so busy in my life and had had innumerable impressions, I "had not had time" (how incessantly one hears the phrase here) to develop a single idea.

It is often said that New York is not America, and I should try some of the smaller places—New Haven, Cambridge, or others. The first statement, of course, is true, but there is also another thing to be said. New York *is* our American metropolis. Compared with it, all these smaller places are provincial, however delightful in many other aspects of living. The only city of our own which we can compare with London is New York. These smaller places must be compared with the provincial towns of England, such as Manchester, Bath, or, if you will, Oxford and Cambridge. In the provincial towns of both countries you miss some of the things that only a metropolis affords—the sense of being the centre of the country's life, the possibility of infinitely varied social and intellectual contacts, music and the theatre, the succession of exhibitions of art. It seems to me to be a national calamity that in our own greatest city, which possesses these things in abundance and with high excellence, the increasing difficulty of leading a sane, comfortable, comely life should be becoming insuperable for many of us. Only the young can stand it.

After some weeks of New York I fled to Washington, known of old and this time even more heartily hospitable than ever. It may be that Washingtonians are no kinder than the dwellers in our other cities, for we are essentially a kindly and helpful folk, but assuredly there can be few who surpass them. The city is also the most beautiful I know in our own land. The mere fact that it contains more trees than any other in the world, with Paris second, is in itself something for which to be deeply grateful. As I sit in my large old-fashioned room, with a gingko tree swaying at one window and with wistaria vines drooping over the other, both affording a view of Lafayette Square with its forest wealth of unusual species, I realize, after the horror of almost treeless New York, what healing of the spirit there lies in the balm of mere leafage.

Moreover, there is in Washington an institution which perhaps should be a source of more legitimate pride than any other in our whole country. The Library of Congress, under the singularly far-sighted administration of Dr. Herbert Putnam, aided by generous grants from Congress, has achieved a unique position in the world of learning. It is not merely that in the substantive value of its material and its serviceability it now ranks with the British Museum and the Bibliothèque Nationale but that, thanks to the rare vision of the Librarian, it has become something far more than a mere collection of books. In the spirit which animates the entire staff, in the ease of access provided to the materials, in all the facilities and amenities offered to the visiting scholar, it is unlike any other institution, and, with its accompanying social and intellectual contacts, offers as great an inducement to the man of letters as can be offered by any institution in the world.

Washington also is fortunate in the countryside which lies about it. As I sat yesterday afternoon on the wide verandah of a private house overlooking a long and peaceful reach of the Potomac below Mount Vernon, the temptation was strong to ask, "Why care about anything else? Why not slip easily into so easy a life?" In another respect, however, Washington illustrates all too clearly an unfortunate feature in our national culture. In London or Paris are centered the business, artistic, intellectual, and political activities of their countries. Although Washington is the capital of ours, after some months in it one begins to feel somewhat cut off from most of the currents of living America other than the political, and this in spite of the constant flowing in and out of distinguished American specialists in many lines. One meets them, and they are gone. If in New York one feels one is living in a great business establishment, one similarly comes to feel here, to some extent, that one is living in a government bureau. The mere government in all its branches and departments overshadows all else as a college overshadows the rest of life in a "college town." Although Washington is far more humane than New York, one does not lead a fully rounded existence here any more than there. One wants, after a while, *when* one wants it, and not on some rare occasion only, to go to the theatre, or hear some music, or rest one's mind by looking at a great painting, or amuse oneself by dropping in at an exhibition of current art, or to be able to rummage around in such bookshops as one may find even in such small cities as Amsterdam or Stockholm.

It is this lack of general cultural background which makes our smaller American cities appear thin after a while in spite of so much that is delightful in them otherwise. All these things, which should be part of the daily food for our minds, come to seem far off and impossibly remote. What happened to Lord Cecil in another regard when some time ago he came over here to lecture on the League of Nations, is what happens to most of us in this. Meeting a man I know here, Lord Cecil was asked, before he started on his western tour, why he was so keen on the League. He answered, "All through the war, even in England, I could hear the guns. Since the war I have still, in my mind, heard those guns. That is why." On his return from his tour, my friend met him again, and Lord Cecil said he felt he had made a failure. "I could not put my heart into my appeals," he said, "because I could not be so keen myself. In the great Mississippi Valley I was so far away, everything was so far away, I could no longer hear the guns." It is so with all of us. We go abroad where our starved cultural emotions can feed in daily ease on so many of the things that help to make us fully rounded human beings. We fondly think that, in spite of every effort required, we will not let them go out of our lives again. And then we come home, and to a great extent these things are not to be had; life is insistent; and we no longer hear the guns.

I find it so in my own case, and am not merely casting stones of reproach at others. I find myself tending to amass impressions and facts, and to be enormously busy assembling them in the fashion of a Ph.D. thesis, rather than in pondering them and thinking. The apparatus for doing just that sort of thing is tremendous in our country, but I do not find it transforming myself in any way, just as I do not find the American college transforming its students. It is all too much on the surface. I am told, and it may be so, that Shakespeare is one of the idols of the American people, yet one rarely hears anyone quote a word of his in conversation or give expression to a thought that would indicate familiarity with him. Most of us over here do not somehow assimilate to our spirits even the culture that we derive from books. It remains at best a sort of "knowledge."

The hurried, confused, tiring life we lead is itself a proof. As for the absence of the other cultural experiences I have mentioned, its cramping effect is well illustrated by the remark of a young Italian in the foreign service whom I met at luncheon the other day. He said it was all pleasant and interesting here but that he had not realized how he was missing something vital until a few weeks ago he happened to be in New Orleans, in an old café in what is left of the French quarter. "There," he said, "was a little of the atmosphere of the Latin and unconsciously I began to sing. I suddenly felt reinvigorated all through me, as though I had been starved and had been given a glass of wine, and realized that I had not sung before in America." We are all of us more or less starving one side or another of our beings here. In the four months I have been home I have talked with innumerable people, educated and delightful and interesting. But as I look back over the conversations I can recall in only very few cases, and those in a somewhat special group, an allusion to music, painting, poetry, or any of the arts. Leaving aside a few people, more or less directly concerned with these things professionally, it has been almost as though I had come to a world where they were non-existent. Of course, they do exist here, and some of them in admirable shape, but the point is that they do not, so far as one can judge from general talk, form a really integral part of our lives.

The conversations have usually dealt with facts or anec-
dotes, and those generally confined to the major interest
and occupation of the person talking, though there are,
of course, delightful exceptions. One is all too likely, however, if one wants to change the topic, to have also to
change one's companion.

For myself, as for others, much that was my simple
daily fare in Europe has disappeared over here. For one
thing, the past seemed somehow to drop below my horizon
with the sudden completeness of a setting sun at sea.
What has become of Goethe, Dante, Milton, the classics,
and all the rest of the reading that came so naturally and
seemingly inevitably in London? In the four months past
the only reading I have done outside of my day's work
has consisted of a few poems of Masefield. Like so many
here, I have "no time." Thanks to the kindness of a Washington friend, I have just spent an afternoon at Monti-
cello. Jefferson, with his wide and versatile culture, could
be happy on his marvellous hilltop. But Jefferson had
spent five years in Paris. It is possible to live long on food
that does not contain the right ingredients in the right
proportions. One can make out even if some of one's organs are under-nourished. It is the same with our
spiritual life, but neither condition is a healthy or a happy
one. The accumulation of neither facts, paid bills, nor
even a few bonds can permanently satisfy us.

That there is deep dissatisfaction with such a life is,
as I have said, amply apparent about us to-day, as it is
in the letters which come to me in a constant stream from

strangers. That even those who disagree with much of my comment on America believe down in their sub-consciousness that it is true would seem to be indicated by the evident irritation aroused by the fact that I have lived a year in England and may live there some more, for some months each year, before settling here at home for good. It clearly indicates an inferiority complex. A country that feels sure of its own culture and its value looks with equanimity upon any of its sons who choose for a while to live out of it. Neither Germans nor English nor Japanese become deeply aroused by a compatriot's going abroad for a few years, but I have been amazed at the strength of the irritation caused in many cases by my living fourteen months in Europe, even though I have no intention of a permanent stay there. The resentment is much like that which might be expressed by a crowd of boys towards one who went to play some afternoon with another "gang."

We are incredibly rich in every sort of educational institution and huge endowments and "foundations," and we are so energetic that we burn ourselves out by forty-five or fifty. A visiting foreigner told me that one of his most insistent impressions here was the absence of old men and the great numbers of middle-aged or young widows. In spite of all our institutional apparatus we somehow miss the heart of the matter. It is the old tale that knowledge comes but wisdom lingers. What is to be the end? Is New York a portent? It had a magnificent site, between its two rivers and looking down its unsurpassed harbor. It was a pleasant place of habitation in my boyhood, not so far distant. Yet with what seems like insane frenzy for mere bigness it has sacrificed every advantage it possessed and has made itself such an uncomfortable place in which to live that people who can do so are fleeing from it as they would from a plague spot. Some of the younger people I know, although by no means all of them, who are strong in nerves, still enjoy its excitement, but, on the other hand, I could count nearly a score of older men in my own acquaintance who have left it with resentment and vow they will go back to it as seldom as possible.

The country is so vast that no generalization or prediction is possible. One desponds, and then one thinks of the Library of Congress. So far, however, our machinery is more in evidence than our product. In Washington, the building of the Folger Memorial is slowly rising to house the greatest collection of Shakespeareana in the world, with a princely endowment, but Shakespeare is on no one's tongue, and Walter Hampden played "Hamlet" here to a half empty house. The Lincoln Memorial is raised in austere beauty, but the people ruin the beauty of every road leading out of the city with filling stations and signboards and litter.

And so I wonder as I prepare, not without many regrets, to leave Lafayette Square for another stay in Kensington Gardens, whether it is, after all, so reprehensible that some of us who can should submit ourselves for a time to those cultural influences that are less easily attainable here, to learn something of the good of many lands and many peoples in order that so far as we can and in our own way we may perhaps render better service to our own.

LAFAYETTE SQUARE, WASHINGTON,
JULY, 1930

2. EMERSON RE-READ

EXCEPT IN TALES of romance it is not given to us to be able to pass through postern doors or forest glades and find ourselves in lands of leisure where it is always afternoon. If one seeks the King of Elfland's Daughter it must be between the pages of a book. Nevertheless, one can change one's stage and ways of life and amplify one's days. Some months ago by a simple shift in space I so wrought a change in time that, for a while at least, I have been able without sense of haste or pressure to browse again among the books I read and marked as a boy, books which for more years than I like to count had stood untouched upon my shelves, open apparently to the reaching hand, but in reality, owing to lack of time, as remote as boyhood's days themselves.

A week ago, I picked up one of the oldest of these, oldest in possession, not in imprint—the *Essays* of Emerson. In an unformed hand there was the inscription on the flyleaf, "James Truslow Adams, 1896." I was then seventeen, and had evidently read him earlier, for at the beginning of a number of the essays, notably "Self-Reliance,"

are marked the dates of reading, "1895, '96, '96, '96."
The volume, one of that excellent, well-printed series
which in those halcyon days the National Book Company
used to sell for fifty cents, is underlined and marked with
marginal notes all through. The passages are not all those
I should mark to-day, but at sixteen and seventeen it is
clear I was reading Emerson with great enthusiasm, and
again and again.

In the past few days I have gone through five volumes of his work and found the task no light one. What,
I ask myself, is the trouble? It is obviously not that Emerson is not "modern," for the other evening I read aloud,
to the mutual enjoyment of my wife and myself, the
Prometheus Chained of Æschylus, which antedates Emerson by some twenty-five hundred years. I turn to Paul
More's *Shelburne Essays,* Volume XI, and read the statement that "it becomes more and more apparent that Emerson, judged by an international or even by a true
national standard, is the outstanding figure of American
letters."

I pause and ponder. "International," even "true
national," standards are high. Whom have we? Lowell as
a critic? One thinks of, say, Sainte-Beuve, and a shoulder
shrug for Lowell. Lowell as poet, Whittier, Longfellow,
Bryant? *Exeunt omnes,* except as second-rate by world
standards. The troop of current novelists and poets are
much the same here as in a half-dozen other countries.
Hawthorne? A very distinctive, and yet a minor voice, in
the international choir. Poe? Again a minor, and scarcely

distinguishable as a "national." Whitman? One thinks of Whitman five hundred years hence in world terms, and shakes one's head. The choice is narrowing fast. Is Mr. More right? Yet the Emerson who evidently so stirred me at sixteen leaves me cold to-day at fifty. It is something to be looked into. I try, at fifty, to reappraise my Emerson. I take up the volumes again to see wherein the trouble lies.

First of all it occurs to me to test him by his own appraisals of others, and I turn to his volume on *Representative Men*. The list of names is itself of considerable significance—Plato, Swedenborg, Montaigne, Shakespeare, Napoleon, Goethe. Four of these are evidently so obvious as to tell us nothing of the mind choosing them. The case is a good deal like that of the Pulitzer Jury in biography, which is forbidden to award prizes for lives of Lincoln or Washington. The essential point is, what has Emerson to say of these men?

I confess that, when after these thirty years or more I turn from reading about Emerson to reading him himself, I am rather amazed by what seems to me the shallowness of these essays. In fact, I believe that even Mr. More considers the Plato a very unsatisfactory performance. Emerson babbles of "the Franklin-like wisdom" of Socrates, and, indeed, I think we could look for as sound an essay from an intelligent undergraduate. The Shakespeare is almost equally naïve and unsatisfying, and Emerson's final judgment is that the dramatist was merely a "master of the revels to mankind," the purveyor of "very superior pyrotechny this evening," and that the end of the record must be that with all his ability he "led an obscure and a profane life, using his genius for the public amusement." This essay throws much light on Emerson if little on Shakespeare. Nor does he show more real understanding of his other great men. He can say that Napoleon left no trace whatever on Europe, that "all passed away like the smoke of his artillery." Of Goethe's greatest poem, the *Faust*, Emerson notes mainly its "superior intelligence." One suspects that he chose these four names unconsciously because they were high in the world's record of the great, not because he understood the men or their work.

When he turns from these names, almost imposed upon him, to another of his independent choosing, it is illuminating that the one he dwells on with greatest admiration is Swedenborg. This fact is significant. For him, the Swedish mystic is "a colossal soul," the "last Father in the Church," "not likely to have a successor," compared with whom Plato is a "gownsman," whereas Lycurgus and Cæsar would have to bow before the Swede. Emerson quotes from him as "golden sayings" such sentences as "in heaven the angels are advancing continually to the spring-time of their youth, so that the oldest angel appears the youngest," or "it is never permitted to any one in heaven, to stand behind another and look at the back of his head: for then the influx which is from the Lord is disturbed." Nor should we forget that entry in Emerson's *Journals* in which he noted that "for pure intellect" he had never known the equal of—Bronson Alcott!

It is true that these essays are not Emerson's best, but they were written when he was over forty years old and at the height of his fame and mental maturity, and they help us to understand our problem. They are typical products of the American mind. Conventional praise is given to the great names of Europe, with comment that indicates lack of understanding of the great currents of thought and action, while Mrs. Eddy and Brigham Young peer over the writer's shoulders. We begin to see how deeply Emerson was an American.

His national limitation is noteworthy in another important source of influence in a mature culture, that of art. Music appears to have been outside his life and consideration. Of painting he could write that, having once really seen a great picture, there was nothing for one to gain by looking at it again. In sculpture he finds a "paltriness, as of toys and the trumpery of a theater." It "is the game of a rude and youthful people, and not the manly labor of a wise and spiritual nation," and he quotes with approval Isaac Newton's remark about the "stone dolls." Art is not mature unless it is "practical and moral," and addresses the uncultivated with a "voice of lofty cheer." All art should be extempore, and he utters a genuine American note in his belief that it will somehow come to us in a new form, the religious heart raising "to a divine use the railroad, the insurance office, the joint-stock company, our law, our primary assemblies, our commerce, the galvanic battery, the electric jar, the prism, and the chemist's retort." "America is a poem in our eyes; its ample geography dazzles the imagination, and it will not wait long for metres." A century later, and we realize that something more is needful for the imagination than an ample geography.

His doctrine that art should be extempore stems from his general belief that knowledge comes from intuition rather than from thought, and that wisdom and goodness are implanted in us—a fatally easy philosophy which has always appealed to the democratic masses, and which is highly flattering to their self-esteem. Wordsworth had led the romantic reaction by making us see the beauty and value in the common things of everyday life, but the philosophy of Emerson has a different ancestry. The two when joined are a perfect soil for democratic belief, and democratic laxity in mind and spirit, far as that might be from Emerson's intention and occasional statements. The more obvious inferences are dangerous, for although a cobbler's flash of insight *may* be as great as the philosopher's lifetime of thought, such is of the rarest occurrence, and preached as a universal doctrine it is a more leveling one by far than universal suffrage.

*

As the ordinary unimportant man, such as most of us are, reads Emerson, his self-esteem begins to grow and glow. "The sweetest music is not in the oratorio, but in the human voice when it speaks from its instant tones of tenderness, truth, or courage." Culture, with us, he says, "ends in headache." "Do not craze yourself with thinking, but go about your business anywhere. Life is not intellectual or critical, but sturdy." "Why all this deference to Alfred and Scanderbeg and Gustavus? As great a stake depends on your private act to-day as followed their public and renowned steps." "We are all wise. The difference between persons is not in wisdom but in art." "Our spontaneous action is always the best. You cannot with your best deliberation and heed come so close to any question as your spontaneous glance shall bring you whilst you rise from your bed."

There is a kernel of noble thought in all this, but it is heady doctrine that may easily make men drunk and driveling, and I think we are coming near to the heart of our problem. The preaching that we do not have to think, the doctrine of what I may term, in Emerson's phrase, "the spontaneous glance," is at the bottom of that appalling refusal to criticize, analyze, ponder, which is one of the chief characteristics of the American people to-day in all its social, political, and international affairs. Many influences have united to bring about the condition, and Emerson cannot escape responsibility for being one of them.

On the other hand, a new nation, a common man with a fleeting vision of the possibility of an uncommon life, above all the youth just starting out with ambition and hope but little knowledge or influence as yet, all need the stimulation of a belief that somehow they *are* important and that not only may their private acts and lives be as high and noble as any, but that the way is open for them to make them so. This is the one fundamental American doctrine. It is the one unique contribution America has made to the common fund of civilization. Our mines and wheat fields do not not differ in kind from others. With Yankee ingenuity we have seized on the ideas of others and in many cases improved their practical applications. The ideas, however, have largely come from abroad. The use of coal as fuel, the harnessing of steam and electricity for man's use,—the foundations of our era,—originated in Europe. Even the invention of the electric light was only in part American. But the doctrine of the importance of the common man is uniquely an American doctrine. It is something different, on the one hand, from the mere awarding to him of legal rights and, on the other, from the mere career open to the talents.

It is a doctrine to which the heart of humanity has responded with religious enthusiasm. It, and not science, has been the real religion of our time, and, essentially, the doctrine is a religious and not a philosophical or scientific one, equally made up as it is of a colossal hope and a colossal illusion. This does not invalidate it. Like all religions it will have its course to run and its part to play in the moulding of man to something finer. It is one more step up, and we need not deny it merely because of the inherent falsity of that gorgeous preamble which proclaims to the world, "All men are created equal." In spite of the self-assertion of the so-called masses, that is a statement which, deep in their hearts, it is as difficult for the inferior as the superior genuinely to believe. It is an ideal, which, like every religious ideal, will be of far-reaching influence, but which must be made believable emotionally. Emerson's greatness lies in his having been the greatest prophet of this new religion, an influence that might well continue to be felt on the two classes that need the doctrine most—the common man striving to rise above the mediocre, and the youth striving to attain a courageous and independent maturity.

Another strain in Emerson, that of the poet and mystic, has also to be reckoned with in making up the man's account. His insistence upon values in life, culminating in the spiritual, is one sorely needed in the America of our day as of his. We are, perhaps, further from the ideal he drew in his "American Scholar" than were the men of his own time. His large hope has not been fulfilled. There is a delicate beauty in his spiritual outlook on life, a beauty akin to that of many an old fresco in Umbria or Tuscany. Unfortunately, there were fundamental flaws in the work of the Italian artists, flaws not of spiritual insight or of artistic craftsmanship, but of wet plaster or of wrong chemical combinations in materials, so that little by little their painting has crumbled and faded. If Emerson's mysticism led him too easily toward Swedenborg rather than toward Plato, and if the beauty of his spiritual interpretation of the universe does not carry that conviction or mould his readers as it should, may we not wonder whether there were not some fundamental flaws in the mind of the man that may explain his decreasing influence, just as in examining a wall where a few patches of dim color are all that remain of a Giotto we have to consider, not the artist's love of the Madonna, but his lack of knowledge of the mechanics of his art? Of this we shall speak presently.

The quintessence of Emersonianism is to be found in the first and second series of *Essays,* and it may be noted that it was these, as my pencilings show, which I myself read most as a boy, and of them, it was such essays as "Self-Reliance," in which the word is found in its purest form, that I read over and over. What do I find marked as I turn the old pages? "Trust thyself: every heart vibrates to that iron string." "Whoso would be a man must be a noncomformist." "Nothing at last is sacred but the integrity of your own mind." "I do not wish to expiate, but to live. My life is not an apology, but a life. It is for itself and not for a spectacle." "What I must do is all that concerns me, not what the people think." "The great man is he who in the crowd keeps with perfect sweetness the independence of solitude." "Always scorn appearances and you always may. The force of character is cumulative." "Life only avails and not the having lived." "Insist on yourself; never imitate." "Nothing can bring you peace but yourself."

This is high and worthy doctrine, the practice of

of which will tax a man's strength and courage to the utmost, and such sentences as the above have proved the strongest influences in the making of literally count- less adolescent Americans, stimulating their ambition in the noblest fashion. Unfortunately this part of Emerson's teaching has had less influence than the other. The aver- age American soon slips into preferring "we are all wise" to "scorn appearances." Insisting on being one's self is strenuous and difficult work anywhere, more so in Amer- ica than any other country I know, thanks to social opinion, mass ideals, and psychologized advertising of national products. Emerson deserves full meed of praise for preaching the value of individualism, but it may be asked, granting that nearly all intelligent, high-minded American youths for nearly a century have, at their most idealistic stage, come under the influence of Emer- son's doctrine, why has the effect of his teaching been so light upon their later manhood? Does the fault lie in them or in the great teacher, for, in such sentences as we have quoted above, I gladly allow that the sage of Concord *was* a great teacher.

The answer, I think, is that the fault lies to a great extent in Emerson himself. His doctrine contains two great flaws, one positive, the other negative, and both as typically American as he himself was in everything. That he had no logically articulated system of thought is not his weakest point. He once said that he could not give an account of himself if challenged. Attempts have been made to prove that his thought was unified and coherent. One may accept these or not. It matters little, for it is not, and never has been, as a consistent philosopher that Emerson has influenced his readers. It has been by his trenchant aphorisms which stir the soul of the young and the not too thoughful, and set the blood to dancing like sudden strains of martial music. It is in these, and not in any metaphysical system about which philosophers might argue, that we find the fatal flaws and influences I have mentioned.

The first, the positive one, in spite of his high doctrine of self-reliance and individualism, is that Emerson makes life too easy by his insistence on intuition and spontaneity. The style and construction of his writings deliberately emphasize the import of the aphorisms. The occasionally qualifying context sinks into insignificance and out of memory as does the stick of a rocket in the darkness of night. We see and recall only the dazzling shower of stars. If this is now and then unfair to Emerson's thought, he has himself to blame. He took no pains to bind his thought together and loved the brilliancy of his rocket-stars of "sayings." We have already quoted some of these on the point we are now discussing. All teaching is "Intuition." In "Spontaneity or Instinct" he finds "the essence of genius, the essence of virtue, and the essence of life," "It is as easy for the strong man to be strong, as it is for the weak to be weak." "All good conversation, manners, and action, come from a spontaneity which forgets usages, and makes the moment great." "No man need be perplexed by his speculations.... These are the soul's mumps and measles and whooping-coughs. Our moral nature is vitiated by any interference of our will.... There is no merit in the matter. Either God is there or He is not there. We love characters in proportion as they are impulsive and spontaneous. The less a man thinks or knows about his virtues the better we like him." A page or two back we noted his theory of spontaneity in art and intellect.

*

This, as we have said, unless the occasional qualifications are as greatly emphasized as the sayings themselves, is extremely dangerous doctrine. Of all the youths who have read Emerson in their impressionable years, a certain proportion have subsequently retrograded in the spirtual and intellectual scale, and a certain proportion have advanced. Of the difficulty with the master felt by the latter we shall speak presently, but for the first group this doctrine of spontaneity, so emphasized by Emerson, offers all too soft a cushion upon which to recline. Act and do not think. Culture is headache. Perplexities are the soul's mumps and measles. Radiant sentence after sentence, graven with clear precision on the cameo of the mind. It has been said that, of all the sages, Emerson requires the least intellectual preparation to read. He is, indeed, in some respects, and those in which he exerts most influence, fatally easy. Fatally easy and alluring to the busy hundred-per-cent American is this doctrine of intuition and spontaneity. It is a siren voice, a soft Lydian air blown across the blue water of the mind's tropical sea. For a century the American has left the plain hard work of life to his foreign serfs. The backbreaking toil of digging trenches, laying rails, puddling iron in the furnaces, has been delegated successively to the Irish, the Italians, the Slavs. But thinking is intellectually, willing is spiritually, as backbreaking as these. The ordinary American prefers also to abandon them and to take for himself the easier task of solving the economic problems and puzzles in which he delights. Intuition and spontaneity—fatal words for a civilization which is more and more coming to depend for its very existence on clear, hard, and long-sustained "thinking-through." It is this positive flaw in Emerson's teaching that has made the effect of his really noble doctrines of so little influence upon the boys who have worshiped him this side idolatry at sixteen and then gone into the world and found every invitation to retreat from the high ground rather than to advance.

What now of those others, those who also worshiped Emerson in youth, who have fought the world, and who find him declining in influence over their lives the more they advance? With them we reach Emerson's negative flaw.

What a gulf between the man of fifty and the boy of sixteen! As one has in those intervening years studied the history of the past, watched the daily life of the people of a score of nations, seen wars and famines take their toll of millions, and, nearer one's own heart, watched the physical pain of those closest to one's self, stood at grave after grave, found, too, perhaps, that one has wrought evil when most striving to do good, one has come to feel the whole mystery of that problem of Evil—of sin, of suffering, of death. One yet may carry a brave heart and hold one's self erect, but one is no longer content with a philosophy of shallow optimism, a "God's in His heaven—all's right with the world."

I think that here is where Emerson fails us as we grow older and wiser. The trumpet blasts of self-reliance which so thrilled us at sixteen sound a little thin and far-off now. We needed them when they first smote our ear and we are deeply grateful, but we have fought the fight, we have tried to be ourselves, we have tried to live our life for itself and not for a spectacle, and now we are older. We have lived, loved, suffered, enjoyed, fought, and to some extent won. The world has been rich in interest—and in suffering. There are hopeful signs on every side. There is sunlight as well as darkness, but there *is* darkness. One has been close to failure and looked it in the eye. There have been the brows we could not soothe through years of suffering, the waxen faces we kissed for the last time before we laid them away, the mysterious darkness coming toward ourselves like the shadow of a cloud on a summer landscape, but inevitably to overtake us. When we turn again to the great teacher of our youth, what does he say to help or hearten us? Nothing.

Owing largely to material circumstance and a vast and uninhabited continent, the prevailing mood of the American people came to be one of shallow and unlimited optimism, the waves of which flowed over even the sectional Calvinism of New England. Nature ceased to be the evil enemy of man's spirit and gave him her fairest gifts, as Mephistopheles bestowed his Helen on the tortured Faust. With material abundance, spiritual evil ceased to appear important and a golden age seemed dawning, as youth came to Faust in that most un-American legend.

For its hundred and fifty years America has been scarcely touched by suffering. Pestilence? None. Think of the Black Death and other great plagues that have swept over Europe. Famine? None. Think of India and China. War? Scarcely more than one. In the Revolution only an infinitesimal part of the population was in the army for any length of time. The War of 1812 was a ripple, almost all at sea, and the deaths were negligible to the population. The Indian Wars? Skirmishes by paid troops. The Mexican War? A junket which never came home to the people. The Civil War? Yes, but even that did not come home to the whole civilian population, except in the South, as have the wars which have flowed in torrents over Europe. Compare it with the Thirty Years' War, in which, to say nothing of the rest of Europe, the population of Germany, from the ravages of the sword, famine, disease, and emigration, sank from 16,000,000 to 6,000,000, and in which of 35,000 villages in Bohemia less than 6,000 were standing at the end, and in which nine-tenths of the entire population of the Palatinate disappeared. The Spanish War was a holiday affair except for a few homes. In the last Great War we lost by death a mere 126,000 as compared with 8,500,-000 in the Old World. In civil life our history has been one long business boom, punctuated by an occasional panic, like a fit of indigestion for a man who continually overeats. We have never suffered like the rest of humanity, and have waxed fat without, as yet, having to consider the problems forced upon others, until we have ceased to believe in their reality. The dominant American note has thus been one of a buoyant and unthinking optimism. America is a child who has never gazed on the face of death.

Emerson somewhere speaks of the nonchalance of boys sure of a "dinner." Can any words better express the American attitude toward the universe, and, in spite of his spirituality and the somewhat faded fresco of his mysticism, does Emerson himself really give us anything deeper? Man, according to him, "is born to be rich." Economic evils trouble our sage not at all. The universe, for him, is good through and through, and "success consists in close application to the laws of the world, and, since those laws are intellectual and moral, an intellectual and moral obedience." One thinks of Jay Gould and the career of many a magnate of to-day! "In a free and just commonwealth, property rushes from the idle and imbecile, to the industrious, brave, and persevering."

As I am certainly not idle (I am working on a holiday to write this), and as Americans would not admit that theirs is not a just and free commonwealth, imbecility is the only third horn of the trilemma on which to impale myself if property has not rushed toward me. "Do not skulk," the sage tells every man in "a world which exists for him." At fifty, we have found, simply, that the world does *not* exist for us. "Love and you shall be loved. All love is mathematically just, as much as the two sides of an algebraic problem." One rubs one's eyes. "There is a soul at the center of nature and over the will of every man, so that none of us can wrong the universe." Man may, he says, "easily dismiss all particular uncertainties and fears, and adjourn to the sure revelation of time the solution of his private riddles. He is sure his welfare is dear to the heart of being." Is he so sure? Alas, no longer.

*

As I think over my most recent visit to Rome, where two thousand years of human history, happiness, and suffering have left their monuments, and Heaven knows how many thousand unmarked before, I contrast it with a visit to Emerson's house at Concord on an October day many years ago. It is a charming, roomy old house, and in it Emerson was able to live with a large library and three servants on two thousand a year. In the ineffable light of an American autumn, as I saw it, it was a place of infinite peace. Concord in 1840 was an idyllic moment in the history of the race. That moment came and passed, like a baby's smile. Emerson lived in it. "In the morning," he wrote, "I awake, and find the old world, wife, babes, and mother, Concord and Boston, the dear old spiritual world, and even the dear old devil not far off."

It is true that he has very occasional qualms and doubts. He even wonders in one essay whether we must presuppose some "slight treachery and derision" in the universe. As we turn the pages, we ask ourselves with some impatience, "Did this man never really suffer?" and read that "the only thing grief has taught me, is to know how shallow it is. That, like all the rest, plays about the surface, and never introduces me into the reality, for contact with which, we would even pay the costly price of sons and lovers."

One ends. Perhaps Mr. More is right. Perhaps Emerson *is* the outstanding figure in American letters. Who else has expressed so magnificently the hope, and so tragically illustrated the illusion, of our unique contribution to the world? My own debt to the sage is unpayable. He was one of the great influences in my early life, as, in his highest teaching, he should be in that of every boy. It seems almost the basest of treason to write this essay, and I would still have every youth read his Emerson. But what of America? What of the hope and the illusion? A century has passed. Is no one to arise who will fuse them both in some larger synthesis, and who, inspiring youth, will not be a broken reed in maturity? Are our letters and philosophy to remain the child until the Gorgon faces of evil, disaster, and death freeze our own unlined ones into eternal stone? Is it well that the outstanding figure in American letters should be one whose influence diminishes in proportion as the minds of his readers grow in strength, breadth, and maturity? And, speaking generally, is this not true of Emerson? Does any man of steadily growing character, wealth of experience, and strength of mind find the significance and influence of Emerson for him growing as the years pass? Does he turn to him more and more for counsel, help, or solace?

There is but one answer, I think, and that is negative. Unlike the truly great, the influence of Emerson shrinks for most of us as we ourselves develop. May the cause not lie in the two flaws I have pointed out, flaws in the man as in his doctrine in spite of the serene nobility of so much of his life? If with all his wide and infinitely varied reading, noted in his *Journals*, we find his culture a bit thin and puerile, is it not because he himself trusted too much to that theory of spontaneity, of the "spontaneous glance," rather than to the harder processes of scholarship and thinking-through coherently; and if we find him lacking in depth and virility, is it not because he allowed himself to become a victim to that vast American optimism with its refusal to recognize and wrestle with the problem of evil? One turns to Æschylus and reads:

146

. . . affliction knows no rest,
But rolls from breast to breast its vagrant tide.

One does need to be a pessimist, merely human, to find here the deeper and more authentic note.

If Emerson is still the outstanding figure in American letters, is that not the equivalent of saying that America a century after the *Essays* appeared has not yet grown to mental maturity, and that the gospel it preaches is inspiring only for unformed adolescence,—of whatever age,—without having risen to a comprehension of the problems of maturity? In Europe, the past has bequeathed not only a wealth of art, but a legacy of evil borne and sorrow felt. Perhaps American letters, like American men, will not grow beyond the simple optimism and, in one aspect, the shallow doctrine of Emerson until they too shall have suffered and sorrowed. Emerson, in his weakness as in his strength, is American through and through. He could have been the product, in his entirety, of no other land, and that land will not outgrow him until it has some day passed through the fires of a suffering unfelt by him and as yet escaped by it.

3. SWEETNESS AND LIGHT—
SIXTY YEARS AFTER

THROUGHOUT LIFE we always, I think, maintain a peculiar interest in the men and books that deeply influenced our earliest and most formative years. No later work, however influential or revolutionary in our thought, ever attains to quite the same intensity of reality as those which helped to stir our minds in boyhood, when the whole world was opening before us, when thought was the great adventure, and when prophets commanded whole-souled homage. As it chanced, my own first decade was that which is generally accepted as the turning point between the old and the new worlds of thought. In America the Civil War was scarcely less recent, in Europe the pregnant Franco-Prussian War was more so, than is the Great War to-day. Carlyle died when I was three, Darwin when I was four, John Richard Green and Karl Marx when I was five, Matthew Arnold and Sir Henry Maine when I was ten, Browning when I was eleven, and Cardinal Newman and Tennyson a few years later. Dickens was but eight years gone when I was born, and Thomas Huxley and John Ruskin were writing when I was in college.

I have barely touched my half-century, yet these names sound like a long-bygone age. In my boyhood, however, when I was keen on every new intellectual trail, their works were not classics or "required reading," but living voices to which I listened with the same sense of contemporaneity with which to-day we read Eddington or Harvey Robinson, Einstein, O'Neill, or Aldous Huxley. The life, however, which has embraced both Darwin and Einstein, Thomas and Aldous Huxley, has straddled, as it were, two eras in thought and civilization. A straddle is generally considered to be neither a dignified nor a determined position, but if it entails certain discomforts it also offers certain advantages, certain piquancies of comparison. Just as a man who knows only one country cannot be considered to know even that, so a man who knows only one era cannot savor its peculiarities with the same biting relish as one who has been a wider traveler in time.

Time, however, in a busy life is apt to pass imperceptibly, and I confess that it was with a good deal of a shock that I happened to note, when engaged in the scholar's equivalent of big-game hunting, the glancing over of secondhand-book catalogues, that Matthew Arnold's most influential work, *Culture and Anarchy*, was published just sixty years ago. I had the sudden sense of being caught in the swift current of a river. I walked to my study window to look out and ponder.

In these present years of wanderings, my windows open on many scenes in many countries in the course of a twelvemonth, but at the moment my study overlooks

Kensington Gardens, in which Arnold wrote one of his well-known poems:

I, on men's impious uproar hurl'd
Think often, as I hear them rave,
That peace has left the upper world,
And now keeps only in the grave.

If Arnold found "impious uproar" in 1869, the very mid-year of the Victorian reign, what would he find, I wondered, to-day? What change, if any, would he feel called upon to make to-day in his philosophy, and how has the world moved with reference to it in those sixty years gone? Dickens, Darwin, Huxley, Green, Maine, and some of the others have conquered. The world has moved in the directions indicated by them. How about Arnold, who seemed to the cultured youth of the late-Victorian period perhaps the greatest prophet of them all?

One recalls his simple and singularly lucid prognosis and prescription for his own age, an age that to us now looking back it seems itself singularly lucid and simple. One has to recall, however, a fact easily forgotten, that every age has its own "uproar." We have to be in it to hear it. Getting into an "age" is a good deal like getting into a railroad train. As we see it first approaching, far down the track, it seems very peaceful. There is no sound, no tremor, only the ease of swift motion. It is only when we are traveling in it ourselves that we feel the jolts and jars, hear the whistle shriek, the brakes grind, the roar of the wheels, and the babel of unedifying conversation in the club smoker.

Even, however, if we are justified in conceding to our self-esteem that we have raised a good deal more of an uproar than was confusing the ears of Arnold, and that there may be more raving now than there was in 1869, it is to misconceive his philosophy to think of him as having given a simple solution for the problems of a simple age. His age was by no means as easy-gliding as the distant railroad train, by no means as stodgy and unstirred as the Georgian retrospect among the younger generation would make out. Arnold's doctrine, in spite of his emphasis on "sweetness and light," in spite of its being the mid-Victorian equivalent of "highbrow," was not intended for the scholar cloistered in an ivory tower, but for the man of action in the turmoil of a transition era.

That doctrine may easily be condensed to two chief points—the eternal contest between Hebraism and Hellenism, and the mediating function of culture, of "sweetness and light." The final aim of both Hebraism and Hellenism Arnold found to be the same, man's perfection or salvation, in spite of the fact that they approach the problem by utterly diverse routes. Hebraism lays the whole stress on doing, on the importance of the *act*, on religion, on strictness of conscience. On the other hand, Hellenism stresses knowing rather than doing, the whole rather than a part, spontaneity of consciousness. The "uppermost idea with Hellenism is to see things as they really are; the uppermost idea with Hebraism is conduct and obedience." Ideas of action and conduct fill the space of the Hebraist's mind. "He is zealous to do battle for them and affirm them, for in affirming them he affirms himself, and that is what we all like." The Hellenist, on the other hand, tries to apprehend the whole of life, to let no part of it slip, to stress no part to the exclusion of the others. He insists upon a flexible activity of mind, and so attains to that clearness and radiancy of vision, that intelligence and tolerance, which Arnold called "sweetness and light." Nothing, he states, can do away with the ineffaceable difference between these two approaches to the problems of life.

Both of these disciples, as we may call them, Arnold saw were necessary for the development of man. If the tendency of unimpeded Hellenism was toward rather a weakening of the moral fibre, that of Hebraism was no less inevitably toward an extreme hardening and narrowing of man's whole nature. Man's only salvation from swinging helplessly between these two poles was to be found in culture, which should not be a mere dilettante toying with art, but a disinterested aiming to see things as they really are, the effort to cultivate the best in all sides of man's nature. I do not think it has ever been noted that, whether Arnold was aware of it or not, his doctrine was exactly that of Kant, who in his philosophy placed the æsthetic consciousness at the centre to mediate between reason and will. Feeling, however, that in his own time the whole tendency was to stress the Hebraic side, the side of unthinking action, Arnold stressed the other, the side of "sweetness and light," and throughout his life in one form and another preached his doctrine of the saving grace of a mediating and all-embracing culture.

*

Amid the complete confusion of our present-day social, intellectual, and spiritual life it is certainly not necessary to bring out in any great detail the evidence that Arnold, unlike some of the more fortunate Victorian leaders of thought, did not point in the direction in which the world was immediately to move. Thanks largely to America, where the forces of the modern world have had their freest sphere of influence, Hebraism has conquered Hellenism with an appalling completeness for the time being.

Arnold clearly saw and constantly preached the essential difference between the machinery of life and life itself. It was not that he merely questioned the utility of physical machinery, although it is easy enough to do so. We may well ask, for example in what lies the great advantage of being able to travel thrice as fast as our grandparents if, arrived at our destination, we do not know how to occupy the time "saved" to as great advantage as they did? It was rather that Arnold saw all the institutional life of our time as machinery—our state constitutions, our churches, universities, libraries, and organizations of every sort. All these he found, of course, essential to life, but merely the tools of life, valuable only for their results, and not for themselves.

In this respect we have obviously gone directly counter to his teaching. We have come to worship our social machinery as an end in itself. Not only is every possible activity organized, which perhaps is to some extent unavoidable in our great modern masses of population, but, what surely is avoidable, we have come to lay more stress on the machinery than on the product, on the means than on the end.

Perhaps we may consider the five great educative influences for the life of the spirit to be one's daily toil, social intercourse, travel, education in its more technical sense, and religion. What of these to-day?

One's daily toil has always of course had for a main object the earning of a living, but it should have an addition an interest in itself. It is a mistake to think that such an interest can be aroused only by intellectual and not by manual work, but, in order that it should be, the worker must feel that he is creating something which he can see grow and develop as a result of his toil. In this respect there was never before, perhaps, a period in which work had less spiritual value for most people than it has to-day. The worker himself has been lost in the complicated machinery of production, and in our worship of efficiency the machinery has come to be considered somehow such a desirable good in itself as to warrant any sacrifice in its name.

Social intercourse in the same way has succumbed

to the machinery ostensibly provided for it. Clubs and organizations of all sorts for bringing people together are legion, but conversation has almost as completely disappeared as has letter writing between friends. We are so busy and wearied in rushing from one meeting to another that our minds themselves have almost entirely ceased to meet. It is not only in the hurry of great cities that there is no longer opportunity for friendly communion. For the inhabitants of innumerable Main Streets throughout the country, Monday night is for Grange, Tuesday the Red Men or Daughters of Pocahontas, Wednesday the Junior Mechanics or the Eastern Star, Thursday the Masons, Friday the Lions, Saturday the Rotary, to mention only a few of the provisions for social intercourse that have ended by destroying all real intercourse itself. There is no genuine depth or value to such gatherings—merely a sense of physical proximity to one's kind. For the life of the spirit they are utterly useless.

Travel, again, as its means have become multiplied and more accessible to all, has largely ceased to have the educational value it once had. Because one can make two hundred miles a day in a motor, people make it. Because one can cross to Europe and pass through half a dozen countries and back in a month, people do it. Let it not be thought that I am exaggerating. Ask any number of people what sort of motor trip they had, and all too frequently the answer will be, "Fine! We did a hundred and eighty miles the first day, two hundred the second, and so on. No trouble. We were gone only two weeks, and covered nearly twenty-five hundred miles!"

An excellent guidebook to London, lying before me on my desk as I write, tells how one may see the city in one day. In the morning one is to go to the National Gallery, the National Portrait Gallery, Houses of Parliament, Westminster Abbey, London Museum, St. James's Park, and four other places. One is to lunch near Piccadilly. In the afternoon one goes to the Royal Academy, Wallace Collection, British Museum, St. Paul's Cathedral, the Law Courts, and drives through two parks and three important thoroughfares. If the traveler intends to remain overnight, the guide continues, he should visit the Embankment and attend a theatre.

This is not a joke. It is intended as a serious guide for present-day travelers in search, presumably, of education and culture. Comment would be superfluous, but it is evident that the end of travel, the broadening of our minds, the development of our natures, has become lost to sight in the mere machinery of travel—that is, the physical transporting of our bodies from place to place.

Is not the same transfer of stress on, and interest in, the end to the mere means shown daily in our educational and religious systems? If one drops in to see a clergyman and inquire about his work, is not one, nine times out of ten, immediately shown over the "plant"— the new parish house, the gymnasium and the swimming pool, the men's clubroom—or offered statistics? If one goes to a college, one is shown with pride the new "J.

Jefferson Jones" dormitory or the "Simeon Smith" laboratory, or the new stadium or business college building. If we turn to the teaching from desk or pulpit, we find the same immersion in the machinery of life rather than in life itself. The body, the "plant," is superb, but one too often looks in vain for the spirit of either Christ or culture.

Is not the reason for all this the fact that in taking the road that Arnold pointed out would surely lead to destruction, to anarchy, we have lost, with the loss of Hellenism, the power to see life steadily and see it whole? We see only parts, the physical part, the machinery part, and have failed to see the end of all these things, the full rounded life of the spirit for the growth of which alone these other things have any validity or value. Of what possible use is a machine, whether it be a dynamo or a university, unless it is to produce something of essential value for human life? Why waste that life on tending machines that produce nothing? Why travel sixty miles an hour if one sees nothing of the landscape, towns, or people on the way? Why go to five picture galleries, two museums, and two cathedrals in a day if one adds nothing to one's spiritual impressions—as one cannot—by doing so?

*

In seeking the reason of Arnold's failure more to influence his time and ours, I think we may trace it to the extraordinarily rapid increase in the influence of one force in the modern world to which he paid curiously scant attention—science, with its offshoot, modern business theory and practice. It is true that Arnold stood only at the threshold of the changes that science was to bring. In *Culture and Anarchy,* at least, he, in striking contrast to Tennyson, seemed wholly oblivious of the dangers threatening from a new quarter.

Science, which from one standpoint may almost be considered a traitor in the Hellenistic camp, would seem to have deflected the world toward Hebraism in two ways. In the first place, through the products of applied science, and business, it has provided man with an infinity of things of all sorts. Whatever may be the ultimate result, the dream that control over the forces of nature would at once make life easier for man and increase his leisure for the things of the spirit has to a great extent been proved wrong. It is true that in very many cases the mere physical labor entailed in an occupation has been lightened by the new inventions. On the other hand, however, man has been overwhelmed by the very multiplicity and variety of his new goods. These new goods differ in one marked respect from the old range. The old goods, such as enjoying the beauty of nature, reading, expressing one's self in one's work, "making things," playing music, conversing intelligently, looking at pictures or statues, studying, friendship, love, social intercourse, could all be had for little or no money, in civilized communities. The new goods, however, those provided by applied science and business, can only be had in exchange for money.

The consequence is that whoever turns from the old goods to the new at once increases enormously his need for money, and the financial pressure upon the individual becomes so great as in most cases to result in his complete absorption in providing the mere means for living, the accumulating of the things that belong to the machinery of life. So far from increasing the leisure for thought, feeling, and emotion, not only has the time for leisure been greatly decreased, but with the abnormal condition of exhausting one's energies in preparation to live and enjoy, instead of actually living, comes an abnormal mental condition which finds relief only in an excitable activity instead of a normal savoring and enjoyment of existence.

Aside from the new inventions, such as motors, aeroplanes, and so on, of which the prime object is speed, the pressure of modern life due to science and business working hand in hand has greatly increased the whole tempo of life. We used to measure the hours. Now we live by the second hand. The spirit, however, cannot be hurried. We may get more quickly to the Grand Central and the 4.50 by the subway, but not to Heaven. Quiet and time are essential for the fruits of the spirit, whatever a Burbank may do with bulbs. I think it was Daniel Webster who once said that the most valuable thoughts he had ever had came to him while jogging on his nag from place to place on his court circuit. No such deep reflections could come to a modern judge covering the same distance in a tenth of the time at sixty miles an hour in a high-powered car. It has recently been well said of our age that it is "restless, wide-ranging, enjoying pleasure and novelty, but moving in space rather than in time, dwelling on the surface rather than in the depth of things." These characteristics we can trace, I think, clearly enough to that applied science that disturbed Arnold so slightly.

In another and equally important way science has deflected us from that Hellenistic attitude which, in one of Arnold's definitions, is the effort to see things as they really are. To do this is precisely what, until almost the present day, science has claimed for itself, and what even to-day most people think it does. The now deeply in-grained belief that not only has science a peculiar validity, but it gives us the entire truth regarding all aspects of the universe, has acted as a corrosive upon a very large part of the content of culture and the things that have con-tributed to man's highest life—literature, art, and religion. Much of all this has come to seem mere moonshine fancies when contrasted with the "facts" of science, of which not only the validity, but the completeness, is not to be ques-tioned whatever happens to any side of man's nature or whatever in that nature they leave unaccounted for.

A whole vast range of beliefs and values that were essentially human were wiped off the slate in the name of science. It is needless to catalogue them. The Hellenistic effort to see life steadily and see it whole on the human plane was replaced by an effort to follow a dance of atoms on the scientific plane. Human values became an irrele-vant phantasmagoria. The universe was reduced to pure

act. In place of the old dangerous error at the upper end
of the Hellenistic scale of "art for art's sake," we reached
the no less dangerous one at the lower end of the Hebraic,
the "act for the act's sake." Hebraism, always more
potent among the mass of men than Hellenism, has thus
found itself since Arnold's day strengthened to a remarkable degree in both the practical and the theoretical
spheres. Not only have the Hebraistic battalions been
heavily reënforced, but in science, in the eyes of the
public, they have apparently gained a recruit from the
Hellenistic camp. The whole scene has shifted since Arnold. And yet was he not right? Is not culture, in its best
and broadest sense, our only salvation? Can the present
materialistic welter of confusion, if unchecked, lead
eventually to anything but that anarchy that formed the
half of Arnold's title for his work? If so, what of the
future?

*

It seems to me that our civilization may take either
of two courses. The first may be indicated by a suggestion
made to Arnold by an American sixty years ago. This
was that "we should for the future call industrialism culture, and the industrialists the men of culture"; and then
of course, as Arnold ironically adds, "there can be no
longer any misapprehension about their true character;
and besides the pleasure of being wealthy and comfortable, they will have authentic recognition as vessels of
sweetness and light." We must confess that to a great

extent our leaders in religion and education have seemingly chosen to follow this suggestion in their teaching of the American people. The Christian spirit has got so mixed up with "drives" and gymnasiums, and culture with cost accounting and business English, that it takes a wise young man indeed to disentangle them in the face of the strenuous and muddle-headed efforts of his elders.

In many directions at present, however, we are getting suggestions which are not put forward by business men, clerics, or professional educators, and which for that reason, and because they are clothed in a semi-scientific language, may claim more consideration from many. Thus a few weeks ago the noted French architect, Le Corbusier, speaking of bridges, steamships, and other engineering works, said they once provoked æsthetically a "violent antagonistic feeling. They were deemed ugly. Yet these works to-day are acclaimed as admirable. A miracle has been accomplished, a spiritual revolution—'the spirit of the age becoming conscious of itself.' " Others suggest that art is an affair of the whole organism and that the art of any age is intricately bound up with the nervous organization of the people of the age. Others, again, hold that the essence of art is one thing and the form another, and that for the future the essence may be permanently passing from pictures, poems, and statues to engineering works.

There is no reason why an engineering work or any other utilitarian one should not be beautiful. They frequently have been in the past, from kitchen pots to bridges. But one cannot help the feeling, in reading such suggestions as that the age is becoming conscious of itself in the sense of admiring its own works, that their authors are unconsciously engaged less in finding new beauty than in condoning our lack of it, though the suggestions are worth pondering. A friend of mine claims not only that a finely made carpenter's tool has a beauty of form of its own, which is true, but that he can get as much pleasure out of studying it as he can out of a Rembrandt. Our race has behind it a long history and a far longer development. From the days of the Quaternary epoch in Europe we have been making both pictures and tools, but it has remained for our own epoch to claim that a tool, however beautifully made, has the same spiritual value as a picture. It is true that the populace of Athens enjoyed spending its leisure in listening intelligently to a play by Æschylus, Sophocles, or Euripides, whereas the populace to-day prefers the horseplay or sentimental slush of the movies, but I do not think the way out of the difficulty is to say that watching a slice of pie jump across the screen, or kisses in a close-up, is as culturally or æsthetically valuable as the unrolling of fate in Greek drama.

The fact would seem to be that for the time we have lost our scale of æsthetic values, because we have lost our scale of values for the whole of life itself. An age which cares only for the speed of its locomotion and nothing for its purpose or destination is not likely to distinguish between a gasoline station and the Parthenon. We obviously cannot have a scale of values unless we consider the whole of life, consider all the possibilities of man's nature, and reckon one against the other; unless we attain to that perfection which Arnold considered the end of culture—which is "an harmonious expansion of *all* the powers which make the beauty and worth of human nature, and is not consistent with the over-development of any one power at the expense of the rest."

*

Of course, the anarchy suggested by Arnold as the final outcome of a democracy devoted to a philosophy of doing, not of being, of action rather than of thought, of developing only one side of man's nature at the expense of all the rest, is not impossible. It has overtaken mankind many times before, and in our busy lives immersed in intense activity we need not believe that what has been can never be again. We cannot rely too blindly upon a moderate distribution of baby bonds, savings deposits, and a share or two of stocks among the populace. It is conceivable, in a civilization based on tensions between its members, resulting from trying to secure each for himself the largest share of material goods possible, that as the gap between salary or wage earners and billionaire proprietors increases it may some day, in an economic debacle, prove too wide to be bridged even by a baby bond.

On the whole, however, I do not think this is the direction in which we are going to travel, though I trust to neither the applied scientist nor the business man to divert us from it, useful as are the functions which each otherwise performs. It seems to me, however, that there are not a few signs in the social heavens that the times are changing and that Arnold's doctrine may come into its own at last.

For one thing, the constant stream of self-criticism that arises from the vocal and more thinking part of the American people at present, morbid as it may seem from one point of view, does indicate a deep dissatisfaction with life as it is now being lived by us. There is a widespread feeling that there is something radically wrong with that life, which feeling appears to centre in the demand that we should have more scope for the development of our own individuality, that we should somehow, vaguely as people may yet apprehend it, have a chance to *be* something rather than eternally to be *doing* something, whether for ourselves, posterity, or the Lions Club. In many households this is taking the form of refusing any longer to be dragooned by advertising and high-powered salesmanship into buying every new device that promises even the least contribution to amusement or efficiency. The very activity of the inventor and the business man may itself help in time to bring about our salvation.

For a while we lost our heads. The novel goods offered by the wonders of applied science have been like the glass beads and red cloth offered to savages. We have bestirred ourselves to unwonted exertions in order to get something to trade for them. But we are not savages. We have a long cultural history behind us. We have deep in us desires and cravings that cannot permanently be satisfied with beads and cloth; and there is a limit beyond which we cannot and will not work. If in the future applied science spawns out purchasable goods which business offers us at a rapidly accelerating rate, we shall, instead of trying to have every new thing that comes along, begin to exercise choice. Once we have discovered that among such a multiplicity of objects choice is inevitable from all standpoints, such as capacity or willingness to work, room space, or even time to enjoy them, we shall become more individual, use our minds again, and once more take pleasure in expressing our own personalities. In trying to choose, in deciding what we really want, we shall discover that a great many things worth having are those that do not cost anything to speak of, such as reading, making our own music, conversation, and other old-fashioned things of the mind. Once the strike is on against working to the limit in order to buy to the limit, we shall begin once more to try to see life steadily and see it whole. With the dawn of that day, the pendulum will begin to swing again toward Hellenism.

Intellectually, also, I believe the way will be made easier by a better understanding both among scientists and among the public of just what scientific truth is as an interpretation of the whole of the universe. That understanding, as I have recently said elsewhere, is making rapid headway among many leading scientists, although the public may be long in following their lead. Once, however, the way is open for the reinstatement, not only in a human world but in the universe, of the purely human *values*, the door toward Hellenism will be swung wide. We shall once more see life whole after a dark night of the spirit.

In that day Matthew, or some new Arnold with more contemporaneity of reference and style, will become our prophet, for as I turn from his works to glance at the books on my shelves on economics, sociology, psychology, and science, with their sprinkling of Freuds, Watsons, and Heaven knows how many other "modern" voices, I cannot see that there is, after all, any saner doctrine being preached to-day for the salvation of society or the inner peace of the individual than that preached by the apostle of culture sixty years ago. That doctrine is simply that if democracy is to be saved from anarchy it must be permeated through with "sweetness and light," understood as intelligence and tolerance; that this can be attained only by culture, and not by ceaseless economic activity; and that, eventually, people will not consider that life worth living or that society worth saving which does not allow them to live normally and fully with all sides of their being.

Arnold believed his doctrine worth fighting for through a lifetime. It is assuredly worth fighting for to-day, with far better chances of success, as I see them, from the probable trend of thought and history in the next sixty years than in those which Arnold faced. But if our leaders—our clergy, our educators, our industrial captains, our statesmen, and our writers—continue to preach the contrary one, that our satisfaction and salvation are to be found in *busyness* and things and a unilateral warping of our nature, then Arnold will indeed have been a prophet, for the second half of his title and thesis will have come to pass.

III

1. NEW MODES IN BIOGRAPHY

MAN'S CURIOSITY as to his fellow-man is perennially insatiable, often vulgar, sometimes cruel. It extends from the patient deciphering of a cuneiform text by a lonely scholar in order to discover facts about some Assyrian, dead these seventy centuries, in whom no one but a few other scholars will be interested, to the colossal mob-hunt of a whole nation to eavesdrop on a Lindbergh during his honeymoon. The satisfaction of this curiosity is, perhaps, the most paying function of the daily press. In book publishing it has swollen the department of biography to gigantic proportions. From 1900 to 1915 over 500 biographies a year were published in England alone, and the stream is steadily swelling. Although I have not the figures at hand, it would probably be conservative to estimate the daily average output of England, America, France and Germany at half a dozen volumes a day.

No man can keep up with this enormous output, but as one tries to bring some order out of the welter of new volumes, he can classify them with considerable ease. We may divide them into the "debunking," the "psychological," the "psychoanalytic," the "jazz-impressionistic," and so on, if we choose. Such classifications, however, lie rather obviously on the surface. They are descriptions of form or type. I prefer, myself, to divide them into those which derive from superiority and inferiority complexes, to adopt the current and convenient Freudian jargon.

One claim made by all of them, however unfounded it may be, is that they portray the *true* and the *real*. The first question, of course, is, What is true or real? Those who write and read with a superiority complex find these qualities to lie in a "scientific" treatment and interpretation of their subject. Those, on the other hand, who write and read with an inferiority complex first establish for themselves a scale of values and then pick out those qualities or acts in their subjects which fit into or illustrate values in that scale. However much individual volumes in these two classes may resemble each other on the surface, I believe that they differ profoundly in motive and origin.

The subjects themselves may cover the entire history of the race—biographies of anybody and everybody from Tut-ankh-Amen to Al Smith—but in spite of the infinite heterogeneity of, say, 4,000 volumes published in the last year, they form, from another standpoint, but a single biography. They may be regarded as a single work reflecting the mass mind of the moment.

The first class of biographies noted above derive from the enormous preoccupation of the present age with science and the belief that such facts as can be studied "scientifically" possess a superior validity. The possession

NEW MODES IN BIOGRAPHY

of the trifling knowledge of the present day in psychology, endocrinology and other sciences has induced an amazing superiority complex, or, if you prefer, a "swelled head." Harry Elmer Barnes says that all biographies written before 1900 are "rhetorical goose eggs" because there was "no valid psychology" before the last generation. More recently he has gone further and told us that a historian or biographer must master physiological chemistry, the glands, arterio-sclerosis and all the rest of disease and physiology. Harold Nicholson predicts in his *Development of English Biography* that, in the future, biography will become a branch of science and we shall have, among other forms, biographies based on the influence of endocrine glands and the internal secretions. If I may say so, this is sheer drivel. As usual we have to go to France for sanity. *"Que savons-nous sur l'histoire médicale des grand hommes du passé?"* (What do we know about the medical history of the great men of the past?) writes Maurois in his *Aspects de la Biographie. "Que saura-t-on dans l'avenir sur ceux du présent?"* (What will be known in the future about those of the present?) "Who," he continues, "at this moment is making notes on the internal secretions of Einstein, studying the endocrine glands of Paul Valéry or recording the dreams of Bertrand Russell?"

*

Thus far, for the most part, our new scientific, superiority-complex biographers have confined themselves to interpreting their subjects according to the "science" of psychology and, more narrowly, psychoanalysis, which are among the least firmly established, it may be noted, on a scientific basis, of all our branches of knowledge. Among the psychological school of biographers the unquestioned leader and by far the most influential practitioner is Lytton Strachey. In many respects his work is as admirable as it is entertaining. In his latest work, *Elizabeth and Essex,* he shows scant sympathy with the medical school. Of few figures in the past do we know as much physiologically as we do of his subject Elizabeth, but, he says, "our knowledge, both of the laws of medicine and of the actual details of her disorders, is too limited to allow of a definite conclusion." He is an extremely able interpreter of character, and his portraits of Elizabeth, Victoria and others *may* be the truth, but I deny that they possess scientific validity, once beyond the realm of attested fact.

It is obvious that in writing the life of any one regarding whose life and acts there is a large mass of available material, selection is inevitable. On this selection the nature of the biography depends. Strachey develops in his own mind a psychological character for his heroine and makes his selection of facts fit into this character. Psychologically, his Elizabeth, his Victoria, his Florence Nightingale are merely these people as they are envisaged by him. The thesis remains purely personal. What we get is Strachey's reaction to his sitter. When, for example, for four pages, he recounts the thoughts that pass through

Elizabeth's mind, we are getting fiction as pure and unde-
filed as anything Thackeray tells us about Becky Sharp.
His best disciple, Nicholson, says that biography is distinguished from history as being the story of an individual, and from fiction as being truth. Such re-creating
of another person's thoughts is not truth. It is, at best,
a shrewd guess, though it *may* closely (and, again may
not) approximate the truth when done by a master of
character analysis.

There is, however, only one Strachey, and his influence has been little short of disastrous. The public cares
nothing about distinguishing between his fact and his fiction. As soon as he leaves established facts, he works in
exactly the same way as any competent master of character drawing in fiction, and because he is a master, he has
achieved enormous popularity. The school of vastly inferior writers that has sprung up about him are for the
most part engaged in writing what are merely biographical novels. Rarely, however, like Maurois in his *Ariel,* do
they have the intellectual integrity and decency to call
their work a "Shelley Romance." For the most part, they
play on the public's belief that it is getting "real" biography scientifically interpreted, and so combine the bene-
fits to be derived from the markets for both fiction and
biography. The historic background gives an illusion of
reality, and the authors claim for their imaginary conversations and their tracing of thoughts a scientific validity
in modern "psychology" that is utterly unfounded. That
Cæsar crossed the Rubicon is a fact, but the greatest

psychologist living, possessing what no biographer can possess, complete knowledge of the "science," could not, with scientific accuracy, reconstruct Cæsar's thoughts before he decided to return to Rome. It is doubtful if he could even make any shrewder guess at them than any man these past nineteen hundred years who had had wide experience of life and men. To say that any one who wrote biography before this generation laid only rhetorical goose eggs is to talk superiority-complex tommy-rot.

For most practitioners of this "scientific" school of psychological biography, it is far easier to imagine what a person may have *thought* than to weave the facts of what he *did* into a readable (and salable) narrative. The public gets all the "kick" of fiction with the soothing sense that they are dealing with something "real" and "scientific." That many of the biographers are not even thoroughly grounded in psychology is patent enough. As for careful study of their subjects from this most difficult standpoint, it is merely necessary to figure how much time they could have had for consideration when turning out a big volume every year or so, or even oftener. In one case I happen to know of, a biographer was sent for by a publishing house. He was told a life of So-and-so was wanted in so many months. The biographer remarked that he did not know a thing about the man. He was told he would be given a list of what to read, a check for $5,000 was passed, and in due course the "true" life came out.

✳

As to having any scientific validity, the psychoanalytic biography is even worse off than the psychological. Clothed in Freudian jargon, a book is considered by the mob as having a claim to be considered ultra-modern and eruditely scientific. Unfortunately for my purpose, the noted biographical attempt made by Freud himself is not allowed to circulate in America, and this book would not get through the mails if I discussed the work in frank detail. In a word, it is an effort to reconstruct the life of Leonardo da Vinci, even to the smile of the Mona Lisa, by means of interpreting a fantastic memory he records as having had of an incident in his childhood. As the author proceeds through "it is quite possible," "we consider it probable," "we further assume" and a whole phantasmagoria of incredibly unscientific assumptions, he grows gradually more certain in his pronouncements until he sums up at the end as facts concerning Leonardo what he has been able "to discover concerning the course of his psychic development." This psychoanalysis has proved a most dangerous tool in the hands of all who have used it. Barnes, for example, considers that it is very easy to see why Hamilton and Jefferson emerged as leaders if we consider the factors surrounding their childhood, factors no different, as he gives them, from those surrounding the childhood of hundreds of other children who did not become leaders. Harlow traces Sam Adams's part in the Revolution to an inferiority complex, forgetting that thousands of other men of the time had the same. O'Higgins explains Mark Hanna by a clash between an impurity complex and a biologic urge to secure the esteem of his fellows. And so the game goes on, the biographers utterly blind to the fact, first, that they are dealing with mere guesses, and, second, that whatever *influence* certain factors or traits may have had, they cannot explain the *whole* of these men and their careers. If ever half-baked knowledge paraded under the name of science it does so in psychoanalytic biography.

We know, definitely and conclusively, as yet, little or nothing of these things scientifically. As applied to persons long dead, they are merest guesses in any case. One of the leading psychiatrists in the United States told me that the author of one of the finest biographies ever published in America sent to him for criticism two chapters in which the author had attempted to prove that at one time his subject was suffering from a certain mental disorder. The psychiatrist told him that even with the living subject before a specialist for personal examination it was no easy task to diagnose, and that in the case of a person who could not be personally examined it was utterly impossible. The chapters were omitted, but had they been included the public would have hailed the book as a "scientific" biography of the "new" school.

*

As I have said, every biographer, like any historian or artist, has to select the facts that he shall include. The "new" biographer and his readers of the superiority-com-

plex school smile at the older biographies or at such recent ones as Beveridge's *Lincoln,* which are in reality far
more scientific than their own, in so far as at least they
will have nothing to do with facts that are not completely
and soundly authenticated. What the new biographers of
the school I have noted are doing is to select such facts
as fit the taste and interest of the public in the present
age, clothing them in a pseudo-scientific form to appeal to
the most powerful cult of the age, the cult of science. It
will be long before science will allow us to predict or trace
human conduct. Human nature and the web of circumstance in which every human life is enmeshed are infinitely complex. Cæsar and Napoleon were epileptics, but
does that explain their careers? So have millions of other
men been, without bestriding the world. All this medical
biography is too general to signify, and psychology at
present is in so inchoate a state as a science as to be in
danger of being laughed out of court if it does not mend
its ways. It is about as useful in the hands of an ordinary
biographer as a stick of dynamite.

When we come to the other school of biography, that
which I have described as springing from an inferiority complex, we are dealing with quite a different aspect of
our age. Democracy and universal education have combined to bring into existence a vast new public capable
of reading. It is a public without cultural standards, whatever it may be in time to come. It has merely suddenly
become literate. For the most part it has no desire to submit itself to the hard work and intellectual training that

culture entails. It wants to be amused and have its ego fed. Above all, it wants to consider itself as good as any other class or any other age. In its soul it may know that it is not cultured, that it is not mannered, that it is not great, but no one cares willingly to admit that he is inferior. In an Oriental society of permanent castes or at certain periods of Western European civilization when society was ordered and stable, the sting of inferiority has been to a certain extent removed. In a society in which change of position in the scale is not possible, there is no personal stigma attached to an inferior position. It is fate, kismet. In a society where any position, social, economic, intellectual, ethical, is theoretically possible of attainment, inferiority of status does carry a stigma, which is equally resented whether due to circumstance or to mere personal laziness or inefficiency. In the complete instability of modern society, a sense of inferiority has become intolerable.

It is not thus intolerable merely to the so-called lower classes who feel this new need to assert their own equality with the best. To a certain extent large sections in all of society are parvenus in the new world created by applied science. We have our radio, telephone, luxurious liners, our public hotels as sumptuous as royal palaces. We have harnessed the lightning, and the waterfalls do our bidding. We make our voices heard ten thousand miles. We have crossed the ocean in a day. We weigh the stars. But with it all has come a spiritual malaise. In growing all-powerful, man has lost his own sense of greatness. We have lost the dignity that at least religion gave to life. Our ethics have dissolved. Science in the popular mind has made man a mere animal, if not a mere automatic switchboard of incoming and outgoing "calls"—impressions and reactions.

With all this has come, for the time being, an unconscious sense of inferiority. We are rich and powerful beyond any previous age, but the other ages had a sense of dignity, of possible greatness in life and conduct, of values in life that we have not. We know it, and, like every class which has felt that some other class possesses qualities of value that it lacks, we tend to defend ourselves by emphasizing our own vulgarity while throwing mud at the others. These two great groups, the utterly uncultured but literate lower class and a good part of the so-called upper but now disillusioned class, have, in my opinion, together called into existence the vast flood of biographies that come under the inferiority-complex type.

Was there in the past a statesman who was really great and incorruptible? Was there a poet or painter who believed in the greatness of his art? Were there scholars who cared nothing for the world? Were there men who, human enough and failing often for that reason, yet kept a sense of the intrinsic dignity and worth of human nature? Are there such today? Then away with them! Crucify them! Or show us that they not only sinned but were hypocrites, little men, smaller even than ourselves! Let us bolster up our self-esteem not by slowly working out for ourselves again a new philosophy of life but by pulling down all men of all times to our level. Set up the "debunking" school of biography and be quick about it.

The school has had an enormous vogue because its public is naturally the largest. That there should be a re-action against the old filiopietistic school both in history and biography was right enough, but the new debunking school has now gone far to the opposite extreme. In what purports to be, for example, a complete biography of Franklin, scarcely to mention his elaborate plan for a union of the Colonies while giving, as I recall, five pages to a smutty skit, is to paint as wholly false a picture of the man as to pretend that he was an asexual saint. In the foreword to the latest life of Cæsar "we see the hun-dred-per-cent Romans brawling drunkenly in their Forum —hurling execrations at one another in their Senate house —lying on the cushions of their litters * * *—gloating sadistically, in their amphitheatres and circuses, over the butchery of unhappy gladiators with starved wild animals. They are fat, heavy-joweled men with greedy, cruel eyes. To make the picture perfect all they need is big cigars." That there were plenty of Romans of that type is true enough, but to explain and paint the Rome of the period of Cæsar as solely made up of that sort is not to explain it at all. It is as far from being "scientific" as it is to explain Thomas Jefferson, as has been attempted, from an inferiority-anti-authority complex due to his father's having died when the boy was fourteen and of his having been brought up with a mother and six sisters.

Again, we come to the problem of selection of material. In this type of biography it is evidently selected solely with a view to picking the last vestige of greatness off all humanity, past as well as present, when the selection is not simply, though not frankly, pornographic. Many of these biographies remind me of the tourist who found himself on the ground-floor room of a hotel in a mining camp with no curtain to the window. Having hung up his undershirt to afford some shelter from prying eyes, he soon found it drawn aside as a man looked in. When the intruder was asked what his business was, he answered, "I jest wanted to see what was going on in here that was so damned private." Descriptive of others we might quote the anecdote of John Fox, Jr., when he read some of his stories about mountain whites to them themselves. A storm broke loose, and a voice shouted, "If he's tellin' the truth, he ain't no gentleman, and if he ain't, then by God, he's a liar."

To class any of the new biographies as more scientific than the substantial scholarly type is, as we have tried to show, an utterly hollow pretense. They either express, as in the psychological school, a personal point of view and a personal interpretation; or, as in the psychoanalytic school, a half-baked, pseudo-scientific effort to explain character and events from inadequate and, as yet, highly disputable scientific bases; or, lastly, as in the inferiority-complex school, a mere effort all too often to swell the ego of the reader by belittling the subject, under the guise of "humanizing" him.

What is the outcome likely to be of the present confusion in biography as in all other aspects of modern life? If, as I have said, the multifold biographical writing of any period is, from one point of view, merely a picture of the mind of that period itself, the answer is that our methods of writing biography will alter as the mass mind alters, and no sooner. A period that is interested in ethical values will ask to have those stressed in the lives of the people about whom it reads. A period that is interested in what goes on in the bathroom will find biographers willing to pry there for them. But as there are various types of individual minds in all periods, so there are various sorts of biographies written, and we have all types today. And there are not a few signs that the times are changing. As I have written elsewhere, the whole metaphysical basis of science is changing rapidly, and, though it may take some time, the current of popular thought will come to be influenced in its turn. In painting, I have just noted in Paris, there is a decided slump in the vogue of green nudes and other mysteries of the "new art." What is more notable is that the prices have crashed. With all the blurbs about the "real John Doe" and the "true Richard Roe," in biography, it is noteworthy that the sales of Beveridge's *Lincoln* have been simply astounding, and have far outdistanced those of any "new" biography.

*

As long as we have a large class that is literate without having any standards, we shall undoubtedly have biography written that is neither science, art nor literature. Much of it has no more right to be considered seriously than the great mass of movie stuff that is put on the market for a similar type of consumer. Fears have been expressed that the taste for biography that really attains to high standards of scholarship or literature may be vitiated by all the "easy reading" lives with which the shops are flooded. I rather doubt it, although I am not particularly optimistic as to the age. The people who have genuine taste and standards have always been in the very small minority in any age, and although at present, because of the great increase in the number of readers, they undoubtedly form a smaller percentage of them than of old, I doubt if they form a smaller proportion of society as a whole. Possibly the contrary is the case. There have always been people whose taste ran to obscene scrawls on walls, just as there have always been those higher in the scale who were dazzled by paste jewelry of the Guedalla sort.

Perhaps in time, also, the label of science will be better understood, as will also the fact that a man is no more "human"—perhaps, indeed, essentially less so —when he is saying "God damn" than when he is saying *"Pater noster,"* even when he is equally sincere in both expresssions. Meanwhile, one duty that lies before critics is clear, and that is to say the truth about books as they come out; to distinguish clearly for the reader between the genuine science, in the sense of exact knowledge, of a book like Beveridge's *Lincoln,* and the pseudo-scientific balderdash of, for example, most of the psychoanalytic school; to distinguish between the scholarly presentation of facts, and the personal interpretation of states of mind, even when the latter are made with all the skill and charm of style of a Strachey. As for much of the rest, it is as little worth a competent critic's attention as any other form of passing amusement devised for the mob. These latter books have, perhaps, to be chronicled, but to treat them seriously is merely to give them an unmerited importance. In the present state of current criticism in America, however, I doubt if even the compiled scribblings on a Pompeian latrine would fail to find *some* reviewer who would hail it as a "profound psychological study, a human document of the first importance."

Literature of any genre is but the reflected light from that of the life of its period. As the light of life itself brightens or darkens, as it turns red or blue or white, so does the literature that reflects it. We cannot predict the future of biography without knowing the future of the mind of society, and he would be a courageous prophet who would forecast that, even a decade at a time. Interest in material, taste in form, shift and alter, but it is not likely that *The Hairy Ape* is greater than *Macbeth* or *Prometheus Chained*. It is different. Nor is it likely that any biography written now is greater than ever before merely because its selection of facts and its mode of expression have changed. It is different. And, except in so far as it refuses to take account of any but proved and accredited facts, it is, in any example that has come my way, assuredly no more "scientific."

2. BIOGRAPHY AS AN ART

IT IS POSSIBLE that the simple naturalness of the biographic art, originating in personal narration or casual gossip, has prevented it from being considered as esthetically artificial and idiosyncratic as the epic, lyric, drama, novel, or essay. At any rate, with all the pother about other forms, almost nothing has been written about biography as an art. James C. Johnston in his volume, *Biography: The Literature of Personality,* has made the first elaborate effort to establish it as a separate one worthy of critical analysis and study. In his whole review of the literature in three languages dealing with biography as a form he is, however, able to list only fifteen essays, several of which are merely short articles of a few pages each and others of which deal with autobiography rather than biography proper. In no other field of literary endeavor are we so in need of careful and sanely critical analysis of all the problems involved.

But if biography as a literary form has never attracted the serious attention of the literary critic, it would nevertheless be a mistake to think that any of its manifestations are new. Literary currents ebb and flow, and partly because of the multitudinous changes in the mere mechanics of living and partly because of the substitution of science and the modern languages for history and the classics in education, our new collegians are too apt to measure by decades rather than by ages. If there is any word which more than another is coming to send a shiver down the susceptible spine of a man who has an historical background, it is the word "new," so sweated in literary shops,—the "new history," the "new freedom," the "new biography." There is nothing fundamentally new in any form of biography written at the present time.

It is true that the school which has practised biography for what a recent reviewer has called "monumental or exemplary purposes" has been the most prolific in all periods. Plutarch in his *Life of Pericles* wrote that "our intellectual vision must be applied to such objects as, by their very charm, invite it onward to its own proper good. Such objects are to be found in virtuous deeds; these implant in those who search them out a great and zealous eagerness which leads to imitation;" and for that reason he decided to persevere in his writing of biographies. On the other hand, one must be ignorant of or merely ignore a vast amount of writing in the past to say, as does Robert Morss Lovett, that "only under the influence of modern realism has the biographer been permitted to approach his public on the side of its strongest interest—that in human experience—and to make use of the most exciting part of his hero's experience—that in which he departed from the accepted *mores.*"

Such a sentence makes one both question and wonder. Has Mr. Lovett never read the *Lives of the Cæsars* by Suetonius? Certainly no "new biographies" have been franker in revealing the most secret sins of their subjects. Or has he forgotten the autobiography of St. Augustine in which he recounts, among other things, his abnormal sexual longings and practices with an openness that only a hardened "new biographer" would compete with? As compared with a few decades ago, we have adopted new methods of selection and emphasis in writing lives, but that is the mere ebb and flow of style as measured by a generation or two, not by the history of the art. Both Woodward and Parson Weems, in their lives of Washington, were heirs of long lines of different methods in the practice of the art. One line of traditional method produced most examples a generation ago; the other produces more today. That is all. The real question comes back, in its only critical sense, to the validity of the two methods and a question of standards.

*

Is biography, by presenting a noble life in its noblest aspects, to serve, teaching by example, to incite readers to emulate such lives, or is its chief purpose to be, as Sir Sidney Lee said, to "transmit a personality"? A good deal more may be said, perhaps, for the first view,

that of Plutarch and his school, than our present icono-
clastic and cynical age may be willing to admit, but as
few people at the moment do admit it, we may pass to
an analysis of the second biographical goal.

"To transmit a personality." Here we have the
crux of the whole problem of biographical writing as
most practised today. What *is* a personality?

In spite of the deliquescence of so many of our old
ideas and standards, people are still more or less agreed
as to what is noble and fine, or at least as to what was
noble and fine before 1914. The Plutarchian biographer
thus has his selection of data fairly sharply defined, but
the Suetonian of the twentieth century is completely at
sea, as is shown by dozens of biographies published in
the last five years. Many of these have been announced
as "the true" so and so or as showing us "the real man."
The writer of this school does not have to decide merely
what is a noble deed but the far more complex problem
of what is a man. In addition he has the two technical
problems of what facts to select among the mass he finds
relative to his subject and how to present them.

I have read and reviewed a very considerable proportion of the biographies of recent years and I am convinced that scarcely one of the writers—there are
exceptions—has posed and answered to himself the fundamental question what is a man, that is, what are the
human qualities which may be considered of the highest
intrinsic worth or which serve best to etch in the outlines
of a personality? We will, therefore, in part leave aside

this question and consider it only obliquely by examining the technical methods employed of late. In the case of practically every modern biographical subject there is a wealth of material relating to the sitter, from among which a selection has to be made by the biographer. It would seem philosophically impossible to make such a selection in order to portray the "true" or "real" man without having settled first the problem of what "a man" *is*. Nevertheless, the publishers assure us that the trick is constantly turned. On what basis do I find the selection usually to be made? Exactly on that predicated by the reviewer already quoted, namely, that the most exciting part of a hero's career is that in which he departs from the accepted *mores*. But could there possibly be a cheaper or more absurd standard by which to value a man's life? The "accepted *mores*" change from time to time. The complex of *mores* was one thing in the reign of Charles the Second; it was another in the reign of Queen Victoria; it is a different thing, again, in the reign of Calvin Coolidge. Is the serious biographer, whose aim is to transmit to posterity "a personality" or to present for us today a "personality" of the past, to be governed in his selection of facts by counting as most "exciting" or important those which illustrate the points in which his hero departs from the accepted *mores* of his moment? In point of actual practice, what many current biographers are doing is to distort the picture even more by dwelling on the points in which their heroes of the *past* departed from the *mores* of *today*. In a sample of this so-called "modern" biography, (which in fact is often simply unphilosophical, unpsychological, and technically poor biography), Russell's *Benjamin Franklin,* I found that five pages were devoted to Franklin's hoaxing skit on the trial of Polly Baker for bastardy whereas less than one page was given to his plan for the union of the American colonies; that some of his most important writings were ignored in order to give space to his "Advice to Young Men on the Choice of a Mistress;" and so on in similar proportions throughout his career.

Do I claim that such matters have no place and that the subjects of biography should be draped in togas and not depicted in every-day clothes? By no means. I have myself dwelt in my writing on episodes which many people would suppress, and have praised highly certain biographies which have probed deeply into the hidden and unpleasant parts of men's hearts and lives. Where then are we to draw the line? It seems to me that there are two distinct and clear cut standards of inclusion of what we might call damning facts. One of these has to do not so much with the subject himself as it has with the biographies of his contemporaries in the case of a historical character. For example, if the biographers of John Hancock should paint him as a saint, they will make it appear that such of his distinguished contemporaries as distrusted him have been animated by jealousy or some other ignoble motive. The fact is that Hancock was not a great character, that, among other things, it was contemporaneously well known that he embezzled the funds of Harvard University while treasurer, and that, for various other reasons, the leading men of the time had a right to distrust him. To whitewash Hancock, is, *ipso facto,* to besmirch his distrusting contemporaries. In the same way, if one paints all Washington's generals and subordinates as faithful and efficient officers and patriots, their biographers rob Washington of the glory of having worked and won with many inefficent and unworthy instruments. It is obviously unfair to take away deserved glory from the deserving in order to give undeserved glory to the undeserving.

*

Where such a problem does not exist and it is merely a question of what to include in a private life, I would say that the test to be employed is whether the facts in question had any real and lasting influence on the man himself, his career and personality. The main object of biography is not to serve as an exhibit in a medical clinic. The physicians should gather and tabulate their own cases. What the biographer has to do is to present a personality. Take, for example, the question of sex, which seems to be all-absorbing at present. Suppose our subject had had a single episode with a girl of the streets when nineteen, that shortly after that he married and lived happily with his wife ever after. Suppose, on the other hand, that in another case in a man's later career he had a *liaison* lasting for years which pro-

193

foundly affected his whole life and work. In the one case, the facts may be of the deepest significance; in the other of no significance whatever. The sole test should be, not the pornographic or even emotional interest of the episode in itself but the importance of it as one of the items selected by which the biographer is trying to build up a picture of an idiosyncratic personality. It is this love of the episode for the episode's sake that damns so many current biographies and distorts the subject into no resemblance of the original. In the earlier lives of Franklin, one gains the impression of a grave philosopher; in the latest, of a somewhat ribald and obscene-minded old roisterer. Both are wrong but I am inclined to believe the older distortion comes nearer to the truth than the later. It is right to paint Cromwell with all his warts, but to give the warts an ounce more of weight than is called for by their influence on the man's career or personality is to paint the warts and not the man, and the business of a biographer is to paint the man.

Of course, we are always led back to the fundamental question, *what is a man?* A biographer who aims to be anything more than a quick-selling journalist must face and solve this problem. Many current biographers do it implicitly by assuming that "intimacy" and "human interest" consist in watching the man perform his lowest physical or mental acts. This is in itself a phase of that profound disillusionment which came from the discovery that the earth was not the center of the universe and, some centuries later, that man was not created but evolved. Having accepted the as yet by no means proved theory that man is of no lasting or cosmic importance, the tendency is to consider that there is no difference in value between the operation of the bowels and those of the brain. If there is not, then why bother about either, except for the fact that the biographer must use the one to fill the other—an obvious explanation of much current biographical writing? It is clear that the competent biographer has got to think out a philosophy of man and nature before he can select his facts.

*

Once selected, how is he to treat them? For one thing, as we have pointed out, the subject should not be considered as a medical case. In R. V. Harlow's life of Samuel Adams the facts that his voice occasionally rose to falsetto and that his hands trembled were used to explain the whole of his career, and no small part of the American Revolution, as due to the mental states of a neurotic, according to the then current but already somewhat discredited psychology. Each new fad finds its way into biography, and the subconscious, for example, has been made to play its part. To that sort of thing there is no end. If we are to write biographies in terms of unconscious complexes and the subconscious, why not in terms of biology, of chemistry, or even in terms of the aggregate dance of atoms which constitute the "physical" John Smith? Any man may be considered scientifically from many standpoints, but I contest that to consider him from that of the unconscious, of biological functions, of chemical reactions, or of atomic structure is not biography. Once we leave the realm of self-conscious life and of observable and recorded acts, we become lost in a descending scale of possible scientific approaches, and have abandoned the clearly defined field of biographical treatment.

Again, are we to give up the old-fashioned idea of recording the ascertainable facts of a man's life and substitute a biographer's appreciation of his character? This method of presentation, the old "character" under modern names, is no newer than any other form of biography, in spite of the acclaim of certain practitioners today. The difficulty with it lies largely in the practitioner. It is obvious that the mere "facts" may not give us the whole man, the essence of his character, but there is just as much danger, if not more, that the "appreciation" may give us the man, not as he was, but as distorted or refracted through the mind of his biographer, just as a portrait gives us his physical features with the psychological traits imagined by the artist; in other words a composite portrait of sitter and painter. In the case of a superb master of his craft we may gain a deeper and more veracious insight into the soul of the sitter from a portrait than from a photograph but in the case of a poor painter we may gain far less, and there is always the question of how much of what we see is the sitter and how much the painter. A superb biographer may play the artist; an ordinary craftsman had better play the photographer of the obvious. In such a recent work, for example, as Howden Smith's life of Vanderbilt, it is impossible to tell, with all the imaginary conversations and interpretations thrown in, how much of the picture is Vanderbilt and how much Smith, and, in my opinion, for that very reason it is worthless except as Smith's opinion of Vanderbilt, which in itself is a matter of little or no importance.

An entire essay might be written on style as part of the method of presentation, but perhaps nothing I could say would teach the would-be biographer as much as would a careful reading of Smith's book, just alluded to, and Johnson's *Andrew Jackson*. Both authors had to deal with self-made men, rather rough and uncouth in some of their aspects. Smith tries to achieve his effect by filling his pages *ad nauseam* with God Damns, Christs!, and other oaths and obscenity. Johnson without a single oath gives us just as clear an idea that Jackson's language at times was appalling and he conveys all the frontier roughnesses of the man, but at the same time he penetrates to his soul as Smith does not. With all Smith's attempted realism in treatment, Vanderbilt remains at best a generalized type; Johnson, with his artistry, gives us an individual. No other two recent books are more instructive in their contrasted methods, and one has only to think how a man like Smith would have dealt with Rachel Jackson, and then study how Johnson has dealt with her, to realize the difference between journalism and literary art. Johnson's fifteenth chapter—"How a Lover celebrated his Lady by saying Nothing"—is a little masterpiece and might well serve as a model for "new" biographers who study love in Freud and not in life.

The two volumes offer another contrast worth pondering. Cornelius Vanderbilt was an extremely low type of the human animal and interesting only as an economic factor. Jackson, rough and quixotic, was a personality with elements of greatness. This introduces the question of the biographical subject. No great biography can be written about a small man. Here, again, many modern biographers are being led astray by the lure of the episode. Just as in writing the lives of great men they emphasize the unessential or misleading but sensational episode for the episode's, not the man's, sake, so they choose subjects unimportant and uninteresting in themselves merely because they can rake out of their careers enough episodes to sell their books. It has been said of a play that if you can only have the audience sitting on the edge of their seats for thirty seconds somewhere in the five acts, it makes no difference about the rest. This is the theory of such modern biographers as write, not to produce a fine bit of biographical art, but to send Johnny to college or buy their wives a Spanish shawl.

It is impossible in three thousand words to discuss adequately the subject of biography as a form of literature. We have shelves full of volumes on almost every other. It is high time that someone should attempt to treat the biographical, and to clarify both the philosophy and technique of what is rapidly becoming one of the most popular and prolific of all literary forms.

3. IS HISTORY SCIENCE?

IN THE PRECEDING CHAPTER I mentioned that the literature dealing with biography as an art topic was so small, even in three languages, as to be practically negligible. When we come, however, to history, which may be described as a sort of multiple biography, we find a vast sea of controversial books and pamphlets, a never-ending discussion for the past fifty years on what history is and how it should be written. When I first began to read that sort of thing some fifteen years ago, I was stimulated to do some thinking on my own account. Since then I have read a great deal more of it but I have rarely found a new idea. The discussion simply goes on and on on the same lines. In the main it rages around two general topics,—what should form the subject matter of history, and whether history is a science or an art.

The battle over the former was waged with the peculiar bitterness of German scholarship in Germany many years ago and spread to the rest of the world. Should culture or the State form the subject matter of history? We still hear much today of the "new history," that is of history which includes, besides politics and wars, much in the life of the people that used to be thought below the dignity of the second Muse, but this, in fact, has long ceased to be "new." To go no farther back, Greene's *Short History of the English People* was conceived in 1869 and met with a tremendous sale on its publication in 1874. The old straw, however, continues to be threshed out. Naturally a man likes to consider as of unusual importance a subject to which he devotes his life. If he spends it teaching or writing political history he is apt to agree with Freeman that "history is past politics," and look askance at the claims of the man who considers the history of trade guilds as of superior validity.

*

The average man and the less doctrinaire historians would seem to be immovably agreed that history should deal with every aspect of what man has done and thought in the past. I believe this is the common-sense view and the correct one. Why not? All man's interests, motives, and acts are bound together in an inextricable nexus. It is true that we cannot write or think about everything at once. In that sense, we all have "single track" minds. We have to throw the emphasis now here, now there, but why should anyone claim that politics or economics or military affairs or religion or any other strand in man's manifold life must be the proper subject of history and no other? No one could drive twenty horses abreast and there are difficulties of construction in trying to tell too many stories at once in a book, but that is no reason for saying that any one subject rather than another is the only one with which history should deal. If history is merely politics, then to what science or art are we to consign all the rest of man's past activities about which people wish to know? History should disinter and narrate the facts of human activity in the past, facts which may later be used by sociology, economics, or other branches of enquiry.

These other branches may utilize to great advantage the facts provided for them by the historian but in these days it is almost impossible for anyone pursuing any branch of knowledge to keep up with the literature of his own branch. The *reductio ad absurdum* of the idea that an historian should also be an anthropologist, a psychologist, an economist, a sociologist, etc., may be found in such a book as Barnes's *History and the Social Sciences*. There is one sufficient answer to all that sort thing. Man's life is three score years and ten. A historian should, perhaps, know enough about them so as to be guided to a certain extent in his selection of facts to be treated by the historical method, but he can never have the knowledge of a specialist in any of them, and a little knowledge is a dangerous thing. The same set of facts may be interpreted as history, as economics, as sociology, and so on. The historian has plenty of work cut out for him in the discovery, the disentangling, the verifying of the facts. An understanding in general of the whole body of modern knowledge will help him greatly, and incidentally workers in other specialized fields, to select the facts, but their interpretation from the angle of special enquiry would seem to belong to those who make a life study of that specialty.

*

Is history an art or a science? It seems to me that in the controversy over this issue there has been a vast flood of words in which common sense has almost lost its life by drowning. The discussion has been particularly virulent, I believe, in the United States. Perhaps certain qualities in the American make-up account for this in part. For one thing, Americans like high-sounding titles for their jobs. The janitor of a New York apartment house (which itself would be a "flat" in England), is no longer a "janitor." He is a "resident engineer." When I hear a historian insisting that he is a "scientist" I cannot help but think of "realtors" and "morticians" and that the whole (American) world is kin. Moreover, it is hard to maintain an independent attitude in the face of a solid social opinion. America today worships science. I have recently dealt elsewhere with this worship and the "intellectual climate" of the present day. Everything, even barbers, must be "scientific" to be respectable. An artist is a more or less negligible camp-follower of our civilization, to be good-naturedly tolerated (especially if he gets good prices for his work), but a scientist is in the van, he is a "leader." A scientist is supposed to require technical training and to be among the intellectually élite. Our education is becoming more and more scientific. One after another of the humanities has been dropped from curriculums. Latin and Greek were thrown to the wolves of democracy some time ago. If history is not a science, God knows what may happen.

*

It is possible that unconsciously this general "intellectual climate" of the present day has more to do with trying to make history a "science" than has logic or reason. Moreover, the professional influence is very strong even when also unconscious. This has often been recognized in the history of the law. No individual lawyer, perhaps, tries to complicate matters for the sake of restricting business to members of his profession, but the tendency as a whole has been to make legal procedure more and more an esoteric affair so as to create a separate caste to deal with legal matters. If history can be made to appear likewise as an esoteric affair, a science in which only the initiated can participate, the reputation of the historian is increased. To write history well calls for certain qualities of mind and character as well as requisite knowledge but these qualities are as often found in men who have not been through the Ph.D. grind as in those who have, and often in a higher degree. Names at once occur to one. I am not speaking of populizers but of those who have done prime work of the highest importance from all standpoints, including scholarship. Perhaps no other American has a higher international reputation among scholars than Henry C. Lea, but he managed to produce his works of enormous erudition while leading the life of a busy publisher. The history of Parkman has stood the test of a whole generation of critics. The best history of the Civil War period was written by Rhodes, a retired iron manufacturer. Henry Adams's history of the United States from 1800 to 1814 is still the standard after forty years. Indeed, I have come to the conclusion that too long an academic training and career is rather a detriment than a benefit to a historian and that it should at least be supplemented by some years of an active career in affairs among men.

It is difficult to understand just what so many who insist that history is a science mean by it. As Poincaré— perhaps one of the most eminent scientists of our day— pointed out, the universe is spawning milliards of "facts" every second. To do anything in the way of arranging and understanding these, selection is, of course, necessary, and science is possible *only because there are certain kinds of fact which recur*. If it were not for this, there could be no possibility of establishing any laws or creating any science. The fact that two atoms of hydrogen when united with one of oxygen will act the same way tomorrow that they do today, and similar facts, enable us to make predictions and to test them. Now I know no historian today who is so hardy as to say that history can do this. Indeed, most of them say just the opposite. Professor Cheyney, for example, who has made some very interesting attempts to establish "laws" for history, states over and over that history never repeats itself, that he has "no confidence that definite individual historical examples will ever be very useful for present-day decisions," "that the similarity of one historical condition to another will never bear close inspection." It appears to me that what he calls "laws" are nothing but apparent tendencies in periods of time too short to be of much use, but in any case they are very different, as he admits, from scientific laws. What respect would a scientist have for a law which could never be expected to apply to any specific case? James Harvey Robinson in his earlier days claimed that the discovery that history is continuous, and the application of this "law," had raised history "in one sense, to the dignity of a science." There you have it. "The dignity of a science." Has art no dignity? Why has science, which is only one method of approaching certain problems of the universe, so much more "dignity" than other modes of intellectual life or interpretation of manifold reality? Why should more dignity be considered to attach to noting the specific gravity of oxygen, tracing the development of an embryo, or studying through a spectroscope the composition of a star, than to modelling the frieze of the Parthenon, painting the Sistine Madonna, or writing "Hamlet"? It is the "intellectual climate" of our age again.

It is difficult for me to see the reason for all this pother about the "dignity" of science and trying to edge in history, to say nothing of certain other branches of enquiry, where they do not belong. It would appear to come down to this. In the intellectual climate of the present day we think about the universe in certain ways. We believe that things do not merely "happen" but develop, one out of another. We believe that intellectual integrity requires that we should attempt to see and report things as they really are, that truth should be sought regardless of the consequences. These are ways of thinking which have proved enormously useful in developing the sciences and we think of them as scientific. They constitute, however, merely an *attitude of mind* and a *method of approach*. They may be used on bodies of data out of which sciences may be wrought. They may also be used on other bodies of data out of which no science can be wrought, because they consist of acts which are not recurrent, about which no predictions can be made and from which no laws, in the scientific sense, can ever be deduced.

*

The scientist and the historian both have to select a few facts from the milliards available. Science can select those which recur and about which hypotheses can therefore be tested. Facts do not recur in history or only in such general ways and mixed with so much new and various extraneous matter each time as to have no scientific value as recurrences. However careful and "scientific" the historian may be in his study of the facts, he has got to make a selection, and as he cannot select according to known laws he is forced to do so according to his own interpretation of logical and reasonable "causes," "sequences," or "connections." In other words, he is bound to select according to the laws of his own mind, not according to a law capable of being tested by repeated experiment which may exist, so to say, among the facts themselves. I do not see how any historian can get away from this.

I have dwelt on this constant striving to make history somehow, however vaguely, take on the "dignity" of science because it has profoundly influenced our historical writing. It has done this in two ways,—by determining both the choice of subject matter and the style of treatment. One writer, for example, points out that zoölogy no longer concerns itself with exceptional or startling creatures but with general principles. Perhaps so, but what has that to do with history, except for that vague "scientific bond" which is supposed to regulate all sciences? Professor Cheyney says that "history is simply a body of material to be studied, understood, and described, exactly as the biologist has his material, the chemist his, the mathematician his." Yet on the next page he speaks of this material as "the fortunes of humanity, with all its joys and sufferings, its conflicts, its failures, its attainments." Perhaps you can treat that body of material as a biologist or mathematician treats his, but one wonders why one has to do so even if history must be "deposed," as he says, from its position as a form of "pure literature," whatever, precisely, he may mean by that.

The difference between history and pure science may be seen if we take, for example, the story of a coral island. We can study the life of the coral insects scientifically because for that purpose every one of them is like every other. We can treat them as we would atoms. We can thus build up a science of these creatures. Let us suppose, however, that in some way we were suddenly enabled to enter into and understand the personal life of each of them and found that they loved, wrote books, painted pictures, had a science of their own, had leaders—in other words had a *history* to be recorded. Our approach to them would then have to be entirely different. This history of them would have to be quite different from the *natural history* of them. This is the ideal of the scientific historian of the human species but it could only be realized in practice by denuding the human individuals of all their distinctively human traits and making them as impersonally alike as coral insects. If this could ever be accomplished, which I do not believe because of the difference between men and animals, we might have a natural history of man but would it bear any resemblance to what we have always understood by *history*, and if not, why not get a new word to designate this new branch of enquiry?

*

Every generation wishes to rewrite to a certain extent its history of the past. This, in part, is because its tastes and interests change. A monarchical age, for example, will be interested in tracing out the monarchical strains in the past; a democratic age in tracing the beginnings of democracy; an industrial age in tracing the beginning of industry. That is understandable and proper. The subject matter of history will thus alter naturally to meet the needs and interests of each new period. But one wonders why the subject matter of history should be regulated by that of biology or zoölogy or any other "ology." Again we encounter the scientific urge. One writer says, for example, "what are the most striking traits of modern scientific method? It may be confidently replied that an appreciation of the small, the common, and the obscure, and an unhesitating rejection of all theological, supernatural, and anthropocentric explanations, establish the brotherhood of all scientific workers, whatever their field of research." It follows naturally that if historians are to attain to the dignity of that brotherhood and be admitted, they also must concern themselves with "the small, the common, and the obscure." Well, they are doing it to a great extent, partly because it is the spirit of the age. Democracy worships its own image and in every branch of art, as well as science, we are becoming more and more concerned with the obscure and the common and the mean. I am so little of a "scientific" historian that I shall not predict the end, but I firmly believe that most if not all the advance the race has yet made has been due to the uncommon, not the common, man. Six thousand years of recorded history is too short a period to generalize from, and I do not pretend to say whether democracy is or is not the final form of government toward which the race has always tended and under which it will remain. I doubt it, and if some day other forms arise in which interest has again shifted from the common to the uncommon man, I wonder if complete preoccupation with the "small, the common, and the obscure" will appear to be as "scientific" then as now. We may compile statistics and try to deduce laws from the lives of hundreds of apothecaries' apprentices in England in 1820, but one of them, John Keats, publishes a volume of poems, the world receives a new and imperishable gift, and our laws as to apothecaries' apprentices cease to be worth a tinker's dam. I do not begrudge the space now being given in histories to mean and common things and persons. The doing so fits in with many of our interests at the moment and I am myself greatly interested in it, but why so "scientific"?

This insistence upon wearing the cloak of science has affected the style of writing. In the last three years I have served on five historical juries and have had to read every important history which could in any way be considered as competing, as well as many theses and manuscript works. Of course, there must always be an increasing number of scholarly monographs on topics too specialized for the public, bricks to be used in building the historical edifice, and nowhere in this article am I speaking of them, but I do not blame the American Historical Association for having, some years ago, appointed a committee to see if something could be done to improve the style of our historical writers. Parkman could write as he liked. Henry Adams could indulge in Jovian laughter as he recorded the history of our early Republic, but the modern academically trained historian, in whom has been thoroughly inculcated the belief that history is a science, and that he must uphold the dignity of science, is afraid to have a style or step out of his laboratory gown for a single instant for fear lest he be damned as "literary," for one thing "scientific" history must not be—the deadly sin—is to be literature. Its professor has lost his public but kept the faith with his fellow scientific historians and saved his soul and salary.

What has the result been? The public to a certain extent has pierced his pretension. It realizes that history is not science in the same sense as is chemistry or zoölogy or astronomy or anything else that *it* calls science. A small part of the public, God bless it, does want to know something about the past of our race, but it wants to be able to stay awake while it reads. It has therefore, in increasing numbers, turned to men who can keep it awake but who are not good historians. With the insistence that history must be a science, a situation began to develop in which extremely valuable books were written by specialists for specialists. Historians began, so to say, to take in each other's washing, while incompetent popularizers fed the public. Fortunately this is changing. But it has got to change much more, and I believe it will not until historians get away from the idea that history is a science and, as a *non sequitur,* must be completely divorced from literature. They may not, as men, be a timid race, but it is, as I said, extremely hard to go counter to the opinion of one's fellows, and so long as our Ph.D. training remains what it is and so long as men who write have to fear being considered "unscientific" by their faculties, we cannot look for much improvement. The number of men who, when they have found their public, leave their academic associates would indicate something wrong.

I do not see why we need label history as either a science or an art, except that everything has to have a tag, but, on the whole, if one insists on a designation, I believe it safer to consider it an art, and leave it to the gentlemen who write it to tell the truth like gentlemen as they find it, for in this age it is not only scientists who try to think clearly, report honestly, and use every possible source and resource to see how things really were and how they have come to be as they are. I can see no way in which history can approximate science more nearly than that. If that be science, make the most of it.

4. HENRY ADAMS AND THE NEW PHYSICS

IN AMERICA, where so often labels count for more than contents, Henry Adams has always been taken by many for a brilliant amateur. Had he had no money, had he taken a Ph.D. degree, and then struggled along on a professorial salary, he would have much more indubitably ranked as a professional. As it happened, he had, instead of these handicaps, not only one of the most brilliant minds America has produced, but sufficient income to enable him to study as he chose, to do an amazing amount of travelling among varied civilizations, and to enjoy mental contacts of an extraordinarily stimulating sort.

An excellent illustration of the attitude I mean may be found in the essay on Adams written by Gamaliel Bradford in 1920. Bradford's mind is microscopic in its functioning, Adams's was telescopic, and it is not to be wondered at that Bradford was inclined to belittle and rather patronize Adams; but in one of his critical remarks he undoubtedly voiced a feeling common to many Americans. He admitted Adams's vast research among documents and his "consistent effort." "Yet, after all his labor and all his effort," Bradford adds, "I at least cannot escape the impression that he was an author 'for fun.'" That, of course, from a New Englander, is damning. The pecuniary needs of any career being provided for, it may, however, well be asked whether the finest work in scholarship, art, and letters has not always been done "for fun." It all depends on how the individual defines his fun. But for the Calvinistic moralist and the practical man "fun" of any sort is essentially suspect. They cannot realize that work done for the love of it may be better than work done under compulsion. For them duty or the dollar is the motive for serious work. The stigma of the dilettante, a lack of high seriousness, seems to them to hang about the work of the man who is driven by neither of these urges but merely by that of intellectual curiosity. In Europe a man's work is all that counts. In America, with its curious moralistic-materialistic form of culture, the estimate of the work waits upon, and is influenced by, all sorts of subtle enquiries into motives, official position, labels of all sorts. It is for this reason quite as much as from the nature of some of his work that Adams in many quarters is still looked upon as having been not quite a serious person.

So vast has our modern accumulation of knowledge become that any man is an amateur outside of some tiny corner. Adams's work in history, however, unquestionably qualifies him as a historian of the first or almost first rank. In science he was an amateur, but the quality of his mind and the intensity of his interest enabled him to absorb as much knowledge as a layman could. On the whole, perhaps no other American has been so well fitted as he to make the effort to establish scientific law in history, if it be possible. I do not wish to make any invidious comparisons, but in running over the list of possible aspirants I can think of no other American historian or scientist who was or is so well qualified in both fields, fields in which, by necessity, a man must be very much of an amateur in one or the other.

It is the object of this essay to deal mainly with the attempt of Henry Adams to formulate a theory of history rather than with his concrete contributions to the writing of it. Yet in view of what follows in this discussion it may be well to state briefly what contributions he made to the art which he later tried to develop into a science.

In the first place, he was for seven years Professor of History at Harvard, an episode which he himself always belittled but which was singularly rich in results for the teaching of history in America. Always disrelishing labels, he might not have cared to have the informal group, which he taught to a considerable extent around the fireside of his own house, termed a "seminar," but it is unquestionable that he was the first American teacher to introduce that method into this country, a method that is now the basis of the best of our graduate teaching. Among his pupils were J. Laurence Laughlin, Henry Osborn Taylor, and President Lowell.

During these years he had little time for writing, but as soon as he was relieved from what he found the drudgery of this work, he turned to his great *History of the United States*. The publication of the nine volumes, covering the periods of the presidencies of Jefferson and Madison, were preceded by his *Life of Gallatin*, with the three supplementary volumes of his *Writings*, the *Life of John Randolph of Roanoke*, and the editing of the *Documents Relating to New England Federalism*. The *Randolph* may be dismissed as unimportant, but the *Gallatin* was in every way a first-class piece of work, and has remained an authority for over fifty years. Not only that but in the balanced restraint shown in writing, at a time when the style and manner of Bancroft were still powerful influences, it did great service in turning historical writing in America into more scientific courses.

The *History of the United States* was at once, and properly, hailed as a masterpiece by those best qualified to judge. In structure and style it cannot rival such classics as Macaulay or Gibbon, but a generation after it appeared, and with all the research since made, it yet stands unchallenged as the best and most scholarly history of its period, and is likely long to remain so. As Worthington Ford wrote at the time of Adams's death, "it has stood every test and remains an example of the best that can be done in the writing of American history." Such writers in the younger generation of historians as Professor Morison are still lavish in their praise. So far as this work is concerned, no other American historian has yet approached Adams in his own field; none has excelled him in any other.

Two later books must also be mentioned. In the *History* Adams had stuck closely to documents, and although he wrote superlatively well, his method had been that which has now become the more or less conventional one for the so-called scientific historian. As Adams brooded over the problems of history, however, he developed a theory that we shall discuss later. In his attempt to bring the facts of history under a scientific law, it was necessary for him to establish "points of reference" from which to estimate the forces with which he became engaged. He chose two: the twelfth and thirteenth centuries as the period when man was most conscious of unity, and the twentieth when unity had given place to multiplicity. His *Mont-Saint-Michel and Chartres* and his *Education* were intended to establish these "points." In both cases his method broke down, as was inevitable. No one, historian or layman, now reads these books with any reference to the author's theory of history, but in both cases the books remain great and unique. The former has been described aptly as "a series of pictures tinged with feeling and glowing with enthusiasm," and if the whole of the medieval story is not to be found in its pages, it nevertheless remains the best introduction for anyone who would reach to the soul of that period. As a synthesis of the thought and aspiration of one period in history, it would be difficult to find its equal. It has been of great and continued influence in America from the time when, against his wishes although with his consent, it was given to the public by the American Institute of Architects, which also elected Adams an honorary member.

The other volume—the *Education*—is now read as an autobiography, and as such it is *sui generis* in American letters. We may admit, as Brooks Adams did in his comment, that the irony is rather overdone, and most readers will end the volume before the final chapters on the theory of history, though William A. Dunning found in them the most substantial manifestation of Adams's genius. It may be recalled, moreover, that Adams never intended the book for publication and that it appeared without corrections after his death. No other autobiography by an American affords such a rich variety of starting points for deep reflection, and its influence, already great, is likely to grow. From this very brief survey of Adams's substantial accomplishment, we may pass to consider his effort to bring history into line with the scientific thought of his own day.

It is, of course, impossible to treat scientifically idiosyncratic and unique facts. As Henri Poincaré expressed it, science can deal only with such facts as recur, or, in Eddington's words, science has to select from the whole domain of experience that portion only which is capable of metrical representation. By such selection and by study of the facts in such carefully selected fields, scientists have been able to establish certain "streaks of order" in the chaos, as Ritchie says, and to establish certain "laws." That the entire cosmos should be orderly and thus eventually possible of reduction to laws is a matter of inference only, scarcely, indeed, more than a pious hope. Particularly in the last half century, however, the aston-ishing success of applying the scientific method to se-lected facts in carefully chosen fields has so affected our instinctive attitude towards epistemology as to make any knowledge of a sort other than scientific appear as in-ferior if not invalid. The scientists, so to say, quickly be-came the aristocrats in the kingdom of the mind, and whosoever would rise to eminence felt a compelling urge to join their ranks. It may well prove to be the case, as Eddington has recently suggested, that the cleavage be-tween scientific and non-scientific knowledge is not be-tween concrete and transcendental but merely between metrical and non-metrical; but the urge, in our present intellectual climate, is no less compelling to extend as widely as possible the sphere of the metrical, and to ac-cord to the resulting "scientific" knowledge a superior sort of validity, and to its practitioners a superior sort of authority.

History, understood as the sum total of all the acts and thoughts of individuals of the human species, is obviously a part of the cosmos, and the effort is by no means new to try to bring some sort of order into the in-finite detail of even our recorded data. We need not here discuss the Greek theory of historical cycles, the extraor-dinarily modern ideas of Lucretius, nor the more recent efforts made from Montesquieu to Comte. The latest at-tempt I have seen was that of Professor Cheyney in his presidential address before the American Historical Association in 1923 in which, with great modesty and emphasizing the tentative nature of his guesses, he tried to establish six "laws in history." Although the urge to establish "laws" is distinctly scientific, how far historical material is as yet from being susceptible to scientific treatment is clearly shown in Cheyney's sixth law, which he calls the law of moral progress. Such a law is obviously based on *values*, and values have no place in science. Yet values undeniably have their place in history.

The various schools of determinists, geographic and climatic from Buckle to Miss Semple, or economic like Professor Seligman, while usefully pointing to influences that must be taken into account, cannot be considered to have established "laws in history" in the genuine scientific sense. So far, indeed, as I am aware, only one man has ever attempted to subsume the multitudinous data of human history under a strictly scientific law, and that man was Henry Adams. It is true that we hear a constant babble about scientific history and scientific historians, but in my opinion this is misleading nomenclature. The modern effort to record facts truly without bias or prejudice, is merely a step towards intellectual integrity. In time such effort may provide the raw materials for science, but it is not yet science, the very essence of which is predictable results based on law. Adams is, I believe, the only man who ever attempted to formulate a law in history that should be sufficiently scientific as to permit of its use in predicting the future, and so to use it. It is still impossible to know whether history can ever be a science, that is, whether its data are rhythmical or non-rhythmical, whether it will prove to be one of the "streaks of order" in the cosmos or whether it will not, but if it ever does prove so, Henry Adams must be accorded the first place in its establishment. It is this that gives unique interest to his, in my opinion, unsuccessful attempt.

The form which that attempt took was predetermined by the period in which it was made, and its expression would have been different twenty years earlier or ten years later. Adams wrote in 1894 that "any science of history must be absolute, like other sciences, and must fix with mathematical certainty the path which human society has got to follow." In 1900 he wrote his essay on *The Rule of Phase Applied to History*, not published until after his death, in which he tried to establish history on a mathematical basis.

Adams's initiation into science had taken place by means of biology and geology, and I think that the two men who had the most influence upon his thought throughout his life were Darwin and Lyell. Just in the period, however, when he was occupied in trying to link the data of history with the growing body of scientific knowledge, the other sciences were gradually being overshadowed by physics, which threatened, like Aaron's rod, to eat up all the others. The same trend of mind that made scientific knowledge appear to be, not merely, perhaps, more useful but more valid than non-scientific, made it also appear that in physics we could at last track the secret of the cosmos to its inmost chambers. In its atomic structure, based on mathematical laws, we seemed at last to have struck rock bottom, and in the prevailing view that the whole universe was mechanistic, the vision opened of the possibility of reducing the whole of its multitudinous phenomena, human and other, to formulæ concerning atoms. The problem, of course, was of enormous complexity, but its insolubility would be based on its complexity only and not on its essential nature. In the twenty years during which Adams was working, the whole of the Newtonian physics and its concepts were still intact. Just at the very end, indeed, the atom yielded to the electron but without, as yet, disturbing the general mechanistic basis of the cosmos. The entire universe was atomic in structure, and atoms were still, for all practical purposes, tiny billiard balls whose actions and reactions could be predicted with mathematical certainty. Larger and larger fields of phenomena were being subdued to this conception. The inference was almost irresistible that it was only a question of time when the whole would thus be subdued, including the realm of mind. If, therefore, history were to be made scientific, and if the whole of science were to become physics—a mere expression of mechanistic relations in mathematical terms—it was obvious that the data of history must be submitted to some such expression.

The Adams mind, ever since its change of phase with the first John in the eighteenth century, has been characterized by a desire to arrange phenomena under law, to transform its outlook upon the spiritual, political, or natural worlds from multiplicity to unity. The Adamses have been daring creators of hypotheses rather than laboratory plodders. It was inevitable, given Henry's intellectual inheritance and the scientific climate of his day, that his effort to make history scientific should take the form of a sweeping mathematical formula utilizing the current concepts of physics.

We may observe three stages in his progress. First comes the belief that history must be treated as a physical science, and a good deal of toying with vague thoughts of the *Pteraspis* and *Terebratula*. Then his mind becomes colored by physics and mathematics, and he tries to apply to history the first and second laws of thermodynamics. We need not concern ourselves here with this second stage, which was given full expression in *A Letter to American Teachers of History,* although we shall refer to one or two points later. The only one to be noted at once is that in dealing with these laws of the conservation of energy and of entropy, or the degradation of energy, Adams assumed that "social energy" (the whole, apparently, of human functioning) was subject to the same laws, that is, was of the same type as physical energy. William James strenuously objected to this identification. As he wrote to Henry, "you can't impress God in that way." Much might be said as to the present status of these two laws, but they are not of prime importance in Adams's theory. Granted the truth of the law of entropy, the beginning of the universe is utterly inconceivable (as it is anyway), but even so the effect upon making history a science is negligible. The main point is whether "social energy" can be identified with physical energy as Adams identified it.

About 1900, apparently, Adams ran across Willard Gibbs's work on the *Equilibrium of Heterogeneous Substances*, including the essay on "phases" of matter, and this gave a new direction to his thought. Adams's own essay, *The Rule of Phase Applied to History*, was the result. In this he took as his starting point the assumption that "Thought is a historical substance," and argued that "the future of Thought, and therefore of History, lies in the hands of the physicists," and that history must be reduced to "the world of mathematical physics."

So far, Adams had been indulging in generalities. He had simply given a characteristic expression to the prevailing belief that somehow the world of mind would sooner or later have to fall under the legislation of the world of atoms, and he had played with some of the implications of such a theory. Now he was to make a genuine effort to extend the laws of physical to the realm of "social" energy. If the effort appears fantastic, it is only fair to say that he himself was, of course, aware of that aspect of his essay.

Carrying forward his list of phases beyond solid, fluid, and vapor, he postulated those of electricity, ether, space, and pure thought, assuming that "every equilibrium, of phase, begins and ends with what is called a critical point," and that the passage from one to another can be expressed by a mathematical formula. In physics he found the three variables in change of phase to be pressure, temperature, and volume. For his purpose he changed pressure into "attraction," temperature into "acceleration," and retained volume, though what he meant by the last is uncertain. In history he found that an attractive force, like gravitation, drew trickling rivulets of energy into new phases by an external influence which tended to concentrate and accelerate their motion by a law with which their supposed wishes or appetites had no conscious relation, and that "if the current of Thought has shown obedience to the law of gravitation it is material, and its phases should be easily calculated." As the nearest analogy to mind he took the comet, arguing that "if not a Thought, the comet is a sort of brother of Thought, an early condensation of the ether itself, as the human mind may be another, traversing the infinite without origin or end, and attracted by a sudden object of curiosity that lies by chance near its path. If such elements are subject to the so-called law of gravitation, no good reason can exist for denying gravitation to the mind." What he intended to mean by "attraction" appears to be indicated on the very last page he wrote on the subject when he speaks of "the attractions of occult power. If values can be given to these attractions, a physical theory of history is a mere matter of physical formula, no more complicated than the formulas of Willard Gibbs or Clerk Maxwell."

He himself experimented with the simple and far-reaching one of the law of squares. In his opinion, history had already experienced three phases, corresponding to solid, liquid, and gaseous, the phase of instinct, that of religion, and the present mechanical one. In order to get some starting point, it was essential, as we have noted above, for him to locate one of the "critical points" that marked a change of phase. This he finally located in 1600, the change from the religious to the mechanical. He suggests as the end of the mechanical phase the year 1900, with the discovery of radium. Working by his law of squares, backward, he found that the second, or religious phase, of man would have an indicated length of 90,000 years, and the first, or instinctive, phase an incalculably long span. Working onwards from the mechanical phase, the same law would give us a period of about seventeen years, until 1917, for a fourth phase, which he calls the electric, and about four years for the next phase, which he calls the ethereal, which would "bring Thought to the limit of its possibilities about 1921." Selecting some year later than 1900 for the end of the mechanical phase would slightly prolong the later phases. "Thought in terms of ether," he adds, "means only Thought in terms of itself, in other words, pure Mathematics and Metaphysics, a stage often reached by individuals. At the utmost it could mean only the subsidence of the current into an ocean of potential Thought, or mere consciousness, which is also possible, like static electricity."

Before analyzing Adams's effort further, we may apply the pragmatic test. The result is extraordinarily interesting, although it does not alter my belief in the impossibility of Adams's historical physics. It must be recalled that he was writing in 1909 and that the future was then a sealed book. His first prediction arrived at by mathematics applied to the historical process was that thought would enter upon a new phase about 1917. As a matter of fact, this was precisely what happened. In 1911 Rutherford brought about what Eddington calls "the greatest change in our idea of matter since the days of Democritus." In 1913 Bohr elaborated the quantum theory of atomic structure, and two years later Einstein extended his doctrine of relativity. The supremacy of Euclidean geometry, Newtonian physics, and a mechanistic interpretation of the cosmos crumbled. As far as we can judge, still so close to the event, a change of "phase" in Adams's sense, comparable only to those at preceding "critical points," had occurred.

His second prediction seemed more incredible of fulfilment. To have said in 1909 that less than half a generation would "bring Thought to the limit of its possibilities" and to attempt to prove it by mathematics, was assuredly to sacrifice one's reputation to the gods of common sense, and yet this prediction also has been fulfilled in a way that no scientist could have dreamed possible when Adams wrote. In 1925 came Heisenberg's new quantum theory and in 1927 his principle of indeterminacy. The law of cause and effect simply evaporated before a world of dumfounded scientists. As Professor Bridgman of Harvard has recently confessed, the physicist now finds himself in a world from which the bottom has dropped out. Nor, as Eddington has pointed out, is the new difficulty merely a dialectical one. It lies in the very nature of human knowledge itself as revealed by the new atomic discoveries. At the very height of its achievement and intellectual pride, science has been brought up against the limit of knowledge. "We have reached the point," says Bridgman, "where knowledge must stop because of the nature of knowledge itself: beyond this point meaning ceases.... No refinement of measurement will avail to carry him [the physicist] beyond the portals of this shadowy domain which he cannot even mention without logical inconsistency.... As we penetrate ever deeper, the very law of cause and effect, which we had thought to be a formula to which we could force God himself to subscribe, ceases to have meaning. The world is not intrinsically reasonable or understandable; it acquires these properties in ever-increasing degree as we ascend from the realm of the very little to the realm of everyday things; here we may eventually hope for an understanding sufficiently good for all practical purposes, but no more." Perhaps no one would have been more stunned than Adams himself at this extraordinary success of the application of his formula. Obviously, however, this test bears no resemblance to the three astronomical tests of Einstein's doctrine of relativity. It proves the correctness of neither Adams's formula nor his method. Indeed, the very advance in physics which has brought about the fulfilment of his prediction in one direction at least, has also done much to invalidate his method of thought.

It would be an easy task to pick to pieces one by one Adams's concepts in the light of the new physics. Take one of his fundamental ideas, gravitation. So long as it was conceived of as a pull or a force or an attraction it was much easier to play with such transpositions as Adams made, and to consider the "attraction" of the earth for an apple and the "attraction" of occult power for mind as obeying similar laws, but when gravitation becomes a function of curved space, the situation becomes different even for the most easily satisfied mind. But this line of criticism is hardly worth while. I think that Adams is entitled to very high credit for making the attempt, by means which he himself knew were rather absurd in detail, to bring history within the genuinely scientific field, that is, of predictability, and to do so in the line of the promised advance in science, that is, along physical and mathematical lines. I believe, however, that his method was entirely wrong, although in a way it was the method that has been used by such scientists as Faraday and Maxwell. In other words, he tried to build up, in a field beyond previous experiment, a structure which had been found to work in other fields of tested experience.

Always questionable, the validity of that method is now more open to criticism than ever in the light of recent developments. As is shown clearly by Bridgman in *The Logic of Modern Physics* and by others elsewhere, we have got to have a thorough overhauling of our concepts, whether or not they are finally to be defined, as Bridgman wishes, in their operational significance. What we have distinctly learned is that not only are the concepts, such as time, space, mass, and others, in a state of flux as to their meanings at present, but their meanings are not universal. Sidereal "length" is different from terrestrial "length" or atomic "length," and, more especially by penetrating into the realm of the infinitely little, we have found that such concepts as cause and effect lose all meaning. Adams assumed that concepts and laws were necessarily valid throughout the whole realm of reality, and that mind, although three phases more subtle than electricity, would be found to conform with the same laws as controlled the lowest physical phase of "solids." If, however, our "laws of nature" and such fundamental concepts as cause and effect, even human reason itself, break down before we have got beyond his *third* "phase," how are we even to think by the time we are dealing with his *seventh?* Is it not evident, if our reason irretrievably breaks down, as the physicists now tell us it does, in dealing with the atom of matter, that if mind is of more subtle essence than matter its nature must be forever hid from us by the essential nature of knowledge, that is, of the mind itself? It would seem at last to be clear that "mind" has got to be "materialized" at some grosser stage than the electron or remain forever unknowable "scientifically."

On the other hand, the problem of mind is becoming more insistent than ever, even from the standpoint of the scientist himself. Whatever scientist one reads now, above the level of the mere laboratory experimentalists and observers, who are mostly twenty years behind present thought, one is continually reminded of the subjectivity of the whole scientific structure. In this respect, men so different in many ways as Bridgman, Eddington, Whitehead, and others would seem substantially to agree. One does not have to be a mystic to ponder what the rôle of mind may prove to be at the last. With the physical universe dissolving into "point readings," mathematical formulæ, or a selection from "the patterns that weave themselves" in our minds, we are evidently getting a long way off from being able to assume with Adams that we may treat mind like a physical stream or a comet's tail.

We cannot, indeed, say that mind is not subject to the same "laws" as matter for we know no more of mind than did our first ancestor on passing out of the phase of instinct. Moreover, in attempting to subsume both aspects of reality, matter and mind, under the same "laws," it is somewhat disconcerting that we have now come to recognize that the "laws of nature" are not modes of behavior imposed on nature but merely modes in which the recognition that something outside (possibly) of us is doing something comes home to us. The "physical" world, ranging from the stars to the atoms, "obeys" those laws, that is, the phenomena arrange themselves in uniform patterns in our minds. Those in the sub-atomic world do not. Is there any reason to believe now that those of the mental world will?

There would seem to be no answer to this except experience. Certainly there is nothing to lead us to believe now that the application of concepts applicable to the super-atomic world would necessarily or even likely work, as Adams tried to make them. Leaving out the biologists from this discussion, though their contribution would be an interesting one, and keeping to the physicists, the tendency is now away from simplification. Bridgman, for example, considers it evident that the laws of nature cannot be reduced to those of mechanics or even electricity. Among some, indeed, there is a growing tendency to admit mind or even to find "mind" and "matter" two aspects of some underlying reality. Having been, so to speak, slapped in the face and told to go home while we are looking at the electron, it may be that we shall never penetrate the mystery further, and can only speculate mystically about it. In doing that we might conceive that both "mind" and "matter" in truth did obey the same "laws," that is, that their modes of behavior would weave the same patterns in a super-mind capable of observing and reacting to the behavior of each in the same way. If the human mind can weave similar patterns for reality in the scale between the sidereal universe and the electron, stopping there, it is conceivable that a greater mind, God, or what you will, might be able to do the same thing for a wider scale, embracing our knowable range, the sub-atomic and the mental, bringing them all into harmony in his own mind. It might even be that some of our logical difficulties with the first and second laws of thermo-dynamics might thus be resolved. It might prove that the amount of energy remained constant and that the constant degradation of energy which we postulate in the physical. universe was being balanced by an increase of energy in the mental or spiritual, a process unobservable to science but clearly so to a mind watching both aspects of reality. The difficulty, but necessity, of postulating a universe starting with a maximum of energy and slowly running down, as the law of entropy requires, might be resolved by some vast systole and diastole of energy tensity in what are to us the two aspects of reality— mind and nature. All such speculations, however, are obviously beyond science.

Was Henry Adams then pursuing an *ignis fatuus?* Was he wholly on a wrong tack in his effort to make science of history? I do not think so, but think that he merely made a mistake in trying to erect a sweeping hypothesis with too little data and to transfer to one field of experience the laws and concepts applicable only to another. The "operations," in the scientific sense, employed in studying the stream of history are entirely different from those employed in studying a stream of water, and Adams ignored "the principle that in changing the operations we have really changed the concept, and that to use the same name for these different concepts over the entire range is dictated only by considerations of convenience, which may sometimes prove to have been purchased at too high a price in terms of unambiguity."

On the other hand, I think he rendered a service in brushing aside the prevailing conception of history as "scientific" when all that was implied was a painstaking unbiassed investigation, with much critical apparatus, of some particular eddy in the historical stream. The facts of history are susceptible of scientific treatment or they are not; that is, they recur or they do not, they are rhythmical or they are not. If *not*, then history is not and never can be a science. If they *are* susceptible of scientific treatment then it will be possible to establish laws based on recurrence, laws yielding predictability of results. Until some such laws have been discovered, I personally believe that it is sheer snobbery to speak of history as a science, a pretense springing from the desire of the practitioners to rank themselves among the popular aristocrats in the kingdom of knowledge. Adams at least had the courage to try for something better, and he followed the path along the only way in which history can become scientific, however easy it may be to criticise the structure he raised.

It is rather beyond the scope of this article to speak of possible methods by which more successful efforts might be made to reach the goal, but perhaps a few words may be added. I wish to avoid the pitfall of transfer of concepts, but it is not without its suggestiveness that although cause and effect and determinism have completely crumbled in the world of the electrons, we still find that laws may be predicted of larger-scale phenomena, whether those laws may eventually be found to have only statistical or other validity. Whether, therefore, we allow free will to the individual or not, it may prove possible to discover "laws" governing the phenomena of history within a certain scale of size. It is probable, apart from their present very uncertain meanings in the field of physics, that the concepts used in that field, such as mass, energy, and so on will lead only to confusion if applied to the field of historical experience and experiment. As a new field of knowledge it will probably require the use of new concepts.

The new physics at least teaches us that we need not be worried by the erratic and unpredictable behavior of individuals. They are no more unpredictable than the electron has now been found to be. The thing to do is to keep away from the individual and to confine ourselves to larger-scale entities and phenomena. (I am speaking now not of narrative history, which must always be written, but of history as a science.) Whether or not history may be rhythmical, certain phenomena on a large scale do recur, although they have never been studied scientifically. We may cite at haphazard two; revolutions and blossoming times for art or intellect. If we took, say, twenty-five instances of such phenomena from the history of all nations, Oriental or Western, isolating them and studying them not as the stories of individual men but as large-scale phenomena, their own characteristics, growth, and decline, and the conditions surrounding each, is it not possible that some form of really scientific knowledge about them might emerge? Is there any reason why the appearance and disappearance of either of these two phenomena should not be studied with the same impersonality as, say, sun spots? It is possible, for all we know, that the individuals who slowly build up a coral island may be moved and motivated by all sorts of emotions which we ignore completely in studying them, but what would the situation of a scientist be, who wanted to study coral islands, if all he had was thousands of volumes dealing with the individual lives, the hopes and fears, the loves and hates, of insect A and B and C and so on by tens of thousands?

Adams was wholly right when, as a preliminary to establishing laws in history, he completely depersonalized it. We must cease dealing with the individual as a unique personality. We must deal only with historical phenomena which fall within the range of rhythmical recurrence and predictability. We must keep above the electron. If we choose phenomena of the scale of revolutions, let us discard all reference to picturesque personalities. Instead of writing in terms of Lafayette, Mirabeau, Danton, Robespierre, Napoleon, let us try what the result would be of treating such individuals as functions of the revolutionary process and give them symbols. In many revolutions that come readily to mind, we can already trace the regularity of the process and the emergence at similar periods of A, A^1, A^2, A^3, or X, Y, or Z, however we may choose to designate them. In this way we could reach a sort of anatomy of revolutions and avoid entangling our minds with personalities. This, of course, would be entirely different from history as it has always been written, and personally, because I do not believe in running off with other people's clothes, I should prefer to leave the term history to what is now so designated and coin a new word for history as a science, if there is to be any such thing. Very likely there is not, but if there is it must surely be as depersonalized as physics or chemistry or biology. We may speak of an atom of oxygen or an atom of hydrogen, but if we began to give the individual oxygen atoms pet names and talked about Jack Oxygen and Jill Oxygen we would not get far in establishing general laws for oxygen atoms. In the same way, in studying, say, revolutions as recurring, and thus predictable, scientific phenomena we must work comparatively through all revolutions and find the elements, the A (Lafayette) at the beginning and the A^5 (Napoleon) at the end of the movements. There are great and obvious difficulties in the way of building up a mass of such studies, but until we can deal with A and A^5 as with oxygen and hydrogen atoms instead of with the individuals Lafayette and Napoleon, I see no hope of "scientific" history.

On wholly inadequate data an Adams may endeavor to establish laws of mathematical precision or a Spengler may try to establish them biologically, but as written now, history, in which the large-scale phenomena alone offer any hope of establishing laws, so heaps and covers these over with a mass of irrelevant personalities as to make it practically impossible for anyone to study these phenomena and isolate them.

In short, the development of physics since Henry Adams made the only effort to establish a scientific law for history that has ever been made would thus seem to point clearly to the direction in which historians should go, if their work is to be brought within the field of "science." In the first place, we have been shown that irresponsibility, indeterminism, or what you will, in small-scale phenomena is not inimical to establishing laws for large-scale phenomena; secondly, that phenomena must lie within a certain scale to be attuned to human reason, and that it is necessary to find that scale; and thirdly, that concepts cannot be applied at random but must be based on operations, and not carried over from one sphere to another. Whether on this basis history may ever become scientific certainly remains to be proved. Others, under the name of laws, have pointed out influences. Others, again, under the same name, have pointed to what may or may not be tendencies. Adams alone made the courageous effort to establish a scientific law with the validity of a fairly accurate predictableness. He was neither a Copernicus, a Galileo, nor a Newton, but until historians realize that mere accurate scholarship is not science, he is likely to stand alone as the sole pioneer of "scientific history."

5. IS SCIENCE A BLIND ALLEY?

IN ALL AGES the opinions and knowledge possessed by the leaders have differed from those of the "men of the market place"; and in spite of all our popular education that same difference holds good to-day. This fact was brought clearly into relief in the popular comment and discussion on the so-called "monkey-trial" at Dayton, which provided heart-searchings for some, amusement for many, and complacent self-satisfaction for hordes of John Does. It was easy to laugh at the Tennesseeans, but was the Dayton trial, after all, merely an uproarious farce—the last stand in the mountains of a dying Obscurantism? Are not aspects of that and other manifestations of what we have come to call "Fundamentalism" worth pondering on broader lines than whales and Jonahs and the first chapter of Genesis? Were the citizens of our cities and graduates of our high schools really so much more intelligent than the shirt-sleeve mountaineers? Do they really know so much more about the universe?

It was pointed out in the seventeenth century that different periods in the history of man have had differ-

ent intellectual "climates," and that the whole mentality
of each period is dependent upon the particular climate
then prevailing. We cannot understand a book written
500 B.C. or 1200 A.D. merely because we can read its
words. We have got somehow to come to understand the
whole "intellectual climate" of that period. No man's
thought can be understood without it; and no man, then
living, was unaffected by it. There was, for example, a
very distinct "intellectual climate" in the medieval
period. in Europe, in which Dante's *Divine Comedy* or
the works of St. Thomas Aquinas flowered as naturally
as the giant ferns in the Carboniferous era. Then came
great "climatic" changes in intellectual Europe and,
later, in the New World, and the climate in which we
live now is wholly different. It can be called, for want
of a better name, the scientific. That is, all of our thinking is of the sort which almost involuntarily rejects any
general ideas or principles which cannot be "verified"
by harmonizing them with a succession of facts tested
by instruments. The only truth about the starry heavens,
for example, which carries any conviction to most men
to-day consists only of such "facts" as are revealed by
the telescope, the spectroscope, and other instruments,
or such hypotheses as seem to be corroborated by other
facts similarly revealed or by mathematical "laws."

Now, this is something distinctly new in the way of
an "intellectual climate." A civilization as a whole is
probably related in some way to the intellectual climate
of its period as the fauna and flora of past ages were

related to the physical climates of their day. Everything at any given moment somehow "hangs together." Nobody has yet satisfactorily defined what we meant by "civilization," and we have no standard by which to judge whether one of the several civilizations that have risen and fallen in human history is higher than another. Man is a conceited creature, and very likely the men of each civilization would consider their own, which they were used to, the best.

The average man in each, however, can no more escape the intellectual influence of the "climate" of the times than he can escape from breathing the physical air of his time and place. Unconsciously he is formed by it. He accepts it as part of the order of nature and cannot understand any other. The average busy man of the present day, and not a few of our minor scientists, may think that they have replaced a worn-out religious faith by "scientific knowledge," when all that they have really done is to replace one childlike faith by another and one bigotry by another.

The "man in the street," whether that street be the Acropolis of Athens, the Forum of Rome, the narrow byways of medieval Florence or Paris, or Pall Mall or Broadway to-day, has never much cared to *think*. He is impressed by practical results and conforms to the current religion or opinion. The practical technological, economic, and sociological results of science have been colossal, impossible almost to overestimate. Had the views advanced by scientists not had these practical results they would have interested the average man as little as do the ideas of Plato or Hegel.

It may yet remain to be determined whether science has proved a blessing or a curse. It is too soon to say, and the problem is too complicated. But certainly it is the fact that scientific "ideas" work so astoundingly in the practical life which has given them such an enormous philosophical validity in the eyes of the people at large. Science in the opinion of the multitude has become something sacrosanct, and the average man to-day is as much a bigot about "science"—as he understands it—as the average man in Europe in the year 1000 was about the dogmas of the Roman Catholic Church, and for the same reason, namely, that he is breathing the air of the intellectual climate of his day. He has picked up the ragtag and bobtail ideas which are floating about, just as his predecessor did. In the Tenth Century Catholicism was the accepted mode of thought, and no sensible person questioned it. It is precisely the same with "science" to-day. If a merchant's clerk in the year 1000 was asked *why* he believed the dogmas of the Church, just what those dogmas were, and on what philosophical basis they were founded, he could not have answered to save his life. They were the only sensible things *to* believe, and he was too busy and too practical to bother about philosophy. He knew that everyone else believed; he knew a lot of practical things the Church did (or might do) for him, and anyone who did not believe was a crank or worse. In the same way, to-day, of the thousands who laughed at the Daytonians how many could have told what is the philosophical basis of science, what are the assumptions on which it is based, and just how far, and why, it is a valid interpretation of the universe?

They know—as the Catholic bookkeeper in the year 1000 knew, about the Church—that science in certain practical ways has done a lot for them. There is the mechanico-materialisic interpretation of the universe, held by some scientists fifty years ago, which has now filtered down to the public and become fixed in its mind. The "average man" of the Middle Ages had his physical flames of Hell and his jewel-strewn Heaven. His modern counterpart has his "scientific laws" and his materialistic interpretation of the universe.

*

And bigotry along the new lines has already set in. If one were not historian enough to know how such things go, one might be surprised to find the "scientific, enlightened" mob who laughed at the Tennesseeans refusing to listen to the leaders among scientific thought. Let us take the case of a man I happen to know. As an open-minded youth, he read Darwin, Huxley, and the other scientists who were leaders in that day. In a sense he is himself a leader in his community, a man of fairly large income, a member of a somewhat exclusive intellectual club, but he says he has time to read only eight or nine books a year. Several of these are scientific, but he will have none of the philosophy of science. He would have no more use for Ritchie or Whitehead or Poincaré on the one hand than he would for the Daytonians on the other. If any "scientist" questions a purely mechanist-material view of the universe, he is to be summarily dismissed. He is as inflexible as the clerk of the Middle Ages. For him the scientific assumptions of a generation ago have become an established dogma, as little to be questioned *by the leaders of science itself* as by the Daytonians. As Poincaré says, "for a superficial observer, scientific truth is beyond the possiblity of doubt. . . . To be skeptical is to be superficial. To doubt everything and to believe everything are two equally convenient solutions; each saves us from thinking."

It is of no use to say to such a man that Poincaré, the leading mathematician and one of the leading scientists of our time, has admitted that science can teach us nothing of the real nature of things, that all it can do, and that only in part, is to elucidate certain relations between them. Moreover, as he explains, science deals with only a very limited number of facts, those which recur with sufficient frequency to enable us to establish "laws," which, as another scientist says, are "hypotheses with a high degree of probability." As Poincaré says again, we have to stop somewhere, and scientists merely work on certain groups of facts so as to establish certain simple rules valid for those groups of facts only.

They have established a good many such rules, and they have had astounding repercussion in the practical applications which have resulted. It is this, I repeat again, which has so deeply impressed the average man. Heaven and Hell are unprovable and very likely unreal. The "good life" was always a matter for the elect and cultured to debate over. But for the common man, the movies and the telephone and the Ford car and a huge increase in population with jobs still going round are realities, and science has brought them about.

But does science give us any satisfactory explanation of the universe? No scientist of any standing would claim that it tells us *why* things happen; it tells us only *how* they happen. Science does not tell us the cause, in the popular sense, of a single happening. It can only tell us that if certain things occur others will follow. And it can do even that for only an extremely limited number of phenomena. The popular idea is that, given time enough, science will be able to explain everything. Will it, even as to the *how* rather than the *why?* A. D. Ritchie, a biological chemist of international note, says, "it seems clear to me that the order in nature of which science reports is really there, and is not a mere figment. But it seems to me equally obvious that the orderliness is not all-pervasive. There are streaks of order to be found among the chaos, and the nature of scientific method is to seek these out and to stick to them when found and to reject or neglect the chaos. It is obvious that we have succeeded in finding some order in nature, but this fact in itself does not prove anything farther. It suggests that, having found some order, it is worth looking for more, but it does not imply that nature is orderly through and through, though, of course, it might be so. Nevertheless, the extreme difficulty and labor of finding laws of nature even when you know where and how to look, much more when it is a question of discovering a new one, suggest that there is not so much simplicity and order about as people think.... The fact that the regions of nature actually covered by known laws are few and fragmentary is concealed by the natural tendency to crowd our experience into those regions and to leave others to themselves. We seek out those parts that are known and familiar and avoid those that are unknown and unfamiliar. This is simply what is called 'Applied Science'."

The reason I claim that popular science has already become a sort of dogmatic religion with the ordinary man, and that he is as much a bigot as the Daytonian, is that he will not listen to this sort of thing even from leading scientists. He has accepted as a new dogma the science of thirty years ago as it has filtered into popular works and he accepts, utterly uncritically, because he has had no philosophical training, any philosophical nonsense handed him by the popularizers of science. He believes that science will ultimately explain everything, because he believes the entire universe is governed by laws to be discovered. This, of course, involves abandonment of any doctrine of the freedom of the will; but many scientists without philosophical knowledge apparently overlooked this entirely, and in the preface to one of the most popular books on recent science we read that we men, owing to science, "have stepped from the rank of Creation's scheme." If science is universal, how are we, any more than anything else in the universe, going to step out of the rank of "Creation's scheme"? Wouldn't that be a colossal miracle, and if an unimportant creature like man can voluntarily step out of the sphere of influence of "natural laws" and begin to control or thwart them himself, what becomes of that all-pervasive "reign of law"? Why be so conceited? If we can step aside from "Creation's scheme" because of what science has learned in a few generations, the universe would seem to be much more loosely governed than popular science believes.

If science is universally valid, it can be so only at the expense of destroying all we have hitherto considered worth striving for, and must theoretically destroy all initiative. Yet science has given us such power over the forces of nature as to stir us to an activity hitherto unknown in the world's history. We have been able to produce and maintain a population undreamed of. We are flying through the air at three hundred miles an hour. We can speak with a person three thousand miles away. We can do all the incredible things we do to-day, and so we, part of an inexorable nexus of laws, are dreaming of annihilating almost every law of nature! There is the paradox, which the popular scientist and the

248

man in the street both ignore, being "practical" men in a "scientific" age.

*

But to get back to our Daytonians and our high-school graduates. As far as thinking powers are concerned, I frankly do not see much to choose between them. The high-school graduates have accepted certain facts the Daytonians did not, but beyond that the High Schoolites are just as bigoted as the Daytonians. They not only refuse to *think* but they have reached the point in accepted and crystallized dogma where they refuse to follow even the leaders of science themselves in their philosophic enquiries. Anyone who does not accept the few established facts which these High Schoolites have accepted, are, in their opinion, ignorant boobs. Any scientist who is philosophical enough to carry on speculations which appear to endanger the simple mechanical scientific ideas to which the High Schoolites have become accustomed is a "crank" and no longer a "scientist."

But, again, it may be asked whether the Daytonians' protest—I cite that simply as an example of a state of mind not confined to the Tennesseeans—is based solely on scientific ignorance and Obscurantism? Are these various protests, in more or less ignorant form and based on positions which, intellectually, are unfortunately taken, the dying gasps of a conflict which is almost passed or the first cries of one new born? It is so hard to get away from the "climate" of one's own age, and so dangerous to be a heretic, scientifically, that the question may seem a foolish one, but I am not sure that it is. I am not so sure that the next century or two are going to be as rigidly "scientific" as our own.

These protests, as I sense them, have to do fundamentally, not so much with certain items of knowledge or ignorance, as with our attitude toward the whole range of values in human life. There are certain questions about life which man has always asked, certain modes of self-expression and enjoyment which he has craved, certain ideals he has entertained, certain forms of experience he has insisted upon. In the ebb and flow of humanity through the ages, in minor changes of modes of thought and social custom, we may sometimes lose sight of these fundamentals; but if we study men in all stages of evolution from savagery to the highest civilizations, we shall find certain aspects of his nature strangely constant. For one thing, he has always insisted on trying to find some real and satisfying explanation of his own nature and that of the universe into which he is born; he has never ceased to ask the *why* of birth and death, of suffering and sin and happiness; he has always expressed himself in art—written poems, painted pictures, carved sculpture; he has always insisted that he was himself a personality, and that the drama of his own life, somehow, had significance. There have been periods when a philosophy or religion arose which ran counter to some or all of these instincts, and for a time, oddly enough, may have seemed to increase the energy of the people believing it, as in the case of Mohammedanism. But sooner or later the people release themselves again, and the religion or other hampering influences become mere forms and lose their significance in practical life.

Now, what is the relation of science to these deep-lying instincts? It can offer us not a single word of explanation or illumination as to the nature of the universe or ourselves. Its "causes" are mere antecedents. It pictures a mere succession of events. Not only must it always be silent as to *why* anything happens, but even as to the *how*, what it really says is merely that if a certain selected group of phenomena is found now, another combination will follow. This is enormously useful to know, and I am not belittling the amazing amount of knowledge of a certain sort which science has accumulated. It is probable that mankind will never find any answers to their many *why's*. That is not the point. The point is that mankind, age after age, has always sought answers, has always refused to remain in a purely agnostic attitude. Has human nature changed so completely and suddenly that it is now going to remain forever content with those answers of science which are no answers?

Moreover, man has implanted in him a peculiar feeling that somehow there is such a thing as value or worth in the universe, that some things, some thoughts, some lines of conduct have more value than others; that a great poem is worth more than an obscene couplet scratched upon a wall; that a noble and brave man is worth more than a puny coward. But, however an individual scientist may ignore the implications of science in private and practical life, science has no place for values. In a universe governed wholly by predictable and inexorable law, value, in its human sense, is an inadmissible quality. The man who sacrifices his life to save women and children in a shipwreck is doing nothing more noble or of more worth than the man-eating tiger who pounces upon a child in the jungle. Both are equally the literally un-*willing* resultants of the entire complex of forces in the universe centering upon them at the time and place, and their acts are as wholly devoid of moral value as the motions of the stars in their courses.

If we adopt sincerely and wholly the popular conception of science we really destroy all values in human life. The arts are already beginning to show this deteriorating influence. In fiction, for example, of what use to write of character if there is no such thing, if personality is a myth, if freedom of action is a dream, and if all we are is merely a succession of states of mind having as little significance as a glow of phosphorescence over decaying wood? The logical outcome is Joyce's *Ulysses*, in which for hundreds of pages we have merely the successive and passive states of mind of one man during a few hours. As an experiment it may have an interest. As the sole form to which the art of fiction is reduced by science, it means the end of art. It may all be true but neither man nor his arts can try to live by it and survive.

It is needless to go on multiplying instances. As to

the immediate questions at issue at Dayton, I believe
the Daytonians wrong and the High Schoolites right,
but as to the larger implications of the whole present
situation I believe the Daytonians were on the right
trail, however clumsily and ignorantly they were groping
for it. If man cannot live by bread alone, neither can he
live on disinfectants or aeroplanes.

As an historian I am skeptical of general laws in
history, but one which does seem to be established is
that man never goes back to revivify old forms. His
civilizations may rise and fall, but he never goes back
to relive the thoughts of an earlier period. I do not look
for a great popular revival of Christianity any more
than of Greek philosophy or Confucianism. Christianity
will probably last for centuries and provide comfort and
hope for millions, but those who have grown away from
it, and their successors, are not likely to be won back.
On the other hand, I do not believe that any body of
doctrine so spiritually and, speaking broadly, intellectually sterile as science will satisfy the many-sided cravings of mankind indefinitely. Its facts are exceedingly
interesting and incomparably useful, but they are too
much on the order of a picture-puzzle to satisfy men
forever. There comes a time when the contemplation of
the unthinkable distances of the stars or the habits of
an electron or even the geological record fail somehow
to move us. It gets a bit too much like reading of Rocke-
feller's millions, because, at bottom, and ineradicably,

man craves spiritual and moral values, and an answer, however crude, to his question *why?*

*

It is obvious that we cannot get along without science. Intellectually it has an interest we shall never again willingly forego. Practically it is essential, not only for our comfort but, as things are now, for our very existence. In fact we have reached the point where in order to support the population brought into the world by science we shall have to have more and more science, more and more inventions almost daily. But, basing my prediction solely on the unchanging nature of man's deepest cravings throughout the entire period of which we know anything of him and his mind, I do believe that science will some day cease to be the sole method of interpreting the universe and that scientists will cease to be the high priests whose words are the sole authority as to what men can and cannot believe about themselves and their environment. It has been said recently that science may some day become a sort of religious cult, with its own hierarchy and its influence on the life and thought of the people comparable to that of the great established churches. I doubt that, for, as I said, it is too sterile. It has appealed to me in general in our day for special reasons, but I do not believe it can permanently satisfy the whole of man's nature, and I believe the "intellectual climate" will gradually alter again—

as it has so many times—and science will come to be considered an extremely useful practical tool, an indispensable one, and an extremely interesting interpretation of certain aspects of the universe, but that it will lose its present high station as the sole interpretation of the whole of it.

Whether in the course of the next few centuries some new religion may be taught, I do not know, but I do not believe that a few generations of scientific teaching have permanently altered man's nature. I believe that before so long he will insist, simply because he cannot help himself, on some restoration of spiritual and moral explanations and values in his world. A philosophy which teaches that there can be no answer to his deepest questionings, that all his spiritual and moral values can be resolved into nothing, that he himself has no personality, not only after death but even in this world, that he is merely a bundle of "states of mind" cannot satisfy him always. When beauty, love, duty, loyalty, and all the rest of what has hitherto given some value to existence have been swept away by scientific analysis, I believe they will come in again by some other door, though where that door may open from I do not know.

In all that I have here said about science I have been speaking of it in the popular acceptation of what it stands for—a conception that unfortunately is entertained also by too many scientists of smaller caliber. Far out on the frontiers of knowledge are scientists who themselves glimpse something different. It may be that they will be the ones to open the door, and if they do, I am not at all sure that the Daytonians may not be more ready to enter than the High Schoolites. The Tennesseeans' science may be negligible but their uncritical sensing of man's deepest needs, of his unchanging nature, and of the values of life is more valid than that of many of the half-educated who got such a hearty laugh out of them, even although the crude protest may have been due to mere resentment against the disturbance of cherished religious dogma. "Intellectual climates" may change; civilizations may rise and fall; our skyscrapers may yet stand deserted; but man will still insist, in the face of every shred of contrary evidence, that he *is* a personality, that there is a scale of values which transcends the useful, that there is more in love and beauty than a complex of instincts and impacts, that there is a mystery and a meaning hidden in the universe, and he will still frame answers to his eternal *why?* The old religions may long linger, but none can be born again. If science cannot lead into some new world of interpretation, it will be thrust aside, except as a tool, and man will turn to some new philosophy of life, for his instincts are stronger than his reason, and man is more than his mind.

IV

1. POLLYANNA, OUR PATRON GODDESS

THE LATEST BIOGRAPHER of General Grant informs us that the hero was never, not even by his own wife, seen naked. In this respect he bears a close resemblance in the American scene to Truth. The case of the General is, I suspect, even yet a fairly common one among the class of Americans from which he sprang, at least of the older generation. Among those of a narrow mind and a narrower religious inheritance, nakedness is something to be disguised and avoided, and all sorts of mental irregularities have ensued from such a wanton attempt to disregard nature and her workings.

It is precisely the same with Truth. A very large proportion of our citizens refuse to look upon her naked, unashamed, beautiful, and normal. She must be cloaked and clothed, and from this fact have sprung, as in the case of our physical life, multifold errors, ugly abnormalities, miserable hypocrisies.

The process begins early in our public schools. Even those of us workers in the field of history who thought they had become somewhat hardened to the general attitude toward their subject were distinctly shocked, three or four years ago, when the head of that department in one of the best known institutions for training teachers came out with the public statement that it was absolutely essential in the lower grades to falsify history, particularly the history of Anglo-American relations.

The prime object of teaching history in the lower grades, he asserted, is to inculcate patriotism. Historical truth is entirely a secondary one. The truth about all the wars in which we have been engaged—the Revolution, the War of 1812, the Mexican, the Spanish, and the World War—must be deliberately sacrificed wherever necessary in order to build up a sturdy one-hundred-per-cent Americanism in the child mind. In high school, he went on, some of the truth might be told, and in college the student might be left to find out as much of it as he chose. His own interest was in the child, in poisoning the stream at its source.

*

The doctrine thus set forth is as clear as a star on a frosty night, and as poisonous as the night air in a swamp. In plain words, it is a pedagogy based on the belief that it is advisable and justifiable to lie to the child, to destroy later his faith in intellectual integrity, in order to induce at the most impressionable age an emotion which is considered desirable in mass life. This doctrine would seem to be the result of two mental attitudes on the part of those, and they are unfortunately many, who advocate it.

In the first place, we detect the effect of an inferiority complex. Is the truth, the real truth, of our national history such that when told to the child it will not produce a feeling of pride, a sane and manly patriotism? Critical as I have been in my writing on much of the American scene, past and present, I deny that this is so. Good and bad have been present, as in the history of every nation, but there is ample material in our history of which any American may be justly proud, and which, without perversion, may be used to beget in the child mind an ideal of what America might and should be, a pride in the efforts of so many Americans to realize that ideal in practice.

I suspect that the chief motive for the advocacy of the perversion and cloaking of truth lies in a second mental attitude on the part of the teacher, that of mere laziness or incapacity. To paint for the child a picture of the past in which there shall never be any question of every American's having been perfect and America's having been solely right in every controversy is a crudely easy thing to do, calling for no critical effort to think on the part of either teacher or pupil. Such teaching, of course, merely produces mendacious emotions and does nothing to develop the power of thought.

On the other hand, to try to make the child see that character and circumstance are not always simplified to that extent, to show that human nature is complex, that there are often questions at issue between classes in society or between nations in which each has a certain portion of right upon its side, is to educate the child mind to begin that process of thinking clearly, of weighing evidence, of judging fairly, that should be one of the prime objects of all education.

Such a process would also initiate the child into an understanding of life and the innumerable problems with which he will be confronted in maturity. Moreover, it would give a greater interest to the subject than the mere beating of the national tom-tom could ever give. Nor do I know of any controversy in which we have been engaged, and which would naturally form a part of the simplified narrative of our general history as taught in the lower grades, in which such explanations of character and situation could not be given in simple and understandable terms. Such a method, however, requires as intelligent an effort on the part of the teacher as on that of the scholar.

*

I speak at length of this deliberate avoidance of truth in the teaching of history because it happens to afford an illustration of a general tendency which I can pluck from the field in which I am most interested, and because of the defense of cloaking and disguising the truth has here its most open advocates. But the fear of the naked truth, and the substitution of emotion for thought, are all too clear in other departments as well.

The envisaging of life and circumstance in terms of emotion and imagination is one of our characteristics which appears most manifest to me when I compare the characteristics of our own nation with those of others as I constantly pass from one to another.

I think there is some historic explanation of this characteristic, and that, like so much else in our outlook and psychology, it stems in large part from the influence of the frontier, from that too rapid exploitation of the continental area which has been the cause of so many of the worst elements in our national life and thought. The conquest of the wilderness called for many qualities, some of which I have noted and discussed elsewhere. Among these, the one which bears on our present problem was the ability, which I may best describe in the vernacular, "to kid oneself."

At that time the ordinary man who could not train himself to see things, not as they were, but as he wanted them to be, would indubitably fail. Unless he had unusual intellectual and spiritual courage, this ability to see only what he wished to see was all that sustained the pioneer in the danger, hard work, ugliness, and hideous squalor of the early days on successive frontiers. Around the lonely cabin in the clearing, or alone on the plain like a ship at sea, he saw a town; in the first ramshackle Main Street of a town he saw the thoroughfare of a thriving and luxurious city.

There was no need for such hasty exploitation. In fact a good case can be made out for claiming that our country would be better off to-day had expansion taken a more normal course at a less furious speed, had we advanced our frontiers more slowly, had our overwhelming prosperity come with less floodlike violence, and had we relied upon our own native labor for the work of nation-building. But, having undertaken the task as we did, the only hope for the individual seemed to be in shutting his eyes to his present surroundings and in seeing others which had their existence only in hope and imagination.

When the individual saw his present plus a possible future, he was not looking at naked truth with a larger vision than the realist, but "kidding himself" with an irrational hope and emotion. In innumerable cases such an attitude led only to destruction and disappointment. The mine was never found; the neighbors never came; the village, instead of booming into a city, dwindled into a deserted hamlet of moldering shacks. On the other hand, taking the whole land and the mass of population, so many times the mine *was* found, so many times the land which cost a few dollars one year *was* worth thousands in a decade, so many *did* win to what they had hoped for, that the reliance upon emotion seemed to find a justification in the order of the universe.

Our American philosophy has always tended toward pragmatism. The "booster" seemed to fit into the ethical and intellectual order of things, whereas the realistic critic was hurled into outer darkness by economic powers. Not to claim that your own ugly town was a city beautiful, that it was bound to become a cultured metropolis in ten years, that everything was for the best, was to become a suspected social pariah. Luck, hope, emotion seemed to be better than critical thought.

Amid the multitude of widely heralded successes, the failures were ignored, forgotten. The universe seemed to set the seal of approval on a crude empiricism and mere emotion. If you only said a thing was so long enough and loudly enough, somehow, half the time, it came to *be* so, owing to illimitable natural wealth waiting to be exploited; and if you were wrong, you were forgotten or you tried somewhere else where luck might land you where you would be.

*

Out of such a training and insistent social pressure for several generations have evolved several traits in the American mind. For one, we have unconsciously learned to be almost blind to our surroundings, as the hideousness of our countryside bears witness. Not so long ago, a man in New York wrote to the editor of a magazine in which I had spoken of crime and armored cars in that city. He deliberately asserted that although his office was at 115 Broadway, he had never seen an armored car in his life, and that I was "seeing ghosts." I do not doubt the honesty of the man, who was a trained scientist. He simply literally did not see the unpleasant or sinister factors in his environment, incredible as this may seem.

Some months ago the statement appeared in the New

York papers that Broadway was "lined" with the most beautiful parks of any city in the world. A stranger, noting that statement, and walking northward for miles from the Battery, would set the description down to an innate love of lying, much as Dickens in *Martin Chuzzlewit* immortalized that "Eden" which he found to be a malarious swamp. The statement went wholly without contradiction or comment.

This blindness and lack of clear thinking, this dependence upon wish and emotion, have naturally destroyed to a great extent our power of critical appraisal. The critic, in the first place, has come to be confused with the mere "knocker," whose name is anathema. The pioneer felt that the critic was at once "highbrow," a putter-on of airs, a claimant to superiority, and that he was a danger to the morale of the struggling community.

Such danger has long since passed, but the feeling persists. Heaven knows New York is big enough, yet if anyone suggests that to-day, in spite of its vast wealth, it is one of the dirtiest, most sordid, and most uncomfortable of the great cities of the world, he is likely to be asked to hold his tongue or move on. He may be allowed to express such opinions in private, but if he does so in public, the old sense of fear—fear lest harm may come to the community by telling the real truth about it—at once rouses antagonism and resentment. The naked truth must be clothed in theatrical costume to create an illusion —the sort of illusion that has done so much to change "bigger and better" in public claque into "bigger and worse" in many an embittered private belief.

This failure of criticism and of the critical spirit has been one of the chief factors in hardening our hearts against looking at Truth in her beautiful nakedness. We have become to-day one of the nations least capable of genuine criticism. All of life hangs together, and a damage in one field is felt in another. Otherwise we might expect that at least in such intellectual matters as the distribution and appraisal of books we might salvage some of our intellectual wreckage.

I do not think we have had, in my memory, such a mass of uncritical book advertising and book reviewing as we had last autumn. Every advertiser's voice seemed raised in print against the others' to prove that his own list of items was composed of impossible masterpieces. To what level criticism has fallen may be noted in a recent publisher's advertisement in which a critic's praise is quoted as "a damned good book." The plain truth no longer suffices, and appeal must be made to the vulgarest and crudest of emotions.

If we linger in this same field, we may note another fact that has much struck me of late. Whereas in England, but more particularly in Germany and France, you will find an ample literature of books dealing in a genuinely critical spirit with the personalities of living statesmen, we find none here at home. Here our statesmen find only campaign biographies or, after they are dead a decade or so, the more careful "life." They are cursed or praised but rarely genuinely criticized. The papers and magazines are full of personalities about them. There are biographical details of the most intimate sort to be gleaned; but no thoughtful appraisals, with the exception of some articles by Walter Lippmann. There is apparently little market for such wares. In the past few months I have asked many otherwise highly intelligent Americans for estimates of many men now in public life, and in only one case have I been met with an effort really to appraise the man.

This refusal to face the truth, or even to search for it, has been notably seen in the pronouncements of the administrations of late years with reference to business conditions, beginning with Wilson's famous description of the slump of 1913-14 as a mere "psychological condition." With the enormous and most damaging amount of Pollyanna nonsense fed to the American people during the past three years by Coolidge, Mellon, and Hoover, I deal in the next chapter and need not repeat here what I say there. By their refusal to think, by their refusal to face the truth instead of wallowing, according to frontier habit, in mere emotional optimism and hope, everyone is now paying a far higher price than they otherwise would have for the cost of a normal and severe trade reaction. Coolidge, with his proverbial luck, escaped the storm; but Hoover is paying with his political, and his fellow citizens with their private, fortunes.

*

This cultivation of emotion in the child instead of the power of critical thought, superimposed on our frontier heritage, is, I believe, a source of the greatest possible danger to us in the modern world, and it is to this that I wish to point rather than to indulge in mere carping criticism of ourselves.

In the first place, it makes us the tools of anyone who chooses to play upon our unthinking emotions and passions. Some years ago the owner of one of our great chains of daily papers, published in many cities, gave as his instructions to his aides the rule to "find out what the local prejudices of your community are and then feed them like hell." The fact that from childhood we are taught to prefer the pleasure of an emotion to the task of clear thinking makes us an easy prey to such a molder of "public opinion," and increases tremendously the danger of that herd instinct which may prove the destruction of the great modern democracies.

The danger extends clearly to the field of foreign relations. So far as I can discover, as far as the man in the street—Main Street or any other—is concerned, his attitude toward such relations is founded in a mere mush of false historical knowledge, emotions, and sentimentality. Take the cases of France and England, both our allies in the late war. It is almost impossible to get an unbiased hearing for the truth about either nation, so strong are our favorable or unfavorable prejudices. Every act of England is viewed with dislike and suspicion;

every act of France is viewed through a haze of sentimental friendship.

The French on their side evaluate our friendship in purely realistic terms. France is friendly when it suits her to be so; the reverse when that suits her better. In the mist of what the old school texts taught us of her "friendship" in the days of the Revolution, in the brilliant light cast by the romance of Lafayette, we forget that she helped us only when and because it suited her general European policy against England; that she tried her best to minimize our fruits of victory; and that in the century and a half that has followed—during the Napoleonic Wars, the Civil War, in the long-drawn out negotiations over the previous war debt (the Spoliation Claims)—we both stood insult from her and threatened war against her.

All these things are overlooked while we splash in a trough of slushy sentimentalism derived from the uncritical accounts in our old school texts of happenings of a hundred and fifty years ago. I have a great admiration for France, and wish to maintain a policy of friendship with her, but I believe the relations we bear to *all* nations should be guided by the light of reason and truth and not mere emotionalism.

Such relations are obviously of prime importance in a world so interlaced in all respects as ours is now. Yet we are willing as a people to do nothing to see the real truth or to make an effort to understand. Trusting solely to emotion and the falsified history of our lower grades, we are the mere victims of such newspaper owners as the one to whom I have alluded, and of that herd instinct which can be counteracted only by clear thought and a doughty individualism.

In England recently, the Simon Report on conditions in India, a serious government document making a volume of about five hundred pages, has sold over forty thousand copies. Imagine any Senate or House report in this country, even on a most serious subject for us all, becoming a best-seller! On the contrary, it is only with difficulty that a popular article dealing in simple, predigested fashion with a foreign country can work its way into a magazine.

*

In our refusal to take the trouble to think seriously, to face the truth, to think critically, we are equally at the mercy of emotional appeal in our domestic politics and economic affairs. The day of the pioneer has passed. In that day, the individual pioneer might fail as a prospector, a farmer, or a cattle herder. Business was largely local and individual. The immense resources and the lack of complexity in life made recovery quick, easy, and almost inevitable.

But to-day the situation has wholly altered. The machinery of production and consumption has become colossal. We are each of us dependent upon forces over which we have not the slightest control as individuals. Our relations with the sources of raw materials and with the markets of the entire world are also of life and death import to us. The America of 1930 cannot afford to trust to a blind optimism, as could the earlier America of the agricultural era. As Sir Josiah Stamp recently pointed out, we cannot live in the golden age of economic organization and the stone age of economic thought.

We are driving a high-powered racing car instead of riding a bicycle. It may prove that the complexities of modern civilization have become too great for all the nations and that we shall ride for as inevitable a crash as would overtake a novice trying to drive his car at a hundred miles an hour. But we shall surely so suffer if we take the same attitude toward the problems of America and modern life that a frontier booster could afford to take toward the problems of his growing town two generations ago. We can no longer trust to Pollyanna as our patron goddess, and refuse to think for ourselves.

Such is the problem. What, if any, is the remedy? I can see only one possible remedy. We must cease to be mentally soft and indolent. We must deliberately train our minds to think as we would train the muscles of our body for hard physical labor. We have shown a tendency to become a nation of uncritical emotionalists. We have to have everything, as they say in Hollywood, "dumbed up" for us. We have largely ruined our minds with headlines, tabloids, and moving pictures. We have no wish to indulge in concentrated thinking. We refuse to search for truth naked.

The hope lies mainly in the next generation. At any cost I would sweep out whole wheelbarrow loads of junk from the curricula of the schools. Whatever else education might be aimed at, I would aim it first and foremost at trying to inculcate in the child the wish and the power to *think*. I would have done with the whole pedagogical philosophy of the easy and the agreeable, the smattering of the all-inclusive, the creation of the ignorantly omniscient. I would come back to the training of the mind as a mind, as an instrument of thinking instead of a scrap basket for half-forgotten facts.

Instead of developing emotion at the expense of truth and reason, making adults who merely desire to have their prejudices pandered to, I would try to develop a generation who would be willing to take the trouble to think, who would learn how to think, and who would realize that emotion and prejudice are but swamp lights in the search for truth, to be avoided at all costs instead of being fed.

The Greeks in their love of nakedness produced not only the most beautiful sculpture the world has ever seen, but in their worship of the nakedness of Truth they began an era of which we are the latest, perhaps the last, of heirs. We owe our inhibiting, warping fear of physical nakedness largely to the Puritans. We owe our dislike of truth largely to the frontier. If we are not to become a race of empty emotionalists, swayed by leaders playing upon the vague wishes and desires of our partly atrophied natures, we must regain the old Greek ideal of the sound mind in the sound body. We must come to worship again with joy and vigorous enthusiasm that one god of all the pagan pantheon who alone can bring us salvation—the naked, the benign, the beautiful Goddess of Truth.

2. PRESIDENTIAL PROSPERITY

IT HAS BEEN SAID that if Machiavelli were alive to-day and were writing a book on the governing of men he would study not "The Prince" but the leaders of the Standard Oil and other great companies—that these are the real lords and barons of our twentieth century. It is true that power and influence to-day are more closely allied with industrial than with political leadership; and many causes and conditions have combined to make it appear plausible that almost the chief concern of the State should now be economic. For one thing, the leaders of a State have always been concerned with the dominant forces of their time; and just as some centuries ago they were forced to concern themselves with religion, so to-day they seem forced to concern themselves with economics. We have passed out of the former stage for the most part, and religion has become a matter of individual belief and practice rather than a great social force which must be controlled and directed by the political leaders for personal and social preservation. Now that business has passed from the individualistic to the national plane, has become a force of national magnitude, it has, like religion of old, grown something to be reckoned with by the political powers.

In some respects the relation of the State to business bears an interesting resemblance to the relation formerly existing between the State and religion. Had religious beliefs remained solely matters of concern to the individual citizens, there would have been no irresistible tendency to merge Church and State. In the same way, had business remained on the small individualistic scale of two centuries ago, there would not now be the strong tendency to merge Business and the State. The period of the Church-State has passed. The period of the Business-State appears to be beginning. Our ancestors experienced the statesman as controller of religious belief. If we are to experience in due course the statesman as controller of our economic practices and prosperity it may be well to reflect somewhat on what may be in store.

The attempt of a government to control the economic welfare and life of a people is not an American invention. We have now been engaged in such an experiment in novel form—for America—for the past several years, but it has been tried elsewhere in other forms. We may mention, for examples, the efforts of Germany on a small scale before the War, and on a great one after it, to deal with unemployment; and what is promising to be a classic example in Russia of an effort to regulate the entire economic life by government control. Our own experiment, however, holds unique interest for us partly because it is our own and partly because, although only four years old, the stages through which it has already passed illuminate many phases of the problem. In the Coolidge-Mellon régime there was merely an extraordinary extension of the old American relation between Republican politics and prosperity. Under the Hoover-Mellon one we are asked to envisage and experiment with a wholly new conception of the Business-State, a Business-State under Capitalism much as the Soviet government is a Business-State under Communism.

Three leading personalities have been involved in our experiment thus far, Mr. Coolidge, Mr. Mellon, and Mr. Hoover. Their interest in economic problems and their relation to them have been widely different. Mr. Coolidge cared little, and perhaps knew less, of the great economic forces and new ideas with which he had to deal. He carried to the White House the ideals and outlook of a hard-scrabble Vermont farm. He held fast to the old ideals, perhaps less outworn than many believe, of hard work, thrift—a getting ahead, either personal or national, by carefully adjusting one's expenses to a point well below one's income. For him the national income was the affair of the one hundred and twenty million citizens. His affair was to see to it that the nation spent less than it earned.

Mr. Mellon is the type of the great modern financier, the man whose vast wealth is in stocks, and whose indices of prosperity are stock prices, hidden assets, and dividends. In a few months of the great bull market his family was reported by the *New York Times* to have made

277

three hundred million dollars by the rise in prices of two of their stocks alone. In carrying out his gigantic public task of reducing the war debt ten billion dollars in a little over ten years, his chief considerations have perforce been low money rates and high security prices.

Mr. Hoover is of a third type. He is typical of the latest stage so far reached in the evolution of the great modern industrialist, that of the efficiency expert on a super-scale, the man to whom the vastness and intricacy of the modern industrial organization offer problems of absorbing interest.

During the years of the American experiment, until the past few months, Mr. Mellon's influence has been dominant; but for obvious reasons, stemming from our old political training, it is the presidents who have been held responsible in the public mind. We have had the "Coolidge prosperity," the "Coolidge market," and were promised the "Hoover market." Before we enter upon larger considerations let us rehearse briefly the relation of these three statesmen to the new theory of economic statesmanship.

*

To understand the conditions surrounding the initiation of the experiment we must first glance for a moment at some of the factors which had operated to make the America of Coolidge so utterly different from the America of McKinley, thirty years before. Speaking broadly, the wealth of the citizens up to that earlier time had been obtained by the exploitation of our vast natural resources combined with individualistic business methods and the old-fashioned Coolidge virtues. New factors in altering the situation, however, quickly succeeded one another. The invention of the modern elevator, for example, which made the skyscraper possible, and the multiplying of rentals from the same plot of ground tenfold added untold billions to the prices of city real estate. With the formation of the United States Steel Corporation in 1901, the era of mergers, billion-dollar companies, and illimitable opportunities to win profits by juggling stocks began. The development of the motor-car industry not only created hundreds of millions of new profits but, owing to its so far unique influence on other industries and the opening up of entirely new ways of making a living (employing to-day, all told, nearly four millions of workers), it largely neutralized for many years the progressive unemployment caused by improved methods of production and operation in many other industries. Owing to constant new ideas and inventions, these improved methods advanced rapidly, adding to the profits of many of the more far-seeing and wealthy corporations. The Great War raised wages to unheard-of levels and brought enormous increases in earnings. The new theory of mass production acted in a similar way, raising both wages and profits, and making spectacular fortunes possible in the stock market. National advertising, to the tune of a billion dollars a year, created new wants. The higher scale of living created new industrial activity. The extension of installment buying to almost every line acted like a forced draft in a furnace. There had been the panic of 1907, the crisis at the opening of the War, and the deflation of 1920; but all the factors mentioned above, and others, proved sufficiently strong to carry the nation by 1926 to a pitch of "prosperity" hitherto undreamed of.

Successively, however, the first great impetus of many of these factors tended to weaken. The strain was becoming great. But what had come to be considered in 1926 as "normal" in business and prosperity for all classes was almost unthinkably higher than that of less than a generation before. In every quarter the great business leaders of the country, realizing that a slackening of consumption would spell disaster on a correspondingly great scale, had assured the people at large that we were in a new era, and that they could buy recklessly without fear that any of the old economic laws would bring ruin to them. The stock market was watched by everyone as the index of prosperity. On December 31, 1926, the average price of twenty leading industrial stocks had risen from $67 to $177 in little more than five years. There were, however, many signs recognized by the more thoughtful business men and business journals that there was a break in sight for this hectic prosperity. Up to this point the prosperity had been non-governmental. From this point onward, it became "presidential."

In January, 1927, the *Commercial and Financial Chronicle*, and certain business leaders, stated that there could no longer be a doubt that a business reaction was well under way. On the other hand, Mr. Coolidge predicted continued prosperity, and Mr. Mellon advised the American people that all was well. The stock market continued to fall, brokers' loans rose, and there was fear of high interest rates. In other words, sanity was beginning to prevail and economic laws were beginning to operate. In March Mr. Mellon gave out a statement, practically implying that interest rates would not rise for at least ten months. The market immediately turned upward, although in about three weeks it again began to sag. Mr. Mellon then issued a much stronger statement, in which he again predicted low interest rates, claimed that brokers' loans were not too high, and predicted general prosperity. The market at once began to climb again. With one recession the twenty industrial stocks had risen to 217 by June, when the advance began to weaken. Business in many lines was distinctly on the down-grade, yet Mr. Coolidge issued a statement giving to the people an optimistic view of conditions and again predicting "satisfactory" business for the rest of the year. The market at once started on a wild climb, rising 26 points in a month.

By this time prosperity had become so "presidential" in the minds of the people that Coolidge's decision not to run again was a severe blow. The market fell on the announcement. However, in spite of such facts as a decrease of 11 per cent in railway earnings, and a marked recession in general, the President stated that the business outlook was better than it had ever been, and, after a momentary hesitation, the market resumed its advance.

Nevertheless, by the beginning of January, 1928, conservative bankers and business men had become genuinely alarmed. During the preceding month brokers' loans had increased over $341,000,000 to a new unheard of total of over $4,400,000,000. When the figures were published, the market broke with great violence. In the *Journal of Commerce*, Parker T. Willis, one of the wisest of American business observers, had written that "there is a great deal of unrest in the banking system and with regard to banking conditions in general." At a meeting in Dallas more than one hundred bankers joined in a protest against the management of the Reserve Banks and the vast expansion of Stock Exchange loans. Thomas R. Preston, president of the American Bankers Association, called attention to the great danger of the situation and noted the over-expansion of credit as one of the great problems to be solved in 1928.

However, on the afternoon when the figures of the loans were given out and the market had broken heavily, Mr. Coolidge issued a statement at the White House in which he said that he did not consider the loans too high and that there was nothing unfavorable in the figure to which they had attained. There is good reason to believe that the opinion thus expressed, to the amazement of the country, was Mr. Mellon's rather than Mr. Coolidge's; but prosperity had become wholly presidential. The statement was published January 7th, and, as the *New York Times* noted, "appeared to cause as much surprise to speculative Wall Street as reassurance." The experiment, started in the preceding year, of creating prosperity by governmental control was now well under way. "Old-timers in Wall Street tried without much success," said the *Times*, "to recall any precedent for Mr. Coolidge's remark," and in the leading editorial on the 11th added that the giving out of such an interview was neither wise nor prudent. The whole question, it said, was in many respects highly technical, and "was partly bound up with the dispute as to whether stock speculation had or had not been carried to excess. These are not matters which a Chief Executive should feel called upon to discuss." The Chief Executive, however, had in the past year voluntarily assumed the job of acting as wet nurse to a wild and unjustifiable speculation and had led the American people to take colossal risks. He had the bear, or perhaps we should say the bull, by the tail and could not let go. Sooner or later a crash was inevitable, but with Coolidge luck it might be staved off for his successor to deal with.

On January 9th, Mr. Willis, in the *Journal of Commerce*, wrote that the President's statement by no means satisfied those who had been worrying, and who "think it queer that the investment market should be so richly endowed with funds when stagnant commercial loans indicate that current business activity is not experiencing a parallel expansion. If new capital for permanent investment is being provided by the public at the rate of over $8,000,000,000 per year, whence is it coming?" The president of the Federal Reserve Bank at Richmond wrote an article asking "Are we living in a Fool's Paradise?" and

concluded that we were, sanely handling the whole problem, so easily disposed of by Mr. Coolidge (possibly as
a "ghost writer" for Mr. Mellon), of loans, credits, and
interest rates.

During January and February trade reaction continued, gold was exported in large volume, brokers' loans
fell somewhat, and the markets were moderately quiet
and declining. The situation was again tending to right
itself in a normal way. On February 29th Mr. Coolidge
announced that he could see no such falling off in business
as to indicate a lack of prosperity. The market again
started to rise, and in the next month brokers' loans increased over $317,000,000, the second largest rise in the
history of the Exchange. In April the market was wildly
excited, rising in face of advancing money rates and gold
exports. On the last day of the month an uncontradicted
despatch from Baltimore in the *Times* stated that Mellon
interests were reported to be heavy buyers of Consolidated
Gas, Electric Light and Power of Baltimore, and of Pennsylvania Water and Power, which had risen to record
prices.

May witnessed another excited rise in prices and an
increase of $366,000,000 in brokers' loans, with continued
gold exports. On June 4th the National City Bank of New
York declared business was good but added that "the
chief jarring note has been the huge amount of speculation in the stock market. Regardless of what may be the
long-time trend of investment values, speculation on the
scale current during recent weeks can only be deplored

as unsound and hurtful to the best interests of the country. Visions of easily made riches are tending to destroy the usual habits of saving, and millions of dollars are being put into the market by many who can ill afford the risks they are taking. Never before has stock speculation involved so many people of all classes, and one hears the frequent complaint that one trouble with business is that business men are paying too much attention to the market and not enough to the conduct of their own establishments. All this can only mean storing up of trouble for some future day, and the danger is that with so widespread a public participation in the market, a decline, which is always a possibility after so prolonged an advance, would affect general consumer purchasing power and so slow up the distribution of commodities." Warning was issued of higher interest rates to come.

The following day the Federal Reserve Board also issued a warning of danger, stating that unless there were a reversal of gold movements or in the policy of the Federal Reserve system the only remedy would be a reduction in the loan accounts of the banks. The care with which the newspapers were warned against premature publication of this statement showed its importance in the eyes of the Board; but when Mr. Mellon, the ex officio head of the Board, was asked to comment, he put off questioners with the mere remark that he had not seen the statement. Broker's loans had passed five and a quarter billions. The market broke badly. On the 14th Mellon stated that the break was without significance, and that

he could not say that stocks were too high or that speculation had assumed undue proportions. The day before,
Hoover had been nominated for the presidency at Kansas
City, and the papers at once began to talk of a "Hoover
market" to begin in September.

General business improved during the summer, and
by September the public participation in the stock market
had become unprecedented, brokers' loans rising over
$462,000,000 in the months. On the 13th the *Times* noted
that "in a market so wild and excited as yesterday's, Wall
Street was ready to believe almost any fantastic yarn . . .
is in a mood to take its tips where and as it finds them,"
and that in spite of denials made as to the values of certain stocks they continue to forge ahead. The public had
gone so mad that a steadying word might have been useful, but Mellon chose the next day to make a report that
the country was prosperous and that he saw no indication
of a slump or depression.

The next month was characterized by "violent and
constantly increasing speculation for the rise." John J.
Raskob announced that stocks were too high, and the
American Bankers Association, at their annual meeting,
took a strong stand against the danger of the speculation.
Stocks broke sharply on October 26th but rallied next
day. On the 31st Mr. Coolidge announced that the foundations of business were very strong.

The presidential campaign was now on. In his
speeches Hoover stressed the issue of good business, saying on November 2nd at Louisville that "the policies of

the government bear an increasing responsibility for continued national prosperity." He thus assumed the obligation of "presidential prosperity."

The new year, 1929, began with a continued advance in stocks; and so insatiable had become the demands for credit to support the market, that nearly every European country was now being drained of gold in a reversal of the exchanges. The steady advance in quotations—17 points for January—gave everyone the impression of unprecedented prosperity, and industrial operations had advanced to a new high level. In the two months of December and January more than $2,240,000,000 of new securities were issued, $256,000,000 of investment trust issues being put out in the latter month. Money ranged from 7 to 12 per cent. The world situation was becoming deranged and at the beginning of February, Norman, head of the Bank of England, was in conference in Washington with the Federal Reserve Board, which, on the 6th, issued a formal warning against the increased use of credit for stock market purposes. Three days later the Treasury Department (Mr. Mellon) "explained informally" that this was not intended to "bring about a sudden slump in stocks." A week later the Federal Advisory Council unexpectedly announced that it approved the tight-money policy of the Reserve Board. Mr. Mellon refused to issue any statement, but on the 15th announced that he thought it an opportune time to buy bonds. "This does not mean," he added, "that many stocks are not good investments. Some, however, are too high in price to be good buys."

287

A week later the Secretary of Commerce, Lamont, stated that business was progressing favorably, only one branch —building—showing a decline.

The tremendous excitement in the market continued through the next few months, nervous and heavy declines alternating with great advances, such as that of over 20 points in June. On May 22nd the public appetite had been whetted by a Pittsburgh despatch to the *Times* estimating the profits of the Mellon family in Aluminium and Gulf Oils alone, on the basis of shares owned, as over $300,-000,000. By the middle of September the stock averages showed an advance since the first of the year of 82 points. The end, however, was in sight. In the annual review of the *Times* on December 31st we read "a Stock Exchange panic of unexampled violence broke out in the last week of October, after several weeks of falling prices. . . . A long list of high-grade stocks fell 25 to 40 points in one day. The crisis of the panic came on Tuesday, October 29, when the outside public's huge speculative account was mostly closed out because of exhausted margins, with disastrous, nation-wide losses." Presidential prosperity had crashed and the nation was lying dead or wounded under the ruins.

*

Hoover, as we have said, is of a different type of mind from either Coolidge or Mellon. The old-fashioned views of the former interested him about as much as an old blacksmith's shop would interest the president of the United States Steel Corporation. Nor did he care about finance, which he had left to Mellon. The President had been paying but the scantiest—if any—attention to Wall Street. He was absorbed in the larger problems of production and consumption, and with vast plans for "stabilizing" business cycles. The crash gave him his opportunity. His calling of the great business heads to Washington for conference and the methods pursued to rebuild the fallen structure of credit and confidence are current history, fresh in all minds, and we need not dwell on them. One of the great heads called was Mr. Henry Ford, and, in view of the news steadily given out by the Administration on business conditions, the comment made by that gentleman was illuminating. "The first thing to do," he said, rather unkindly, "is to correct the impression that the present state of affairs is due to the stock market. . . . The real explanation of the present situation is not to be found in recent stock-market history but in recent business history. . . . In this country the purchasing power of the people has been practically used up."

Psychologically, and for a time, the calling of the great modern Barons into conference and the promise that they would without delay set Humpty Dumpty up again may have had a reassuring effect and prevented large failures and further demoralization. As to the long-run results to be obtained by scientific stabilizing of business by government the issue is more doubtful. Something more is needed than mere desire for a new economic order, as Russia can convince us. The problems are of enormous intricacy, and the curious may find some of them touched upon in the *Papers and Proceedings* of the American Economic Association read at their meeting last December. What would seem essential are extraordinary wisdom and power of forecasting on the part of those responsible for the process. It is not unfair to judge somewhat of these attributes in the light of recent predictions by Mr. Hoover and his advisers.

On December 5th Mr. Raskob announced that "by early spring business ought to be going ahead at its regular rate. The whole economic situation would seem to indicate that." On December 14th Mr. Hoover thought that the volume of Christmas shopping indicated that the business of the country was back to normal.

On January 1st the ever-hopeful Mr. Mellon announced that "I see nothing in the present situation that is either menacing or warrants pessimism. During the winter months there *may be* [italics mine] some slackness or unemployment, but hardly more than at this season each year. I have every confidence that there will be a revival of activity in the spring."

On the 22nd Hoover said the trend of employment had changed in the right direction, and Secretary Davis announced that every major industry was showing increases and that "we can expect a great deal of business in 1930." The following day Miss Perkins sharply disputed the Secretary's statistics of unemployment for the State of New York.

On February 11th Secretary Lamont, of the Department of Commerce, stated that "there is nothing in the situation to be disturbed about. ... There are grounds for assuming that this is about a normal year," and added that the steel plants making steel shapes for automobiles were "filled up" for months ahead. A week later he announced, after a White House conference, that there was every reason to hope that business would soon pick up.

On March 3rd, speaking for the Administration, he said business would be normal in two months [May 3rd] and that "it is amazing how well off we are considering what we went through." It had all, however, amounted to very little in the mind of Mr. Hoover's assistant. "We were going ahead a little too fast," he said, "and got winded. In another month or two [April 3rd or May 3rd] we will catch our breath for a fresh start." On March 8th Hoover predicted that unemployment would be ended in sixty days [May 8th], and in general gave out an optimistic statement.

On March 16th, Mr. Julius H. Barnes, chairman of Mr. Hoover's National Business Survey Conference, announced that "the spring of 1930 marks the end of a period of grave concern. ... American business is steadily coming back to a normal level of prosperity. ... On the whole a note of optimism is apparent among the vast majority of industries." A fortnight later the monthly *Survey* of the Guaranty Trust Company of New York stated that "in spite of the considerable improvement in business sentiment and the definite establishment of some of the fundamentals of recovery, industrial revival has made only very moderate progress." Speaking of the hopeful feeling that recovery may not be long delayed, it made the more than suggestive remark that the "consistently cheerful comment from Washington in the issuance of trade figures has probably helped to create this sentiment, although there has become evident an increasing disposition to discount such views as inspired by a desire to aid business recovery rather than to examine the situation in the cold light of truth."

On April 19th Mr. Barnes spoke of the Business Survey Conference as "a really novel social experiment," and was optimistic about unemployment.

On the 28th the Guaranty Trust Company again introduced a death's head at the feast in its monthly *Survey* when it stated that "aside from the usual seasonal expansion of some branches of industry, little tangible progress in business recovery has thus far been reported." On the same day Mr. Barnes presented facts, not forecasts, to the meeting of the U. S. Chamber of Commerce, and the market started downward, after its three months' wild upward whirl of this year, based on misleading governmental predictions.

On May 2nd Mr. Hoover in a long address said "we have been passing through one of those great economic storms [not merely getting winded, as his Secretary of Commerce had phrased it] which periodically bring hardship and suffering on our people. While the crisis took place *only six months ago* [italics mine] I am convinced we have now passed the worst and with continued unity of effort we shall rapidly recover. . . . I believe I can say with assurance that our joint undertaking has succeeded to a remarkable degree." Poor Mr. Hoover! Had he not told the American people in his campaign speeches that "the victory of the [Republican] party will ensure stability of business and employment"?

The optimistic utterances quoted above had misled the American people into staging a remarkable "comeback" in stock speculation. The soberer element had been amazed at the rapid rise since the beginning of the year. But, as the Guaranty Trust Company noted at the end of March, people were beginning to suspect the horse sense and the reliability of presidential predictions. The last utterance of Mr. Hoover was the signal for the biggest crash in the market since the panic of last autumn. As the ordinary old-fashioned business man, not indulging in new social experiments but merely trying to see where he stands, looks about him, he reads of rapidly declining railway earnings, of lowering steel prices, of smashed copper markets, of big decreases in foreign trade, and so on through the rest of our statistics. In the *Times* of May 11th—a date subsequent to all those which the government had set as a return to "normal" prosperity—I read that "it may be that industrial production is now on an upward trend and that unemployment is showing noticeable improvement; but tangible evidence to that effect is unfortunately difficult to obtain."

On the 28th Mr. Hoover was reported to have said that business would be normal by fall. The same day the excellent survey issued by the Union Trust Company of Cleveland, after pointing out that "a very decided improvement in business would be required during the second quarter to bring the general volume of business back to a satisfactory level," added that "no such swift revival is in evidence. Business is therefore resigning itself to the realization that it may have to face a 'long, hard pull' in order to get back to normal." Meanwhile, as pointed out in the financial editorials of the *New York Times* of May 28th and 29th, the exports of wheat for April were the smallest for that month in any year except 1928 since the War; the decrease in railway net earnings for the northwestern regions for April 1930 as compared with 1928 ran from an average of 60 per cent to 80 per cent for some carriers; seventy railroads throughout the entire country showed losses of 33 per cent in net; and the drop in the price of steel billets to $31 in May brought the price of steel to the lowest since 1922, when it touched $28.

Perhaps our ordinary business man sympathizes with Will Rogers, who cried out, when Mr. Hoover's last speech on prosperity was followed by a first-class smash, "the whole thing shows there is none of them knows any more about it than Texas Guinan. If we could just persuade our prominent men to stop predicting! If they must predict, let 'em predict on the weather." On May 8th the last touch was given to what would be roaring farce if it were not stark tragedy, when Governor Young of the Federal Reserve Bank declared that there was "food for serious thought" in the fact that even with our excellent banking system we had come to "the brink of collapse" and were now in "what appears to be a business depression." If we were not also in a Republican administration there would be less doubt among our present leaders as to whether we were in "what *appears* to be a business depression"!

*

I do not pretend that without exception every time the market has given a shiver to the bulls the White House or the Treasury has immediately come to the rescue. The synchronism, however, is clearly too marked to be accidental, although I am not here making a mere attack upon men or any party. I agree with Mr. Hoover that such crises are "periodic" not political. Nor do I blame, as false prophets, any one of the three men with whom I have been chiefly concerned. In that I agree with Will Rogers. None of them knows any more about it than does Texas Guinan. The professors of economics in the colleges, such as Irving Fisher, and the business prognosticators, such as Babson, were all as wrong as our political leaders. Coolidge certainly knew nothing whatever about it all. His autobiography has given us the stature of his mind. In financial matters he could not fail to be deeply influenced by Mr. Mellon. Under the circumstances, for him to have opposed his own mind to Mellon's would have been to take a colossal responsibility. As for Mellon, I believe him absolutely honest, even if his own profits were as colossal as Mr. Coolidge's responsibility would have been. He told the people when to get into the stock market, and, somewhat cryptically, when to get out. It was the novelty of having a Secretary of the Treasury encourage the market for our benefit that probably lost so many people their money. The trouble with Mr. Mellon has been that he was a stock-market-minded financier, and not a statesman. As for Hoover, he inherited a mess left him by Mellon and Coolidge and had had to make rash promises, giving blank checks for prosperity drawn only on the bank of Republican tradition, when his predecessor had largely, though innocently, gutted the institution. The problems raised by the experiment of presidential prosperity are larger than any personalities. We can only glance at them here.

One is, what is to become of the stability of government in its time-honored functions if it is to become a business-efficiency or a tipster's bureau? In the winning of men's respect, the maintenance of civil order, the dispensing of justice, the waging of war, the handling of foreign relations and other problems of the older statesmanship is it likely to be helped by undertaking to create prosperity and guide people in their stock speculations? That "big business" has raised big questions must be allowed. That *all* questions are now tinged with economics must also be allowed. That some experiments in stabilizing business may be needful and eventually useful may also be allowed. But in the present state of our abysmal ignorance about economics is there not danger in handing over the economic lives and welfare of our people to the government, already tottering under the load of the older functions which it is performing none too well, such as maintaining order and dispensing justice? Is there not danger in a government to which we are taught to look for stock-market tips and which is expected to make rightly the hardest of all predictions?

Moreover, it may well be asked, how many different sorts of loads can a president carry? In addition to the burden already on his shoulders, can we expect him to be the super-business man who will manage all our prosperity for us? I doubt if we could have a better man than Hoover as a business engineer; but is he proving a great success? Already prosperity overshadows all other questions in an election; but if the government is made constitutionally, so to say, responsible for prosperity and stock booms, will any other question stand a show at elections? And will not the already natural desire to bend every other activity of government to creating prosperity or the appearance of it warp every other thought in the minds of those anxious for re-election? Is not the comment of the Guaranty Trust Company on the unreliability of the government's pronouncements indicative of what we might expect? Are they likely to give us the facts in the cold light of truth, or will every government department be bent solely on creating a favorable atmosphere?

Again, to what sort of men are we to commit our prosperity? Has our experience with boards in America been so reassuring that we wish to build up new ones, in the government service, to run our business? Is there not danger that if business becomes political it will be run too much as most of our political life is already run? It is true that our best brains have long been drawn away from politics into business, because the real power now lies there, and that if the running of our entire business machinery should come to be controlled by government, the new access of power to politics might make that profession again attractive. That, however, is problematic, and so far our experience has been against such a fond hope. Can we unite, as yet at least, the tremendous power of running business with our present methods of electing public officials? Are we not likely, in the long run, to find we have committed the power either to politicians or to a bureaucracy?

We may look at the question from another angle. Part of the possibility of the government's maintaining order is the willingness of the individual to forego private revenge and to seek justice for himself and to acquiesce in the acts of the government through the police and courts. And so to a greater or lesser extent is it with other governmental functions. If government becomes responsible for prosperity, for stabilizing business or what you will, will it not become increasingly necessary to forego private judgment and initiative in deference to the policy of a Coolidge, a Mellon, or a

Hoover? If a Mr. Mellon, as a government official charged with the creation of a bull market, insists that stocks are going up, would we become bad citizens, "conscientious objectors," if we chose to sell out on him?

If the maintenance of prosperity becomes a governmental function and duty it will inevitably overshadow all others. The maintenance of peace and order, the administering of justice, the following of a wise foreign policy, the dozen other things government does or should do, would count for far less in the mind of the average voter than its ability to guess right on the stock market or so manipulate it and business as to bring him ever increasing "prosperity." The pressure on officials, who may know no more than Texas Guinan, or who may be faced by an inevitably bad business situation, may become impossible.

Moreover, would not the chief desideratum in a president at an election become—as it already has to a great extent, thanks to the fetish of Republican prosperity—the mere ability to bring good business? What of the type of leader that such a situation would be likely to create in our public life? As I have pointed out elsewhere, the business mind has its excellent qualities. It also has its very marked limitations. Would not making the government responsible for prosperity reduce our choice of leaders to the ranks of super-business men, captains of industry, stock-market manipulators; and is that the type which the great American people desire for their future Chief Executives? Is statesmanship to become wholly subordinate to big business, and government merely a branch of economics?

These, among other questions, suggest themselves to the lover of his country as he watches the "really novel social experiment" now being tried. Might it not be better for a while to work through outside organizations in the effort—a noble one—to try to find some method of stabilizing modern industry and employment? Let the government give help in every crisis. Let it look benevolently on every effort of the people to grow in economic wisdom and self-control; but is it wise to make our Chief Executive solely responsible in the eyes of the governed for maintenance of our business welfare at all times? I realize the problems inherent in modern economic development and also that the government must excercise more and more a regulating function, but I see grave danger in a "Coolidge market" and a Secretary of the Treasury guiding the destinies of a frenzied speculation to the very last point before he tells the people to "buy bonds." We have tried the experiment. We are at the parting of the ways. Is there not as much chance of the new theory leading to an abuse of the functions of government and a decline in our national character as to renewed and continuous "presidential prosperity"?

3. LIBERTY OR PROSPERITY?

IN 1765 the American colonies were aflame with resentment against what they felt to be encroachments
upon their freedom by the acts of the British government and its officials in America. In Boston, James Otis
had thundered against the claims of the revenue officers
to search and seizure under cover of general warrants.
In Williamsburg, Virginia, in the old brick Courthouse,
Patrick Henry, denouncing the Stamp Act, made the
address containing the words that every schoolboy knows
by heart, "Give me liberty or give me death."

Scarce five generations have passed. By fire and
neglect, the shrine of liberty in Virginia has not only
been levelled to the ground, but its very foundations
are now impossible to trace. The old edifice is being
rebuilt as an historical curiosity by the richest family
in the world, a family which controls the destinies of
hundreds of thousands of its fellow-citizens. Schoolboys
still repeat the resounding rhetoric of Patrick Henry's
speech, but it, too, like the building in which it was
spoken, has become an historical curiosity. When a
mature American quotes from it it is almost inevitably

with an indulgent and ironic smile. The choice between liberty or death has become an absurd exaggeration, a flourish fit only for school children or a Fourth of July harangue to an uncritical mob audience. No presidential candidate wins either applause or votes by a pledge to defend our liberties; but let him promise prosperity, and a Coolidge or a Hoover floats into the White House on overwhelming majorities.

A great change has evidently come over the mind and outlook of the American people. A century and a half ago liberty was its chief concern, a liberty it was then endeavoring to preserve by bloody war. We disguise the change with a formula. We say that the thought of our new age is economic, not political. But why? Why has prosperity replaced liberty as the catchword and watchword of the nation and its leaders?

In the days of the Founders of the Republic, in spite of the economic interpretation of history, we have to acknowledge that the feeling for liberty was deep and sincere. A very large part of the American people and their leaders believed the truth of the words in which they announced to the world that, "we hold these truths to be self-evident; that all men are created equal; that they are endowed by their Creator with certain inalienable rights; that among these are life, liberty, and the pursuit of happiness." That declaration was wholly political. It was neither biological nor economic. The majority of those who applauded it believed every word of it.

It was the first declaration by a responsible body of

statesmen of the new theory of liberty, and was to have resounding repercussions. The French Revolution followed, and the great English Reform Bill. The repercussions have not yet ceased to be felt, in Europe, South America, Africa, and Asia. But the problem of liberty is in utter confusion. As I write, the King of Spain is fleeing from Madrid, and the populace is shouting for the Republic. They will find the situation is not solved by the expulsion of a monarch. For the new idea of liberty has been a source of confusion in government ever since it passed from the closet of the philosopher to the hustings and the marketplace.

In the medieval period a "liberty" meant something quite different from what it does now. The "liberty" of the king or barons or the Church meant the right to exercise sovereignty within a special field; and when it is said that Henry VIII "took all liberties into his hands" it does not mean that he destroyed all the liberties of the people in the modern sense, but that he merged the several bits of sovereignty into the sovereignty of the Crown. By doing so he destroyed conflicting jurisdictions, made law "common" and justice national. He also raised, however, the modern problem of "sovereignty"; and the people stood face to face with the Crown in any struggle for enlarged rights. Such rights, however, were particular rights, which the people might struggle for and which, if they won them, they would value accordingly.

In the eighteenth century the new doctrine also arose of the rights of man as man, rights which each

THE TEMPO OF MODERN LIFE

individual possessed in virtue of his quality of human being, quite apart from any power or struggle to win them. Liberty, it was conceived, was a gift of nature, of which some men had unlawfully been deprived by their fellow-men. Self-government and an abstract universal liberty were the "right" of all. According to this theory, sovereignty became lodged in the mass of men instead of the monarch and, just as the latter had had to call in the theory of divine right to bolster his claims, so the mass now had to assert the possession of innate good-will and of universal wisdom to bolster theirs. The Voice of the People became the Voice of God. The old dictum that the King can do no wrong was replaced by the assertion that the People can inevitably be trusted.

Society has ever been subject to stresses and strains. Groups, institutions, classes have always been striving for their several ends and individual welfare. In earlier days, all of these groups were fairly clearly delimited as entities, whether they were monarchs, aristocracies, classes with legal privileges or disabilities, the Church, the guilds, municipalities or what not. In the constant shifts of interest some would combine for specific purposes against others. With the rise of the sovereign monarchies, the alignments became simplified. But as a result of many centuries of complicated struggles, certain rights, which our ancestors believed essential to a happy and free life, had been rather definitely won. When peoples like the Americans or the French, substituted their own sovereignty for that of monarchs, they deemed it essential that these rights should be placed in an impregnable position; not that the people feared themselves as untrammelled sovereigns, but that they feared usurpation on the part of those to whom as a practical necessity they might delegate some of the functions of governing. The Declaration of Independence stresses the right to "liberty." Most of the State constitutions, however, as also the early amendments to the Federal one, embodied Bills of Rights for the purpose of forever protecting certain specific liberties, such as freedom of speech, of the press, the right of *habeas corpus,* of freedom from unwarranted search and seizure, and from cruel and unusual punishments.

As a result of long experience, such rights as these had come to appear to men so essential as the basis of civilized life, that both our own ancestors and Europeans of later generations were willing to go through seas of blood to win and defend them. To-day, as the result of a far shorter experience, we seem entirely willing that we should allow ourselves to be deprived, and to deprive others, of practically every one of them.

*

The story of freedom of speech and press in America is that of an almost steadily increasing restriction. In the Civil War under Lincoln, and in the recent war under Wilson, Americans were muzzled to a far greater extent than were citizens of England. The Constitution nowhere provides for the slighest suspension of guarantees under wartime conditions; yet as soon as we have gone to war, such suspension has occurred. In the Civil War not only were many newspapers forced to suspend publication at the whim of the Federal authorities, but in some cases their editors were thrown into jail and kept there without being able to discover the nature of the charges against them. One of these, for example, J. W. Wall of New Jersey, who later became U. S. Senator, was imprisoned for weeks in Fort Lafayette without formal charges, and was released only at the earnest intervention of the Governor of the State. In the last war Congress practically abolished part of the Constitution by passing a law which provided punishment of "not more than $10,000 or imprisonment for not more than twenty years, or both" for anyone convicted of using language intended to bring the Government of the United States "into contempt, scorn, contumely, or disrepute." This could easily be made to cover almost any criticism of even the mere efficiency of the government in conducting its operations. The ensuing wholesale arrests were a scandal in our history, and there are yet men serving their twenty years for having, in the opinion of a judge under the influence of wartime psychology, infringed a Congressional law clearly in contravention of rights guaranteed under the Constitution.

But the steady decline in freedom of speech has not been incidental solely to wars. The right has been increas-

ingly abridged when its excercise has been thought in
any way inimical to the particular form of capitalism
in vogue. An early presage of this occurred before the
Civil War, as early as 1828, when many of the Southern
States abolished freedom of speech with regard to
slavery—a year in prison being the punishment for anyone who might claim, in speech or writing, that slave-
owners did not have a right of property in human beings.
At the present time, the Postmaster General, under the
widely-stretched obscenity statute, has almost dictatorial
powers over the transmission through the mails, and
consequently over the circulation, of printed matter.
Many States and communities are under control of their
more local authorities, and the extent to which freedom
of the press has now become curtailed may be seen in
what used to be considered the most intellectual center
of the nation, Boston. There would seem to be little left
of intellectual freedom in that city when it is illegal to
sell or circulate there certain works of the following
authors: St. John Irvine, Sherwood Anderson, Arthur
Train, Conrad Aiken, Bertrand Russell, Upton Sinclair, Olive Schreiner, Carl Van Vechten, Count Keyser-
ling, Theodore Dreiser, Michael Arlen, Robert W.
Service, Ben Hecht, Judge Lindsey, Warwick Deeping,
John Dos Passos, Sinclair Lewis, H. G. Wells, and others.

It is needless to cite the long list of even the most
notorious cases in which freedom of speech, of assem-
blage, and statement of grievances have been denied
in recent years whenever any question of property or

form of government has cast its least shadow over the situation. The unseating of the Socialists elected to the New York State Legislature, the refusal of freedom of speech in Boston to the sympathizers with Sacco and Vanzetti, the incidents of the Paterson and innumerable other strikes, the disgraceful series of trials and imprisonments in California are but the most striking examples of the increasing denial of Constitutional rights.

What has happened to freedom of speech, the press, and lawful assembly has happened also in many cases to the right to *habeas corpus,* and to freedom from unusual punishments and from illegal search and seizure. The Oppenheimer case in San Quentin penitentiary, for example, reads like a survival of medieval torture. For four days and fourteen hours this man is reported to have been tied up in a canvas strait-jacket, his arms bound to his sides, the brass eyelets of the canvas eating into his flesh, released at no moment for the performance of bodily functions, suffering such tortures as, he said, had induced four prisoners to commit suicide in one year rather than face the ordeal. Yet we are guaranteed in the Constitution against "cruel and unusual punishments." Again, we are guaranteed that we shall be secure in our "persons, houses, papers, and effects against unreasonable searches and seizures," that no warrants shall be issued except upon "probable cause, supported by oath or affirmation, and particularly describing the place to be searched, and the persons or things to be seized." Yet in enforcing the Eighteenth Amendment to the Constitution (the first which limits instead of protecting the liberty of the citizen), these rights have been blown to bits. Motor cars, yachts, buildings are entered and searched without warrant, by uniformed or un-uniformed officers of the government. On June 13, 1929, it was asserted in Congress that one hundred and thirty-five persons, many of them innocent, had been killed by government agents. Yet these murderers are protected by the Federal government. It is no wonder Mr. Wickersham said yesterday in a speech that "law enforcement officers stoop to attain their ends by means as illegal as the acts they seek to punish or suppress."

Such a situation as exists in our country to-day might be understandable if our liberties had been overthrown by a tyrant with an army at his back; but we claim to be governing ourselves and to be the freest people in the world. Another curious feature is that scarcely anyone seems to care. With the exception of some of the wets suffering under the unjust and illegal enforcement measures, it is almost impossible to stir the slightest interest in cases of infringement of personal liberties. In fact, when one tries to do so, one is apt to be voted a "nut" and a nuisance, a "red" or a danger to society. When, not in wartime, the Supreme Court of the United States, Brandeis and Holmes dissenting, sentenced people to twenty years in prison for publishing what Justice Holmes said in his Opinion they "had just as much right to publish as the Government has to publish the Constitution of the United States, now vainly invoked by them," there was not the least ripple of excitement among the public, most of whom probably never heard of the case. Indeed, the public to-day seems to have heard very little of liberty. Arthur Garfield Hays cites the instance of a man who read a section of the Declaration of Independence at a meeting and was arrested by a policeman for doing so. "I didn't say that. Thomas Jefferson said it," the victim replied in defense. The policeman's answer was, "Where is the guy? We'll get him too." Quotations from Lincoln have been hissed by audiences, ignorant of their authorship, as being un-American and revolutionary. Both Jefferson and Lincoln, in their Inaugural Addresses as Presidents of the United States proclaimed the right of the people to discuss or even to achieve by revolutionary force changes in our form of government. Yet the attempt to do even the first to-day is likely not only to result in being blacklisted by such narrow-minded die-hards as the Daughters of the American Revolution but to land a man in jail by sentence of the Supreme Court of the United States. How has this colossal change, catastrophic for personal liberty, come about?

*

There have been, I think, two factors in operation. One has been the working out of the eighteenth-century political philosophy, and the other has been the economic change wrought in the nineteenth. We are getting the results of the new theory as to the location of sovereignty, and of a new scale of values. The eighteenth century left us as a legacy the belief in the goodness, the right-mindedness, and the wisdom of the mass of men as men. It bequeathed to us the shibboleth of a vague general liberty which had been assured to us forever by the choice of a form of government. The nineteenth brought us new economic conditions and aspirations for the masses, and also a new type of leadership inimical to individual liberties. Thus, our modern political world now rests upon a group of illusions. There is, first, the illusion that the Voice of the People, as they are at present, is the voice of God; that they will know and strive for what is best for themselves in the long run; that they will be jealous guardians of their own liberties. Second, there is the illusion that liberty is a gift of nature which has only to be regained and enshrined in a particular form of government to be retained forever; that the form, rather than the spirit, is the essential. Third, there is the illusion that a satisfying and civilized life can be based upon a material scale of values. Both leaders and led have succumbed to all of these.

But such illusions would seem inevitably to lead to the grasping of power by the strong, and to the loss both of individual liberties and of the very concept of liberty itself. The form may remain, but human life is not static, and the forces of society are forever arranging themselves in new patterns, above or beneath the surface, visible or hidden.

311

One of the characteristics of modern life is its impersonality. In earlier days men fought for particular rights to be wrested from the barons, who had their particular bits of sovereignty; from the Church, which had its; from the King, who had his. But following our struggle against England for a generalized "liberty," we placed sovereignty everywhere and nowhere, in "the People." It is clear that in any government much will depend on the character of the "sovereign"; and it has been in the hope of getting rid of such an objectionable character that the Spanish people have just ejected the Spanish King. Just as much, however, will depend upon character when the People is sovereign as when a king is, or when the sovereignty was shared by various persons and classes.

What to-day, is the character of the people, of that mass mind which we have set up as ruler? For one thing, as we pass down in the social and intellectual scale, just as when we descend from maturity to childhood, we find among individuals a steadily increasing demand for conformity, a governing of their conduct by taboos, a desire to be like everyone else and to make everyone else like themselves. Perhaps the two communities in which it is most difficult to be an individualized person, in which the pressure of conformity to conventional standards is greatest, are a small village and a boy's boarding-school. There seems to be something in the immature or undeveloped or uncultured mind which demands conformity for its own satisfaction. A conservatism based on taboos precludes any possibility of individual divergence. Such a mind is also opposed to enlightenment or change. The same instinct that necessitates a schoolboy's tying his cravat in a certain way because all his fellows do, makes the ordinary man of the village resent the holding of moral, governmental, or social ideas different from his own by anyone whom he can control. One of the essential features of a taboo is that is a form without an intelligible meaning. We might expect the People as sovereign, therefore, to be insistent upon forms, intolerant of change and differences, of individual liberties not conformable to their own ways and desires.

Nor has the average member of the mass, or the mass as mass, ever much cared for liberty except under the impulse of a temporary emotion. It may be questioned even then whether the desire has not been chiefly due to mass psychology. At the time of the greatest excitement over freedom—the time of the American Revolution—only one-third of the people, according to John Adams, cared about winning it by actually going to war. They might shout themselves hoarse when Patrick Henry or Sam Adams harangued them in mobs; but, out of the more than three millions which they then numbered, Washington was never able to get more than twenty-five thousand into the army at any one time. The man who will make a genuine choice between liberty and death is not a common man but a most rare and uncommon one. To raise our armies in the Civil and World

Wars we, like other nations, had both to inflame emotions with propagandist lies and to force men into the ranks by the legal compulsion of drafts. What the average man wants is to be able to lead his own small private life with as great comfort as possible. He troubles himself as little as may be with anything which he cannot see concerns him immediately. His views are neither long, broad, nor high. He is oblivious of an attack on anyone else's liberty so long as he himself is not bothered. He is quite ready to deprive someone else of the liberty to do or say something which he himself does not care to. He is even more ready to deprive the other of the liberty to do or say something of which he himself disapproves. He is easily moved by propaganda and by mass-psychology in all its manifestations. If his own interests, coinciding with those of his group or class, are too heavily infringed, he may indeed revolt; but from the above and other reasons it is absurd to think of the mass of the people as a "sovereign" who will be careful to preserve the liberties of the nation.

But the mass today *is* sovereign; and the preservation of liberty has become in some ways more difficult on that account. In 1776 we could hurl defiance at George the Third and tell him in the Declaration of Independence that "he has made judges dependent on his will alone for the tenure of their offices"; that "he has erected a multitude of new offices, and sent hither swarms of officers to harass" us; or curse him "for imposing taxes on us without our consent." But, though we might, after civil war, cut loose from George, how are we to defend ourselves when the sovereign people makes judges dependent on *its* will alone; when through Congress *they* erect new offices and send swarms of officers to harass us; or when five million of us, all of whom might object, are forced by the voters of the other hundred and fifteen million to pay the whole of the Income Tax raised in the country? What is to be done when, unhindered, the officers of this new Sovereign tell us we cannot say this or that, though the Constitution guarantees that we can; when we are told what we can and cannot read among books that almost all the rest of the world can read; when, even supposing that we are evenly divided on the Prohibition question, half of our hundred and twenty million people tells the other half they shall not be allowed to drink a glass of beer because the first half disapproves? In a monarchy the worst despotism has always been "tempered by assassination." One cannot assassinate a despot with a hundred and twenty million heads.

The transferring of sovereignty from a monarch to the People thus did not ensure the preservation of liberty. It merely assured, possibly, that such liberties might be preserved as especially appealed to the desires or narrow imagination of the vast mass at the low end of the social scale. Freedom of speech or press, for example, under the old-time absolute monarchies meant liberty to say or print what otherwise the king might have objected to. Various forms of pressure can be brought, as they always have

315

been, against an individual as sovereign. In a democracy, freedom of speech or press has come to mean, as innumerable incidents have illustrated in America in the past decade, a liberty to say only what the people are willing to allow; and pressure is far more difficult to bring against the mass mind and will than it is against an individual tyrant.

*

There is another element in our present situation. The industrial revolution, following the introduction of machinery, has brought vast changes, both for the leaders and the mass. Throughout all the ages, from the days of the Pharaohs down, whatever may have been the form of society, it may be said to have consisted of three divisions: the men of economic and political power; the artists, writers and thinkers whom we may call the intelligentsia; and the great mass of work-a-day folk. So it was in Egypt. So it is in America. Although the classification persists with extraordinary uniformity, the characteristics of the classes vary with the source of their power. A feudal aristocracy based on land tenure and military service will develop different characteristics and demand different "liberties" from an aristocracy based on selling chewing gum to the mob or manufacturing steel under a protective tariff. So will an intelligentsia which looks for support to "patrons" among the rich from that which is dependent on writing movie scenarios for the crowd. So will the work-a-day people who have automobiles and are "sovereigns" from those who tilled soil for their over-lords.

All three groups, however, have ever striven for the same thing—the power to express themselves according to their own desires. The first group has always had the will to power. The second has been concerned primarily with the discovery or creation of truth or beauty; and the third with leading as comfortable and safe a life as might be. In the long run, it is the second that exerts the most lasting influence. We care nothing to-day about the domestic happiness of a fish-seller in Athens or the power once wielded by the richest Athenian mine-owner, whereas the works of Phidias and Plato, Aristotle and Sophocles are imperishable possessions. Such influence, however, is likely to require time. At any given moment, the power of the few and the mass of the many are of great and, it may be, of overwhelming importance.

At present, in our as yet rather inchoate civilization following the industrial revolution, it would seem hopeless to look for any high regard for personal liberty from either of these two groups. Almost the sole vital concern of our new aristocracy—the Coal Barons, the Meat Barons, the Steel Barons, the Chewing-Gum Barons and whatnot—is with the profits resulting from production, distribution, or consumption. Their fellow-citizens, for them, are workmen or consumers. Regarded as the former, the more docile and less insistent they are upon any liberties, the better. Machinelike efficiency in unlimited supply is what the employers demand. Ford will not even allow the workmen in his German factories to have a glass of beer with their dinner after work at night. In strike after strike the new Barons have shown that they will go to any length to deprive their workmen of their rights under the Constitution. Great corporations have not only ruled legislatures but have issued ultimatums to Federal Courts. What these men openly demand, as in tariffs, or secretly seize, as in control of legislation, courts, or police, are "privileges." As for their own "rights," their power protects them in these, not the Constitution—which, however, by judicial interpretation has been constantly altered in their favor. Delightful as some of them may be in private intercourse, great as their benefactions to public funds out of their incredible surpluses may be, it is quite certain that there is no use in looking to them for guardianship of our liberties. The record is too long and too damning. They have shown too often that they care nothing for either abstract liberty or the individual liberties of others when their own personal interests are at stake.

Nor is there much hope at present in looking to the other group—the mass. This may be divided into two classes—the wage-earners and the salaried, with the small business man attached to the latter. Different as these two are in many ways, they are both influenced by one factor in common—their growing dependence on the great corporations and the comparatively small group at the top from whom the streams of power and influence radiate downwards. In 1776, ninety per cent of the American people were farmers, living for the most part in their own

homes on their own land. They could be fearless and independent to an extent that almost nobody can be to-day.
Wide as may be the gulf that separates an iron-puddler
from the vice-president of a Trust Company there is one
bond that spans the difference—fear of losing a job. What
is largely at the bottom of the extraordinarily reactionary
conservatism of present-day America, with its threat to
all personal liberties, is the sense of dependence and fear.
Scarcely anyone can any longer rely wholly upon himself.
If he has a job he is dependent on his boss, on his Board
of Directors, or on the powers even higher, depending on
the economic stratum in which he works. If, on the other
hand, he is in business for himself, he is dependent on
other business men, on the banks, or perhaps on the
temporary complacency of a competing corporation with
resources unlimited as contrasted with his own. If he has
retired, his property is probably largely in stocks and
bonds, and he is tied hand and foot to prosperity and
stability.

In many ways, prosperity has come to mean more
than it ever did before because we are more dependent
on both the possession of things and a steady acquisition
of money. In the old days, the range of things which most
people might wish to possess was extremely limited, to a
very great extent because they were simply non-existent.
Our forefathers felt no desire for, or lack of, a multitude
of things, such as bathrooms, radios, cars, telephones,
and a hundred others, for the reason that they did not
know of them, just as we to-day do not desire those un-

known conveniences that our descendants may come to look upon as the barest necessities of life in *their* day. The minimum standard of life to-day is vastly above that of a century ago in the demands it makes upon those who have to provide it. Practically all of these new things have to be bought and cannot be made by the consumer. The farmer of 1776 could breed a colt, could raise the oats to feed his horse, could make the rough wagon in which he drove. To-day the workman who goes to his job in a car cannot breed it or make the gasoline which keeps it going. He has to earn money to buy both car and gas. And so it goes with most things. Not only has the standard of living become heavily materialized by the long list of things which have become highly desirable to most people, or necessities under modern conditions, but these things can no longer be directly produced by work but only indirectly by the double process of translating work into money and then money into the things. One's own work no longer suffices. To have that work avail us anything, it must be transmuted into money or credit through the operation of the economic system of the day.

At the same time that money has become essential for all these new things, the earning of money has also become so in order to secure many of the most simple fundamentals of living for which our ancestors were in no way dependent upon it. For that ninety per cent of the population who were farmers when our liberties were fought for and established there was practically no need of money for such necessities as housing, fuel, clothing, or food. These were provided by hard work on the farm. To-day, for a very large proportion of our population, money is absolutely necessary to secure any of these things. In the big cities comparatively few can now own their homes, and the rent for a room or an apartment has to be paid for in work transmuted into money. We cannot warm ourselves in winter with wood cut by ourselves on our own woodlot. We cannot feed ourselves with the produce of our own gardens, cows, pigs, and chickens. We cannot clothe ourselves with cloth spun by our wives and made into suits and hats by them.

The new standard of living has made any fall from it appear like a catastrophe. Apart from having to give up such luxuries as have come to appear, and in some cases are, necessities, the new condition entails the terrifying thought that the moment our supply of ready money is gone, there remains not even shelter, food, or clothing. In the old days the men who fought for our liberties might not see a dollar of money in a year and yet have all these things by virtue of simple hard work. To-day a man can have none of them, however hard he is willing to work, unless he can find some place in the economic system in which he is not only allowed to work but to do so under such conditions as permit of the rapid transmutation of his work into money. Just as his car stops if he cannot pour gasoline into it, so his life stops if he cannot pour a constant stream of money into it. The Declaration of Liberty asserted that we were all entitled to "life, liberty, and the pursuit of happiness." Most men, if they have to choose, will give up liberty more readily than life or the pursuit of happiness.

*

The functioning of our modern economic machinery in making us so dependent has taken away our independence. The man of the earlier day who felt that the welfare of himself and his family derived only from his own hard work and theirs could think in terms of freedom. The man or woman to-day who realizes that the mere will-to-work avails nought unless the economic machinery operates so that the work done can be by it transmuted into that money which has become the indispensable link between work and its results, is likely to think in terms of fear—fear that the machine may stop, fear lest it alter in such a way as to throw them aside, fear that any change may occur to upset what they realize is their precarious balancing between a standard of life far above their ancestors' and a depth of destitution unknown to them.

It is the plain truth that fear has entered into the whole of our life as never before. It has become panic. What is considered "liberal" in Europe is apt to be branded here as wildly radical or even anarchistic. It is unforgivably radical to rise even to the height of thought of our fathers in 1787, to insist either for ourselves or others upon the rights guaranteed in the Constitution. The penalties may run all the way from being considered an

322

undesirable "nut" socially to losing a job or being jailed. It may mean dropping from an extraordinarily high material standard of living to a bottomless pit, the mere thought of which makes us shudder. When we combine the general psychological characteristics of the people at large, and of its present leaders, with the fears produced by our economic system as at present functioning, we can understand that the problem to-day is not of enlarging our liberties in a higher civilization, but of desperately trying to save those which our fathers handed down to us. It is a struggle not against a king who may be dethroned or against any aristocracy which may be denuded of titles and privileges, but one against a sovereign which is hydra-headed, the People as a whole. No force will avail, only, perhaps, a growing intelligence which shall play over all the complexities of the new era. As yet there has scarely been time for mind to work on the new conditions which have been outlined above as resulting from both the political and the economic changes of the past two centuries.

At present the entire world is in flux in trying to solve at once the two problems of stability and liberty. A dozen monarchies have fallen in a dozen years. Republics have passed into dictatorships. The most advanced, radical, and to us detestable experiment in economic regimentation is being tried in Russia. No one can predict what will come; but to despair of democracy is to despair of the fate of man. The eighteenth-century generalized concept of "liberty" has little meaning. There are only "liberties," to be won and held. It is possible in the new world now arising that these will have to be different from those in our old one, but it is difficult to see how those guaranteed in the Constitution can be allowed to lapse without hindering the progress of those elements in civilization which we have come to prize highest. In every class or nation civilization has always been based on reasonableness and a sense of values. There would seem to be only two ways out of our present decadence in liberty. One is to instill such reasonableness and sense of values into our new sovereign, the People, as may result in raising its character, altering its economic system, making it worthy of rule, and driving out fear. The other is to go again through the eternal round, the collapse of society, the rise of the dictator, and the slow winning back once more of the old liberties, the value of which would be proved to us by a bitter experience of lacking them. Either process will be long and discouraging, but, in either, the duty of defending our liberties rests as ever upon the few who remain unconfused by clamor and undeterred by fear.

4. WANTED: PERSPECTIVE

BUSINESS, STOCK PRICES, CURRENT ANXIETIES, AND HISTORY

EVERYONE KNOWS the "close-up" in the movies, the projection of the lovers' kiss, the villain's scowl, or what not. There are several characteristics of the close-up as contrasted with the rest of the pictures in the film. For one thing, there is discontinuity, the interrupting of the story while we dwell on a minor aspect of the whole. There is also an absence of all background, the setting vanishing completely, making the immediate act which we witness unrelated. There is also excessive concentration and exaggeration. The face of the lover or the villain, which in the preceding pictures we have seen in proper proportion to the rest of the body and setting, suddenly becomes magnified and occupies exclusively the entire screen. While we gaze on it it blocks all intellectual consideration of cause and effect, the whole nexus of events with which the drama is concerned. Intellectual attention, mild even as it may be in most movies, is suspended, and the appeal becomes a crudely emotional one.

For the last two or three decades this technic of the

325

close-up which seem far removed from the screen, notably in newspapers, magazines, and even education. As a result, we are tending to look at our world, with its interests and problems, more and more as a series of close-ups than as a casual continuum. We concentrate on the act, the problem, the situation of the moment with ever-decreasing effort to see them in relation to their background, as parts of a whole. Both our educational institutions and the press are pushing us in the same direction. The other day I heard of a boy who has lived his life in a tiny settlement remote from what we call civilization. The college to which he has now gone will give him his professional degree in two years by concentrating every single one of his long working days solely on studies immediately concerned with the profession. There is to be no literature, no history, nothing but the technic of the profession itself. That is not education. It is a close-up, and our oldest and best universities are tending to do the same thing by their students. History, in its broadest sense as including both the events and the thoughts of the past, is the background that is essential if we are not to envisage all our life and its problems in a staccato series of moronic close-ups.

We shall return to this point later but I would say here that for the most part we are indebted to the "practical" men of our day, of whatever social or financial grade, for this dangerous tendency, which is becoming steadily more accentuated. It is considered by them high-brow to deal with relations rather than with things, to consider the past instead of dwelling exclusively on the present. In the famous phrase attributed to the financially most successful of these men, "history is bunk." Isaac Newton, because he was wholly concerned with relations instead of things, would be considered a "nut" by most of these practical men if he were living to-day. If you declared that Newton had done more than any of them for the material development of twentieth-century America because he had discovered the square root of minus one, you would unquestionably be considered a wild nut yourself. Yet to-day the practical transmission of all electric power is daily calculated and based on formulæ which involve that absurd square root which seems such moonshine to the business man, and are impossible to figure in any other way.

But at the moment the most notable instance of our close-up way of looking at things is our attitude toward the business depression and the present level of the stock market. Let us take this for a few moments as a case in my general theme which will assuredly come home to the interest of us all.

*

One hears constantly the remark that this is the worst panic in our history. Newspapers talk about the discount rate as "the lowest in the whole history of the Federal Reserve System," giving a startling impression until one recalls that the Reserve System is only seventeen years old, scarcely of high-school age. People talk of the terrible prices for stocks as though they were un-heard-of and spelled the collapse of our civilization. What are some of the facts? What has happened in our history before, and what is the real relationship level of present market prices?

It has always been our habit to indulge in specula-tion, to overdiscount the future, and then to pay the piper. This present crash is no new phenomenon in our history. We went mad over real estate before the panic of 1837. Sales of public lands by the government jumped from about 4,500,000 acres in 1834 to over 20,000,000 two years later. Between 1830 and 1835 the assessed value of real property in New York City rose from $250,000,-000 to $403,000,000. Just as in 1929 people thought it was their last chance to buy "equities" in the United States through common stocks, so, absurdly, though no more insanely, people in 1835 thought it was their last chance to buy land in the country. It was said that our timber was nearing exhaustion, and wood lots in Maine rocketed from $5 an acre to $50. In the six years preced-ing the panic 347 new banks were started, and all banks loaned money on real estate at fantastic prices, just as they did on stocks in 1929. When the panic broke they all suspended specie payment, and wild confusion ensued. In North Carolina farms could be sold for only two per cent of their supposed value. In Alabama it is said half the whole property in the State changed hands. Slaves recently bought for $1,500 each were offered at $200.

The failure of the great United States Bank in 1839

redoubled the fury of the storm. During the crisis nine-tenths of all the Eastern factories were closed, and the same proportion of their hands idle. The "white collar class" also suffered, and in Philadelphia from one-half to two-thirds of all the clerks in the city were discharged. Book-printing, furniture-making, and some other trades stopped completely. The State of Mississippi repudiated its bonds, and even Pennsylvania suspended the payment of interest. Laws were passed in Western States to prevent property being sold for debt. Early in March, 1837, several of the greatest firms in New York and New Orleans failed. By April 8 ninety-eight firms in New York alone had done so, for the then huge sum of $60,000,000. Within three days thirty more crashed. Commercial paper was discounted at five per cent a month. In all, it has been claimed that 33,000 merchants failed with total liabilities of $440,000,000. While cotton fell from 20 cents to 10, flour rose to $12.50 a barrel, and the seamstresses of New York could make only fifty cents to a dollar a week, not enough to buy bread alone. The poorhouses everywhere were crowded. A mob of 5,000 men attacked the City Hall in Boston. In Mississippi taxes were several years in arrears, and sheriffs would not summon juries. Although the panic started in 1837, the lowest point of employment was 1841.

The panic of 1857 was not quite so severe. There were heavy failures among banks, life insurance companies, and such railways as the Illinois Central and Michigan Central, with suspension of specie payments by all the banks in the country. The crisis had been coming on from 1854, and at its acutest stage in 1857 industry almost stopped for a while with severe distress to labor. All kinds of property fell 25 per cent to 75 per cent in value, and mobs paraded New York with cries of "Bread or Death." There were threats to plunder the banks and the Sub-Treasury in Wall Street, and the latter had to be guarded by Federal troops. Business declined until 1859, making a quick recovery the following year.

The depression of 1873 was much worse, and although there were the usual warnings for those who could see, it burst on the country with great suddenness. In the preceding year the failure of four savings banks in New York had caused runs on others resulting in the withdrawal of $20,000,000. For the most part, however, everyone, including such leaders of business as Jay Cooke, Thomas A. Scott (Vice-president of the Pennsylvania Railroad), and William H. Vanderbilt, was living in a fool's paradise. Indeed, the last named, who was considered far-sighted, was paying $120 a ton for steel rails for his new ventures just before the crash. Every sort of scheme and promotion was being entered upon, especially railway building. With the failure of Jay Cooke & Co., who were compared with the Bank of England for stability, the panic was on. Heavy failures of important houses, such as Fisk & Hatch, Henry Clews & Co., and the Union Trust Company of New York, quickly followed. The New York Stock Exchange was forced to close for eight days. Other great firms went soon after, the noted textile house of the Spragues in Providence failing for a larger sum than the total State and municipal debts of Rhode Island. H. B. Claflin & Co., the largest wholesale house in America, had to ask for four and a half months' time. In one day, eighteen Stock Exchange firms collapsed. Banks failed right and left, and the President of the United States came to New York to confer on the situation.

By the end of 1875 railroads had defaulted on $779,-000,000 worth of bonds, a sum comparable to several times that amount to-day. There was no currency to move the crops, and Southern cotton could not be got to even such market as there was. Ships lay at their docks at New York because merchants could obtain no foreign exchange. In October, 1877, it was estimated that in the preceding twenty months there had been a shrinkage of 25 per cent in the amount of capital employed in mercantile business. In many lines of industry products could be sold only far below the cost of manufacture. Nearly 50,000 commercial houses failed between 1873 and 1878. So quickly had the crash occurred that by November, 1873, pig iron could hardly be sold at any price, and by December 1st half the furnaces and mills in the country had shut down. Six months later there were 175,000 men idle in that industry alone. Building stopped on all railroads, and all hands were discharged from rolling mills and car plants. In July, 1877, railway wages were cut 10 per cent, and the *Commercial & Financial Chronicle* stated that "it is unnecessary to review by detail the unparalleled series of riotous outbreaks which, during the week, have run like a wave of fire along our principal lines of railroad." Rhodes has succinctly described the situation in those five years, which were, he wrote, "a long dismal tale of declining markets, exhaustion of capital, a lowering in value of all kinds of property, including real estate, constant bankruptcies, close economy in business, and grinding frugality in living, idle mills, furnaces and factories, former profit-earning iron mills reduced to the value of a scrap heap, laborers out of employment, reductions of wages, strikes and lockouts, the great railroad riots of 1877, suffering of the unemployed, depression, and despair." The maximum of failures was reached in 1878, after which recovery set in fairly rapidly, the scale of living soon attained thereafter being such as would have exhausted the resources of the country before the panic began in 1873.

The next great depression, in due cyclical course, which I well remember even as a boy, took place twenty years later, in 1893. In a few months 407 public and private banks failed, 47 savings banks, 13 trust companies, and 16 mortgage companies. In 1873, nine out of every thousand commercial houses had collapsed; in 1893, the number was thirteen, with total liabilities 50 per cent greater than in the former crash. Scorching winds reduced the corn crop of Iowa, Kansas, and Nebraska from 548,000,000 bushels to 137,000,000. On the other hand, wheat fell to the lowest price ever touched before

332

or after, 49 cents a bushel. The Reading, Erie, Atchison, Union Pacific, Northern Pacific, and other railroads followed one another into receiverships in endless line, until 169 roads, operating 37,855 miles of road, had become bankrupt, unable to pay their mortgage interest, the amount in stocks and bonds involved being $2,400,000,-000. Union Pacific stock sold at $4 a share and was then assessed $15. Northern Pacific sold at 25 cents for a $100 share, and was also assessed $15. Currency rose to a premium of 4 per cent above checks and was difficult to obtain for pay-rolls.

There was such great labor unrest as to make many fear that anarchy had arrived. In London mass meetings demanded the abolition of the House of Lords; a mob invaded the City Hall in New York; troops were held in readiness to protect the banks in Denver; and President Cleveland ordered Federal troops to suppress the railway strike in Chicago. The *Herald* in August, 1893, reported 100,000 men idle in New York, 200,000 in Chicago, and half of all the working class in Pittsburgh. Exaggerated as these figures may have been, they reflect more or less truly the most serious social disturbance the nation has, perhaps, ever faced. In June, money was loaned on the Stock Exchange at previously unheard-of figures, and one afternoon became unobtainable at any price, although 360 per cent was bid for it. As one runs over the business news of the time day by day, it is a continuous story of the complete closing down of plants

333

of all sorts in every part of the country. Recovery began in 1895, and was extremely rapid. Between February and November the production of pig iron rose forty per cent, and the price of dry goods staples twenty-five per cent.

We will not describe the minor crisis of 1907, as it was much less severe, but may note that even then, in what we have almost forgotten as a mere episode, the production of pig iron dropped fifty per cent in less than a year.

I have not attempted to recount the story of any of these depressions in detail or to discuss their causes. My purpose has been merely to find some sort of standard measure for the time we are passing through now, so that we may view it in perspective. Having done this, let us consider somewhat closely the question of stock market prices.

*

In discussing the price of stocks, for purposes of sane comparison we must discard and forget 1928 and 1929 altogether. The country was insane then, and prices bore no relation whatever to business realities. Let us take a year of sound, prosperous business in the post-war era, say 1925, when business was so good as to satisfy everyone before we ran amok.

I am writing this chapter on June 3, the market having plunged yesterday to the lowest depth yet reached. In making the comparisons of the lows of 1925 and the closing of June 2, 1931, have been employed. The worst showing is being made by the rails, as noted below:

	Price 1925	Price 1931
Atchison	116¼	134⅛
Baltimore & Ohio...........	71	44
Delaware & Hudson.........	133½	108½
Erie	26¾	13½
Illinois Central.............	111	41⅝
New York Central	113¼	71⅜
New Haven	28	64¾
Norfolk & Western..........	123½	142
Northern Pacific	58¼	32
Pennsylvania	42¼	42⅜
Southern Pacific	96	67¼
Union Pacific	133¼	137⅛

In spite of what seems in immediate retrospect like an appalling decline, we find that four of the roads, or one-third of those taken at haphazard among the leaders, are actually above the prices of a recent good year.

The comparison of the public utilities is much better.

	Price 1925	Price 1931
American Telephone & Telegraph...	130⅝	158¼
Commonwealth Edison...........	130½	230
Consolidated Gas (split 2 for 1, 1928)	61	83¾ (=167½)

The last stock named brings up a significant point, one which makes the ordinary comparison of the prices then and now of many of the most important stocks, particularly the industrial ones, difficult and highly mis-

335

leading. This is the fact that owing to the mania for split-ups and stock dividends, chiefly in 1929, the prices of many of these stocks to-day are really several times those shown in the daily list. For example, if a stock has been split two for one, or has had a 100 per cent stock dividend, the present price should quite clearly be multiplied by two to make the proper comparison with the price before the split or dividend. Since 1925, taking merely active stocks, with no wish to make out a case by using extreme examples, Continental Can, Kennecott Copper, and Timken Roller Bearing has each received a stock dividend of 100 per cent; American Smelters and Union Carbide has each been split three for one; Sears Roebuck four for one; International Business Machines received a 200 per cent stock dividend and three subsequent dividends in stock of 5 per cent each; Burroughs Adding Machine had a 400 per cent stock dividend; International Nickel was exchanged for a new stock on a six for one basis; Commercial Solvents was split ten for one, and General Electric, in two steps, sixteen for one. Sometimes, as in the case of American Tobacco, a change in the par value of stocks quoted in dollars per share has had the same effect. United States Steel, which received a stock dividend of only 40 per cent, was unusually conservative. Allowing for these adjusted prices, we may tabulate the comparison as below, recalling the fact that we are comparing prices at the very bottom, so far, of what is considered a major depression with those of a recent prosperous year.

	Price 1925	Adjusted Price 1931
American Smelters	80	75
American Tobacco	170	200
Burroughs Adding Machine...	65	100
Commercial Solvents	76	110
Continental Can	60½	82¾
General Electric.............	227¼	585
International Business Machines	110	368
International Nickel..........	24¼	60
Kennecott Copper...........	46¼	29¼
Sears Roebuck..............	147	200
Timken Roller Bearing.......	37¾	66
Union Carbide..............	65¼	132
United States Steel..........	112⅛	116

I do not wish for a moment to minimize the extreme seriousness of the present situation or the heavy losses people have suffered. I merely wish to put that situation into some relation with the past, in other words, to consider it intellectually and not react to it emotionally as a "close-up." When we compare the situation to-day with that of the good business year of 1925, and consider it in relation to the previous great depressions, I think we may say that, instead of giving way to despair, we have considerable cause for thankfulness. What we are worrying about is that dividends may be cut or temporarily passed, but the fact that the better steel and other industrial bonds and those of public utilitiy companies are selling to yield less than 5 per cent, that many rail bonds yield from 5 per cent down to less than 4, and that good

337

preferred stocks yield from 6 per cent to 4½ per cent, assuredly indicates a very different condition from that which prevailed in most of the great crises of the past.

There may well be a stretch of bad days ahead for us, and often failures increase as business picks up. But we are already two years on our way. In addition to the normal factors present in every crisis, each has its own peculiar ones—bad banking, the currency, undigested securities, or what not. To-day we have our special idiosyncratic factors also, political and economic; but although the factors may be new, the mere presence of of new factors is not itself new. I am making no predictions and do not wish to indulge in Pollyanna nonsense. The government gave us all too much of that in 1928 and 1929, at the very time when I was predicting catastrophe. There is one point to note, however, which is that the very same men who shouted the loudest about the "new era," declaring that there was no limit upward in 1929, are now for the most part the same men who can see no bottom and who declare that the new situation of the world is so bad that there can hardly be recovery in our time. On the other hand, it is the men who, trusting to reason rather than emotion, foresaw the crash who are now the most hopeful about an eventual, though not immediate, recovery to higher levels of business prosperity than the world has ever yet attained.

*

The difference is that between a man with a "close-up" mentality and the man who insists upon background and relations. The former in 1929 could see nothing but the meeting of the lovers' lips enlarged to fill the whole screen; now he can see nothing but the villain's scowl of equal expanse and equally blocking out consideration of all else. Those two years, 1928 and 1929, appear to have oddly extinguished almost all memory on the part of innumerable individuals for all that made normal life and business before. It is said that flyers at high altitudes have a somewhat similar experience, and as they approach the earth it seems strange to them, and they have the sensation of having been away for an incalculably long time. Business, the stock market, and most of us with them, went up even into the stratosphere in those years, and now that we are back on earth again (where we should have stayed unless we had better heads for playing around at ten thousand meters), it seems strange and unrecognizable. Of course all this may be but sorry comfort to the man who jumped overboard from the plane with "City Bank stock at 500" instead of a parachute, but we are not here concerned with sympathy for the individual but with trying to study general trends.

I may also repeat that we are not so much concerned even with the business situation in itself as in using the present panic of mind to illustrate our main thesis, namely the need of escaping from the close-up way of looking at life. It is becoming increasingly difficult for all of us to do so. Just as the movies concentrate on it, so do the newspapers and magazines. It is impossible, for example, to escape the stock market. I am convinced from a considerable number of years in Wall Street and a greater number since as a modest investor, that the only way to make money is to think and act in terms of years instead of "turns," and that the best thing to do, having taken a position for a several years' "pull," is to pay as little attention to daily quotations as possible. It is certainly better for one's sane appraisal of the general situation. But it is next to impossible to do so, and during the part of the year that I am in America I find myself waiting almost as anxiously as anyone else for the evening paper. It is not that I have any more commitments while in America than while in England or Italy, but the American newspapers work up a sense of excitement about it all like the emotional appeal in the movie screen close-up.

This started in 1893. In that year, which now seems almost as far off as the battle of Salamis, although I was fourteen years old, the close-up began for Wall Street. Up to January of that year Wall Street had not been "news." Up to about July the small-type, closely leaded headlines of the *New York Times* and even the *Herald* were much like the *London Times* to-day, except that they were even smaller and less inciting to excitability on the part of the reader. The whole financial and business news of the world occupied less than three columns on a far back page. February 18, 1893, was a day of tremendous excitement for "the Street." Sales on the Exchange reached the unprecedented amount of 888,000 shares (although only forty out of the ninety stocks were traded in for more than 1000 shares each), and 392,000 shares of Reading were dumped on the market. All this got some notice on the first news page of the *Herald* but there was nothing about it in the *Times* except a little fine print on page six, in the regular Wall Street column. The *Herald,* however, was in its full career toward "sensationalism" as it was then considered. The Reading road failed on the 20th, and next morning the *Herald* gave an entire page to the story with pictures, a reproduction of some inches of ticker tape recording the crashing prices, and a write-up about "titanic stock dealings" and "battles of financial giants." The *Times* gave a half column on page one to recording the failure but did not mention the market; and the brooding calm of the headlines was undisturbed. The *Herald,* however, had discovered the sensational value of finance. The public had had its first close-up of the villain or the lover, and the *Herald* continued to throw them on the screen. In the summer the battle of the headlines was on, and the modern newspaper format was emerging.

The magazines were slower to change. During the whole of the crisis of 1893 to 1895 the pages of *Scribner's, Harper's* and the *Century,* for example, were unruffled by articles on any current controversial topic, and for all of them there might have been no such thing as business in the world. The contents were excellent. Never, before or after, have American magazines been so well illustrated. They were full of the works of Church, Frost, Abbey, Parsons, Cole, and others. The reading matter was equally good, largely made up of art, history, travel, articles on foreign countries, and the best of current fiction. This was all changed just before the coming of the Great War, and since then it has been almost impossible for any reader of either newspapers or magazines to get away from the incessant domination of events and problems of the present instant. Journalism, to a very great extent, has become one vast screen on which are thrown only close-ups—close-ups of the stock market, close-ups of the latest murder, close-ups of the high cost of medical service, close-ups of ladies who find their husbands difficult and *vice versa,* close-ups of every conceivable thing. The background has disappeared; the thread of the drama is lost.

As usual, we have rushed from one extreme to another. We probably used to ignore current problems too much. The magazines became a trifle too dull perhaps. They felt the stirrings of a new age, or was it the promptings of the circulation and advertising managers? At any rate, we have now run to the other extreme. We become immensely excited over everything, divorce, psychoanalysis, hospital costs, a ten-point rise in General Utility Preferred or a drop in Consolidated common. We all scramble after every close-up thrown on the journalistic screen, and no dinner party is smartly intellectual without a discussion of it.

Just as even the crudest close-up on the screen has

342

a certain compelling quality and relaxingly relieves us of thought, so has this turmoil of journalistic and literary close-ups in which we have become almost inextricably enmeshed mentally. To react away from it all, to try to see things steadily and see them whole, to search amid the welter of facts and emotional appeals for the abiding and significant relationships intellectually, calls for a genuine act of will and for knowledge with a background, that is, wisdom. Never before has the observer and thinker been able to get so much material from the public press of all sorts, but it is only raw material, and is rank poison unless he can digest it and properly assimilate it.

The only hope would seem to lie in our educational system, which ought precisely to perform the function of training us to see life not in a series of emotional close-ups but in rational and ordered relationships. For this, background and a knowledge of what has been done and thought in the past are absolutely requisite; but more and more the schools, colleges and universities seem bent also on giving us the close-up on to-day and the ideas only of the moment. The decision just announced by Yale to discard the classics as requirements for the bachelor's degree is merely the most recent step in a continuous movement. For the classics as mere grammatical excercises I have no use whatever, but there is an infinite amount to be said for the classics as a means of rescue from the mentality of close-ups. It is not without significance that just at the time when the market started for the stratosphere one of the principal university clubs in

343

New York, pressed for room in its library, removed the entire section of American history to a storeroom out of sight. Whoopee and the "new era." Perhaps a little history would have saved some margins. At any rate, it would seem as though one of our chief problems were to learn how to keep our mental balance by being able to react against the emotionalistic mush of all and every close-up by clear thought in terms of relations and background. I suggest that educators might well ponder, more than they seem inclined to, what they are doing to save their students from supine yielding to the barrage of close-ups which in daily life will be pouring down on them on every side.

THE END